Albania's MOUNTAIN QUEEN

Edith Durham and the Balkans

MARCUS TANNER

I.B. TAURIS
LONDON · NEW YORK

Published in 2014 by I.B.Tauris & Co. Ltd
6 Salem Road, London W2 4BU
175 Fifth Avenue, New York NY 10010
www.ibtauris.com

Distributed in the United States and Canada
Exclusively by Palgrave Macmillan
175 Fifth Avenue, New York NY 10010

Copyright © 2014 Marcus Tanner

The right of Marcus Tanner to be identified as the author of this work has been asserted by him in accordance with the Copyright, Designs and Patents Act 1988.

All rights reserved. Except for brief quotations in a review, this book, or any part thereof, may not be reproduced, stored in or introduced into a retrieval system, or transmitted, in any form or by any means, electronic, mechanical, photocopying, recording or otherwise, without the prior written permission of the publisher.

Every effort has been made to gain permission for the use of the images in this book. Any omissions will be rectified in future editions.

ISBN: 978 1 78076 819 9
eISBN: 978 0 85773 504 1

A full CIP record for this book is available from the British Library
A full CIP record is available from the Library of Congress

Library of Congress Catalog Card Number: available

Printed and bound in Sweden by ScandBook AB

CONTENTS

	List of illustrations	vi
	Note on spelling	viii
	Introduction	1
1	'The Balkan tangle'	14
2	'The other end of nowhere'	33
3	'My golden sisters of Macedonia'	57
4	'God has sent you to save us'	77
5	'A fine old specimen'	97
6	The Great Mountain Land	118
7	'They never all rise in a lump'	136
8	'Boom – our big gun rang out'	157
9	'He is a blighter'	183
10	'For a dream's sake'	204
11	'Albanians will never forget'	240
	Notes	255
	Select bibliography	280
	Index	285

ILLUSTRATIONS

Maps

Map of the Balkans in 1900   ix

Map of the Balkans in 1913   x

Plates

1 Edith Durham as a young woman
   Not to be reproduced without the written permission of the Durham family

2 King Nikola of Montenegro and his family
   Mary Evans Picture Library

3 King Petar of Serbia
   Public domain

4 Ismail Qemali and the declaration of Albanian independence, November 1912
   Public domain

5 William of Wied
   Public domain

6 King Zog of Albania
   Public domain

7 Aubrey Herbert
   Public domain

8 Henry Nevinson
© *National Portrait Gallery, London*

9 Robert Seton-Watson
Courtesy of the British Academy

10 Rebecca West
© *National Portrait Gallery, London*

11 Albanian tribesmen
Public domain

12 IMRO leaders in 1903
Public domain

13 Shkodra in 1897
Public domain

14 Ohrid circa 1900
Photographed by M.E. Durham. RAI 3799. Courtesy of the Royal Anthropological Institute, London

15 Cetinje in 1895
Public domain

16 Resen
Drawn by M.E. Durham. H 388. Courtesy of the Royal Anthropological Institute, London

17 Macedonian freedom
© *Punch Limited*

18 Edith Durham School in Tirana
Public domain

NOTE ON SPELLING

It is hard to be entirely consistent about spellings in a region where so many places have changed their names over the past century, or are spelled in different ways, each sending a different message as to which community 'owns' it. I have opted to use modern names and spellings for most place names, as these probably are now the best known. Thus: Edirne, not Adrianople; Bitola, not Monastir; Thessaloniki, not Salonika; and Dürres, not Durazzo. For the same reason: Kosovo – the internationally recognised name of the republic – not Kossovo (the old-fashioned English spelling), or Kosova, as Albanians usually call it; and Metohija – Serbia's preferred expression. I have made an exception for Constantinople, as this term remains familiar to everyone. Regarding personal names, generally I have used modern spellings rather than English translations. Thus: Petar, not Peter, of Serbia; and Nikola, not Nicholas, of Montenegro. I have stuck with William of Wied, not Wilhelm, because that is how he is normally styled in English. Likewise, on the grounds of familiarity, Nicholas II of Russia and Franz Joseph of Austria-Hungary – rather than Francis Joseph or Franz Josef. With Albanian and Ottoman names, I have followed the same principle. Thus: Essad Pasha Toptani, not Esad Pashe; and Ahmed, not Ahmet, Zogu. Both Abdul Hamid and Abdulhamid are commonly used in English for the Ottoman Sultan. I have opted for Abdulhamid.

Map of the Balkans in 1900

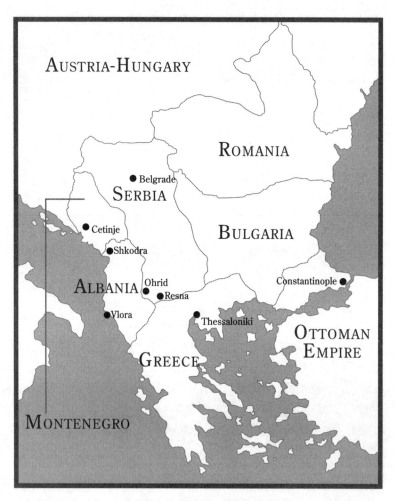

Map of the Balkans in 1913

Introduction

I WAS STAMPING MY feet outside a freezing courthouse in the grim town of Mitrovica in northern Kosovo when I first heard of Edith Durham. A rookie reporter, I had been sent there by a British newspaper in October 1989 to cover the trial of Azem Vllasi, the recently arrested leader of the League of Communists of Kosovo in what then was the Socialist Federative Republic of Yugoslavia. Inside that federation, in which Kosovo was imprecisely linked to next-door Serbia, Serbia's assertive new leader, Slobodan Milošević, had resolved to scrap Kosovo's autonomy and absorb the province into Serbia.[1] With a view to frightening the mainly Albanian population of Kosovo into submission, he was having their leader arrested.

Vllasi, a saturnine man with vaguely matinee-idol looks, was up for the typical communist-era, catch-all charge of 'counter-revolutionary nationalism and separatism'.[2] Outside the chilly courthouse in Mitrovica we didn't see it, but it was the beginning of the end of the Yugoslav state that the Entente powers had helped to set up 70 years earlier, following the end of World War I.

The Serbs, a shrinking and embittered minority in Kosovo, were all for sending Vllasi to prison, if not to the scaffold.[3] Almost all Serbs, not just those in Kosovo, saw Kosovo as an integral part of their own national patrimony, and for years Yugoslav politics had been held hostage to the Serbs' *idée fixe* of bringing the Kosovo Albanians to heel. The 'Kosovo knot' was their term for the ongoing tug of war. What the Serbs did not realise was that by violently unravelling this knot with hard yanks, they would end up unravelling all the other cords that bound Yugoslavia together. The conflict that began in Kosovo in the mid-to-late 1980s spread from one republic to another like fire through thatch.

Vllasi, meanwhile, was on trial in Titova Mitrovica – 'Tito's Mitrovica', as it was styled – in homage to the late Yugoslav strongman.[4] Tito's or not, the town was grim even by the undemanding standards of the Balkans. Mitrovica had been an industrial centre of some significance in communist Yugoslavia, lying close to the important Trepča zinc and lead mines. But, by 1989, nine years had passed since Tito had expired in a clinic in Slovenia, and the industrial and economic boom he had overseen was over. Yugoslavia had been in the grip of an economic crisis since the oil crisis of 1983. Now these economic strains showed in the fractious relations between the six republics and in the drawn, flyblown appearance of towns like Mitrovica.

Jobless or semi-jobless Serbs and Albanians sat stony-faced, puffing away on their cigarettes and sipping grainy black coffees in separate but equally grey cafes that faced one another on the dilapidated main square. The Albanians complained bitterly of the arrest of Vllasi and of Milošević's plans to do away with the autonomy that Tito had granted the province at the end of World War II.[5] They all supported the 1,300 miners from Trepča who had staged an eight-day hunger strike that February, protesting against the Serbian government's plans. Their Serbian neighbours all rooted for Milošević, denounced the strike and talked longingly of Kosovo's reunion with Serbia. Tito's gift of autonomy had been a hateful thing to them, separating them from the broad current of Serbian life and placing them on the same level as a people they despised. With the two communities busy glaring at each other, there was a marked absence of anything in Mitrovica that suggested either cared much about the town's decayed appearance. One of Mitrovica's notable features was the number of old fridges and ovens that locals on both sides of the ethnic divide had hurled onto the banks of the Ibar, the river that bisected the town. Many still lay forlornly on the river bank, smashed to pieces and rusting away slowly.

It was while I was waiting outside the courthouse for news to emerge of Vllasi's trial that a journalist colleague suggested I take a look at his copy of a book by Edith Durham. If I wanted to know more about Mitrovica and the rest of Kosovo, it was all in *High Albania*, he suggested. A much-thumbed Virago reprint of the book, first published in 1909, made its way into my backpack. Later, in the twilit gloom of the Hotel Grand in Pristina, I flipped through it, bypassing Durham's accounts of her journeys through the mountains of northern Albania and encounters with 'sworn virgins', and heading straight for the chapter on Kosovo entitled 'The debatable lands'.

As I read on, I found myself back in the Kosovo of the 1900s, around the time of the 'Young Turk' revolution in Constantinople, which was when Durham had begun assembling the material for her best-known book. What was striking about *High Albania* was not only the vivid quality of these accounts of Albania and Kosovo long ago; it was the unnervingly contemporary feel of her 80-year-old description of Mitrovica, Pristina and other parts of Kosovo. Mitrovica, Durham wrote, was that most dangerous of phenomena, a strategic town bestriding an ethnic frontier. To the south lay the solidly Albanian lands of the centre and south of Kosovo. To the north lay the lands of the Serbs. Two worlds and two competing narratives, Slav and non-Slav, Christian and Muslim, collided in this dreary town on the Ibar. Durham accepted Serbian and Albanian claims to the province as equally deeply held, hence the non-committal title of the chapter, 'The debatable lands'. But she also judged these claims irreconcilable. 'Mitrovitza [*sic*], though it looked so peaceful, is tinder waiting for a spark,' she wrote:

> Here we come to the crucial race question. Exact figures are unattainable but of the general facts there can be no

doubt. Kosovo plain is now, by a very large majority, Moslem Albanian [and...] were it not for the support and instruction that has for long been supplied from without it is probable that the Serb element would have been almost, if not quite, absorbed or suppressed by this time.

She continued:

It has been an elemental struggle for existence and survival of the strongest, carried out in obedience to Nature's law, which says, 'There is not place for you both. You must kill – or be killed.' Ineradicably fixed in the breast of the Albanian – of the primitive man of the mountain and the plain – is the belief that the land has been his rightly for all time. The Serb conquered him, held him for a few passing centuries, was swept out and shall never return again. He had but done to the Serb as he was done by.[6]

When I first read those startling lines, holding such ethnocentric views about delicate Balkan questions was deeply unfashionable. In 1989 both Yugoslavia and the many champions of the Southern Slav idea, in the country and abroad, were very much alive. The prevailing wisdom was that such an important feature of the contemporary map of Europe could not be allowed to disappear. Most western books on Yugoslavia, if only unconsciously, reflected the Yugoslav communists' own conviction that class, not race or ethnicity, was the determining factor between communities. Durham's insistence of the primacy of ethnic and racial issues sounded anachronistic.

Ten years on from Vllasi's trial, her words seemed less anachronistic than prophetic. By 1998–9, Milošević had decided that cowing the Albanians of Kosovo, by abolishing the autonomy of Kosovo and depriving them of access to employment, was not the solution. Confronted by a full-blown uprising, led by a little-known group called the Kosovo Liberation Army, he launched a campaign of 'ethnic cleansing', which by the spring of 1999 had prompted the flight of about 800,000 Albanians and caused the deaths of almost 10,000.[7] Over the spring and summer of 1999, the Serbian police, military and assorted paramilitaries razed whole villages. The military intervention by NATO in the conflict from March to June then dramatically changed the balance, forcing Milošević to withdraw his forces from Kosovo, after which the briefly exiled Albanians returned home. This then prompted the mass flight of most of Kosovo's remaining Serbs. A second wave of ethnic cleansing followed the first. Kosovo effectively became a separate state from the summer of 1999 onwards, although it did not declare independence until 2008. Today it remains unrecognised by Serbia,[8] where many cling to the idea that Kosovo remains 'the southern province'.[9]

In reality, a new international frontier exists in the Balkans. But it does not run along the old border between what in the Yugoslav era were the Province of Kosovo and the Republic of Serbia. Instead, it runs to the south, inside Kosovo, through the town of Mitrovica. More than a century after Durham penned her lines about Mitrovica, the town is still a piece of tinder waiting for a spark.

Years after that introduction to Durham's writings in the Hotel Grand, where I had started with *High Albania*, I discovered that the range of her writing covered far more than Albania, the country with which she is normally associated. In fact, she wrote seven books on a variety of topics concerning the Balkans, from the rise of the kingdom of Serbia to the complexity of the Macedonian question, the horrors of the Balkan Wars of 1912 and 1913 and the question of the responsibility for the outbreak of World War I.[10] Her collected works, including numerous articles and lectures, not to mention unpublished diaries and letters, form a rare surviving account in English of the condition of the Balkan peninsula during the last years of the Ottoman Empire-in-Europe. It is hard to think of anyone else who left behind such an insightful and prophetic account of what would soon become the vanished world of Ottoman Europe.

I now discovered that Durham had not only written about much more than Albania, but that she had been much more than a writer and explorer. While traversing the Balkans between 1900 and 1914, her persona and self-image had evolved and she had added the careers of humanitarian worker, diplomat, politician and national advocate to her earlier career as a writer. Over those years she had become a confidante to the King of Montenegro; had run a hospital and a refugee operation in Macedonia; had explored Serbia, Dalmatia, and Bosnia and Herzegovina, as well as Albania; and had become a war reporter following the outbreak of the Balkan Wars in 1912 – possibly the first woman war reporter ever.

Her opinions and sympathies had also shifted. After starting out a fervent admirer of the Serbs, Durham ended her time in the Balkans an even more fervent partisan of the Albanians. This was partly because she grew to like and admire them and partly because she hated injustice, and feared the Albanian's legitimate interests were in danger of being sacrificed in any carve-up of South-Eastern Europe that followed the collapse of Ottoman European power.

Her impassioned advocacy on behalf of the Albanian cause in Britain, her pioneering exploration of the remotest parts of the mountainous north of the country and her humanitarian work among Albanian refugees during the Balkan Wars of 1912–13 gained her the devotion of many Albanians, who called her the 'Queen of the Mountain People' in tribute.

Durham did not create the new state of Albania, which emerged from the wreck of the Ottoman Empire-in-Europe in 1912; the Albanians did that. But her persistent, targeted lobbying on their behalf assisted the new state's passage into the world, and she deserves some credit also for shaping Albania's southern borders to its advantage; thanks in part to telegrams that she and her journalist friend Henry Nevinson sent to the great powers meeting in London, the important but disputed town of Korça became part of Albania and not Greece. Along with another friend and admirer, the MP Aubrey Herbert, Durham also had a hand in securing Albania's admission into the League of Nations, an important diplomatic coup, which is one reason why her many friends in Albania invited her back to the country for an emotional *adieu* in 1921.

Edith Durham's achievements ensured her a secure reputation in Albania, at least until the communist takeover at the end of 1944. She had once also been well known and respected in Britain as an authority on the Balkans, her books widely read and keenly anticipated. Diplomats from the Foreign Secretary Sir Edward Grey downwards had appreciated her shrewd insights into this turbulent arena of great-power rivalry. For various reasons, following her return to Britain in 1914, she had fallen into obscurity. Yet, it still seems strange, given her former prominence, that she has gone without a biographer. Many of her articles and letters have been collected and reprinted, and she has walk-on roles in recent works on women travellers in the Balkans. But no one has assembled the whole story. This book is only part of that story, for I make no claim to recount all there is to say about the life of this remarkable woman.

Durham did not set foot in the Balkans until her late thirties – a late start in life, especially by the standards of the 1900s. The first half of her life in London, the eldest of nine children of a highly strung surgeon, much of it spent as her mother's nurse and companion, barely features here for one reason: Durham referred to this period only fleetingly and without nostalgia in her published works.[11] Her voluminous correspondence with her family written from the Balkans also provides few clues. Packed with details about travels in Kosovo, Albania, Macedonia, Serbia and Montenegro, and about the politics of the region, these letters were designed as a resource from which she could draw material for books. Apart from conventional greetings and salutations, they shed little light on the internal dynamics of the Durham clan.

It may be because Durham regarded her seven surviving younger siblings – one of her brothers died young – with a degree of resentment.[12] The Durhams were a self-consciously progressive mid-Victorian family. Durham's father, Arthur Edward, and his two brothers, Frederic and Edmund Ashley, all went into medicine. Durham's mother, Mary, was the daughter of William Ellis, the pioneering educational reformer and founder of the Birkbeck schools. The Durhams encouraged all their numerous, often brilliant, children, the girls included, to make maximum use of their talents and go out into the world.

This they did. Arthur Ellis, the next in line to Edith, gained a first at Cambridge in Physiology, went off to study medicine in Paris and returned to work in the London Fever Hospital in Islington, which was where he caught diphtheria and died tragically young in August 1893.[13] Herbert Edward, Edith's junior by three years, also gained a first at Cambridge, went to Vienna on a scholarship in 1894 and was credited with making a notable discovery in the field of cholera before heading off on expeditions to Brazil and Malaya. Edith's youngest brother, Frank Rogers, trained as an engineer and went to work in Germany, Romania and other European countries before returning to become Secretary of the Royal Horticultural Society and Director of Works at the Imperial War Graves Commission.

Edith's sister, Caroline Beatrice, married a rising scientist, William Bateson, in 1896 – making her one of only two of the Durham daughters to marry. After joining him in Cambridge, she became an active assistant to her husband in his evolutionary experiments while immersing herself in family life; she and William went on to have three sons. Another of Edith's sisters, Florence Margaret, a budding geneticist in her own right, joined the Bateson circle in Cambridge, where, Caroline recalled, she 'hybridised mice in a kind of attic over the Museums'.[14] Later she lectured at Newnham College. It must have been with mixed feelings that Edith saw the youngest of all her siblings, Frances Hermia, her junior by a decade, making her way through the Women's University Settlement in Southwark before rising steadily up the ranks of the civil service.

Durham could hardly have followed in Herbert's footsteps and gone off to Brazil. But, somehow, she also missed out on the new academic opportunities for women in England that her younger sisters, Florence and Frances, had seized: they both studied at Girton. Durham never became part of this Cambridge world. Nor was she especially welcome in the Bateson household in Grantchester, even as a visitor. One of her nephews later recalled that neither of his parents cared for 'Dick', or 'Dickie', as the family nicknamed her.[15] Instead, after four years at Bedford College in London, Durham studied art at the Royal Academy. By 1900, her CV contained only one achievement of note: some illustrations of reptiles and amphibians executed for the *Cambridge Natural History*. In comparison to her brothers and sisters, Durham had fallen behind.

What changed matters dramatically for Durham, and for the worse in the meantime, was their father's sudden death from pneumonia at the age of only 61 in May 1895. In certain ways Durham took after the highly strung and idealistic Arthur Edward Durham. 'He was most remarkable for his personal character,' a friend observed following his death:

> The enthusiasm he displayed in his work and the devotion he paid to every case which came before him was extraordinary. There was no shirking his duty. He did his best for everybody, giving no thought to money considerations [...] It seemed as if doing good was the prime motive in his life.[16]

According to his biography in the Royal College of Surgeons, the flourish with which he conducted his surgical operations reminded contemporaries of a true artist. 'His remarkably long fingers, that seemed to have eyes in their tips, his flexible wrist and sinuous movements of the hand made him powerful, searching, and graceful in all his manipulations, while his invention of the lobster-tail tracheotomy tube has proved of great value,' it wrote.[17]

But Arthur Edward was not strong. In his latter years he suffered from deafness, depression, bronchitis and mysterious attacks of vomiting, the causes of which were never explained. A final summer holiday in Norway offered temporary respite, where, 'braced by the Northern air, his enthusiasm knew no bounds and he became the most popular man on board'.[18] But the recovery did not last and he died the following year.

The sudden disappearance of this much loved, charismatic figure created a void in the household at 82 Brook Street in Mayfair, which no longer echoed to the sound of young doctors arguing with their mentor over medical breakthroughs. Instead, there was silence and an ailing mother who required the steady company that her more adventurous children could no longer provide. There was no question of Caroline Beatrice delaying her marriage, which had been kept on hold for years already, and still less of any of the others quitting their burgeoning careers. The task of nursing mother ineluctably fell upon Durham, whose artistic commitments could not be described as pressing.

Durham undertook the role of carer to Mary Durham with grim resignation and a degree of revulsion. She yearned for the same kind of adventures that her siblings were experiencing, and the feeling of being cooped up in Brook Street made her ill and even suicidal. In a rare revealing comment about that desperate period, she wrote later: 'The future stretched before me as endless years of grey monotony, and escape seemed hopeless.'[19] When she did 'escape', at first on temporary leave, she immediately embarked on what looked like foolhardy adventures in remote places because, as she wrote dramatically, 'a bullet would have been a sort of way out'.[20]

The original arrangements in the Durham family had to be changed because after she had spent five years as an involuntary carer in central London, Durham suffered a form of nervous breakdown. Armed with an alarmingly worded doctor's report, in 1900 Durham demanded and obtained leave to take two months away from London each year. The condition was that she would return to care for Mary for the remaining ten, an arrangement that lasted until 1906, when Mary died, after which Durham was free at last to manage her time.

It is hard to tell how her revolt against her appointed role affected her relations with the rest of the Durhams. She wrote assiduously to her mother from the Balkans, which suggests that at some level Mary well understood her unhappy eldest child's desperate yearning to breathe different air. But her brothers and sisters surely did not appreciate Durham's description of those London years, in her books, as the equivalent to a death sentence.

Bit by bit, at first for only a few months a year, later for longer, Durham reinvented herself in the Balkans, a patriarchal society that paradoxically offered a single, financially independent, foreign woman like herself far more freedom than she could ever have hoped to obtain in her own country as a dreaded 'spinster'. This book reflects her own bias towards the arena that from then on consumed her physical and emotional energy. It focuses on the decade-and-a-half that she spent in the region, on her attempt to alert the outside world to the danger of a great war breaking out, and her immersion in the cause of Albanian independence.

I have not disguised my admiration for a woman who defied the conventions of her time and class to escape the few options available in the England of the 1900s to middle-aged, single women. It was no easy choice to give up a comfortable, if unchallenging, existence in London in order to explore unknown lands, write books, assume responsibility for the well-being of thousands of refugees and champion a national liberation movement. The Balkans were not then a short journey away. Geographically, they were far removed from the England of her day; mentally, they were further from most people's minds than India. In his 1880 book, *Turkey Old and New*, Sutherland Menzies wrote that Albania was then so little known that even the landmarks remained indistinct in atlases. Only the Adriatic coast was clearly defined. As for the people of Albania, the governments of Europe 'probably know less [about them] than of the negroes of equatorial Africa,' he wrote.[21]

In acknowledging Durham's courage, I have not attempted to conceal her many contradictions. Single-minded in the pursuit of justice, she was hard to work with and was generally contemptuous of other women. Her numerous Albanian friends and admirers named her the 'Queen of the Mountains', or 'Queen of the Mountain People', in recognition of her services, but she was a true queen also in the sense of brooking no rivals. She had a wicked sense of humour, was sarcastic, and could be incredibly ungracious and unkind to individuals. She was sometimes bigoted towards entire nations, as she was towards the Macedonians whom she helped in material terms but viewed with undisguised contempt.

Complicating the work of any would-be biographer, Durham also rewrote her own history, editing out chapters that had become inconvenient. She dedicated the last half of her life to the cause of the Albanians and to attacking those she saw as their oppressors, starting with the Serbs and the Serb-dominated state of Yugoslavia. At this stage of her life she omitted to mention that she had begun her literary oeuvres in the Balkans as an enthusiastic apologist for what was then the little kingdom of Serbia. She would have hated then to acknowledge the fact, but her first book, *Through the Lands of the Serb*, played a part in positively changing British opinions about that once despised country. She compressed and played down her once intimate connections to the Montenegrin royal family, which had, in fact, endured until the start of the Balkan Wars of 1912–13.

Far from being an embarrassment to her, these contradictions make Durham a more three-dimensional person. The Queen of the Mountains was not a plaster saint, oozing compassion for the downtrodden, but a queen of flesh and blood, torn by her passions and by sometimes violent prejudices, as well as by fast-changing circumstances in the region. What redeemed the whole was her unshakable commitment to justice, which in the Balkans, in the end, placed her on the side of the truckled and abused Albanians. That is all that most Albanians remember, inasmuch as they remember her at all. 'Albanians have never forgotten – and will never forget – this Englishwoman,'[22] King Zog of Albania (whom she did not admire or befriend) wrote on hearing of her death in 1944. It is a sentence that remains true today, and is probably the only tribute that would have mattered to her.

CHAPTER 1

'The Balkan tangle'

There is again a Turkey-in-Europe.
(Benjamin Disraeli to Queen Victoria, 22 June 1878)[1]

WHEN DURHAM STEPPED off a Lloyd steamer in Dalmatia in August 1900, Queen Victoria's reign had six months to run and the Boer War was at its height. The failure of the British army to gain an early victory over a small army of Dutch-speaking farmers had revealed hairline cracks in the British Empire but they were as nothing compared to the fissures opening up in the Habsburg and Ottoman Empires, the two great powers that straddled the Balkans.

Dalmatia, like the rest of Croatia, belonged to the Habsburg Empire, which was not so much a country as an agglomeration of estates united around a family. Austria-Hungary was still counted – just – among the great powers of Europe. A guidebook printed in English in 1914, just before the outbreak of the war that would sweep it away, contained no hint that it might disappear. While conceding that the country was deeply divided, it preferred to dwell on the great love everyone allegedly felt for the Emperor. 'It is not the Austrians alone but the Slavs and Tyrolese and the Hungarians who look with tender reverence on the aged man,' it wrote. 'Whatever else divides the Magyar from the Austrian, and the Austrian and the Slav from the Magyar, here they are all at one.'²

Like the British author of *Austria-Hungary*, until the last year of World War I almost everyone inside the Empire and out assumed its continued existence. Nevertheless, if the Empire was less doomed-looking to contemporaries than we now imagine, it was visibly in decline. Feebler economically than the new, united Germany, or France or Britain, it faced a more serious existential threat in nationalism; the Empire appeared to be slowly succumbing to the strains created by the competing ambitions of its constituent peoples: Germans, Magyars, Italians, Czechs, Slovaks, Poles, Ukrainians, Romanians, Serbs, Croats and Slovenes.

Unlike Britain, France, Germany, Italy or Russia, Austria-Hungary was not a national state, and had no potential to become one. As the great nineteenth-century French historian Albert Sorel wrote: 'There was no Austrian nation and no means of making one.'³ According to Sorel, Austria was the most dynastic state in Europe. For that reason alone it seemed at odds with the spirit of the age, in which nationalism was the coming force and dynasticism was in decline. To Henry Wickham Steed, the unsympathetic correspondent of the London *Times* in Vienna, the dual monarchy was 'like an old tree, full of sap in its branches but with a trunk already hollow or rotting at the core'.⁴

By tradition, the German Austrians were the most faithful, *kaisertreu*, of all the nationalities. And, for as long as the Empire maintained a broadly German character and had aspirations to lead national Germany – for as long as the Germans could think of themselves as 'the people of state' – their support could be counted on. But by the time Durham arrived in Dalmatia, Prussia had pushed Austria out of national Germany and the Austrian Germans felt taken for granted. Outnumbered by roughly two to one in the Austrian 'half' of the monarchy, a shrinking minority in the lands of the Hungarian Crown, they feared marginalisation and looked with longing at united Germany. As for the Hungarians, Romanians, Italians and Slavs, they saw their futures, with varying degrees of clarity, in independent states, or in union with a 'mother' country: the Serbs with Serbia, the Romanians with Romania, Italians with Italy.

That perception of weakness – the smell of death, even – was heightened by two deaths in particular: the suicide of Crown Prince Rudolf in 1889 and the assassination of the Empress Elisabeth in 1898. Neither event had a political character to it; the Crown Prince succumbed to ennui, the Empress to a deranged drifter. But, together, the royal deaths fed a perception that both the Empire and the imperial family were gripped by a fatal malady.

Ironically, this feeling that the Empire was terminally ill, a feeling that reached right up to and through the imperial family, added a desperate, agitated tone to its political life in those last years – as if both the Emperor and his subjects had resolved to confront approaching death by adopting a pose of exaggerated and artificial vitality. The qualities of gaiety and frivolity for which the Empire and the Viennese especially became well known were never so much in evidence as during the last decade-and-a-half of the Empire's existence. And while gaiety and frivolity were not attributes associated with the Emperor, the Habsburg politician, Count Dzieduszycki, held him personally responsible for the feverish tone of the Empire's politics. Franz Joseph 'is an old man in a hurry, who hurries the older he gets [...] He has been turned out of Germany and turned out of Italy and will be turned out of the Balkans if he is not careful,' he told Wickham Steed in 1907. 'But he wants, before he dies, to add something to his realms that posterity will look upon as compensation for his losses elsewhere.' The Count ended on a prophetic note: 'One day [...] he will do something or sanction some wild scheme that will wreck the Monarchy for good and all.'[5]

To prove to a doubtful world that Austria-Hungary remained a power of the first rank became the order of the day. It was the driving consideration behind the decision in 1878 to occupy Bosnia and Herzegovina, an economically negligible asset. Snatching this province from the Ottoman Sultan enraged Muslims as far away as India and did not enrich anyone except the bureaucrats sent to administer it. The addition to the Empire of yet more Slavs heightened the anxieties of both the Austrian Germans and the Hungarians who, unable to agree on much else, shared a dread of the Slavs. The largest community in Bosnia, the Orthodox Serbs, passionately opposed the Austrian occupation. Trouble from that quarter was foreseeable from the start.

While the Habsburg Empire was a fading force in 1900, its condition was infinitely more vigorous and its prospects more hopeful than that of its decrepit counterpart and one-time rival, the Ottoman Empire. The Habsburgs had a formidably efficient bureaucracy that was up to the task of collecting taxes; administering justice; maintaining law and order; and building schools, army barracks, government offices, roads and railways. The physical transformation of the Bosnian capital of Sarajevo after 1878 was testament to their energy.

By contrast, the Ottoman Empire's threadbare, corrupt and badly paid bureaucracy was capable of few of those tasks. The public administration was a shambles, not least because the Sultan's civil servants, like his soldiers, were often not paid on time. Communications remained non-existent in many areas, and whereas all the Habsburg provinces had assemblies, albeit elected on tiny franchises, the various far-flung Ottoman provinces had no elected representatives. Having no means to articulate their numerous grievances the ground-down peasantry in the Balkans regularly rebelled.

It was a revolt among the Serbian peasants in Bosnia in 1875, which then spread to Bulgaria in the spring of 1876, that led to war between the Russian and Ottoman Empires the following year. The conflict would have resulted in the complete demise of Turkey-in-Europe, as the Sultan's Balkan empire was known, had it not been for the British Prime Minister Benjamin Disraeli's footwork at the Congress of Berlin in 1878. His combination of threats and bluffs forced the Russians to abandon the gains they had made in the war with Turkey and allowed the Ottomans to regain most of their possessions in Europe. But, three years after Durham arrived in the Balkans, another revolt broke out against the Ottomans, in Macedonia. Towards the end of her stay in the Balkans the Albanians in Kosovo were in almost permanent revolt.

While the great ace in the hands of the Habsburg Empire was a justified reputation for impartial governance, the Ottoman Empire's only real claim on its subjects was antiquity. The Ottomans had been present in the region far longer than the Austrians. They had begun the slow asphyxiation of Constantinople and the piecemeal conquest of the Balkan hinterland in the thirteenth century. By the time they captured the Byzantine capital in 1453 they had penetrated several hundred miles into South-Eastern Europe, overrunning Bulgaria, Greece, Serbia and Bosnia before moving north to seize most of Hungary-Croatia.

The occupation of Hungary-Croatia was relatively brief by Ottoman standards, lasting a century-and-a-half. After a failed attempt to take Vienna in 1683, the Habsburgs had inflicted a series of game-changing defeats on the Ottomans in the 1690s, which had forced them out of the Danube basin and established a new border to the south along the banks of the River Sava. Following the Treaty of Belgrade in 1739, this river border, leaving Hungary and Croatia to the north and Bosnia and Serbia to the south, had remained relatively stable for the best part of a century.

But the border was not permanent. In the 1800s the Serbs and Greeks revolted, leading to the formation of a small autonomous Serbian principality and an independent Greek kingdom by the 1830s. Turkey-in-Europe again faced a crisis. A third force had now entered the Balkans: independent Christian nation states. But the immediate impact of these two newcomers was not very significant. In the mid-nineteenth century, Greece and Serbia were too small, poor and chaotic to act as magnets for the mass of the Balkan Christians in the Ottoman Empire. In the meantime, Turkey-in-Europe continued on its separate path, a different Europe, cut off from the West. It became increasingly Muslim as the more enterprising Christians migrated to the new independent Christian states only to be replaced by Muslim refugees, victims of ethnic cleansing elsewhere. The percentage of Muslims in Turkey-in-Europe grew significantly in the mid-nineteenth century, from about 36 per cent in the 1840s to over 47 per cent in the 1890s.[6]

All the Sultan's European domains were isolated from the West. But none was as cut off as Albania, a land whose approximate borders were a matter of conjecture, as it encompassed several Ottoman *vilayets*, or provinces. This isolation was partly down to the fact that the Ottomans built few passable roads there. No trader or ambassador had to cross Albania to travel from Central Europe in order to reach Constantinople and the Near East. The key roads ran from Vienna and Budapest through Serbia or Romania, then through Bulgaria and Eastern Thrace. From the late 1870s they were complemented by a rail link that ran to Constantinople from Vienna and Budapest through Bucharest in Romania and then to Varna on the Black Sea, from where passengers travelled by ship to Constantinople. It was the start of the celebrated Orient Express. The completion of the line from Belgrade to Niš, Sofia and Edirne enabled the start of a more direct connection from 1888. The lands of the Albanians remained a black hole as far as railways were concerned during the Ottoman era – and for long after; the nearest railway stations were in Mitrovica, Skopje and Bitola, and the lines from these towns ran west and south-west towards Thessaloniki. Their only real purpose was military: to enable the Ottomans to move troops around and quell disturbances in Macedonia.[7]

The alternative sea routes to Constantinople ran from the ports of France, Spain or Italy through the Mediterranean. To reach Albania by land involved a long and arduous detour that few people thought worth the effort, given the Albanians' reputation for banditry.

Language and religion also isolated the Albanians from the outside world. Most of the Christian subjects of the Sultan in the Balkans spoke Greek or a Slavic language – all familiar to European scholars. The less numerous Vlachs, a scattered people, spoke a Romance tongue close to Romanian. But the Albanians inhabited a linguistic island and spoke a language that had no close relationship to any Indo-European tongue: 'plainly the sole modern survivor of its own subgroup', as the *Encyclopaedia Britannica* put it. Albanian was also split into two very different, usually mutually intelligible, dialects: Tosk in the south and Geg in the north. Very little was written in the language.

Religion was the other barrier separating Albanians from their fellow Europeans. Early medieval Albania had been overwhelmingly Catholic, and the great warrior George Castriot 'Skanderbeg', a name immortal to Albanians, spent his life in the mid-fifteenth century resisting Ottoman conquest. But, after Skanderbeg's death in 1468, Albanian resistance petered out, the Ottomans completed their conquest and most of the population converted to Islam. In the south, towards Greece, part of the population remained Orthodox Christian. In the mountains of the north, around the city of Shkodra, the Catholic Church retained a foothold. But the Catholics of northern Albania were an all but abandoned flock, as a report compiled by an Apostolic Visitor in 1671 confirmed. Pietro Stefano Gaspari wrote that many churches had fallen down, mass was rarely said in those that remained and whole villages had gone over to Islam within living memory as a result of pastoral neglect. The clergy were a poor asset, Gaspari wrote. Some were beggars, others went around armed with knives and guns. Most did not teach, or appear to know, elementary Christian dogmas. Gaspari recalled having met one priest who did not know how to make the sign of the cross. Gaspari's report gathered dust; the Vatican took little interest in Albania until the nineteenth century. Though adjacent to Italy on the other side of the Adriatic Sea, it might as well have been the Barbary Coast for all the notice that anyone took. In the eyes of Italy and of Europe, Albania was a wilderness where most people had become Muslim, and that fact alone distanced it as a concern. The Albanians had in effect ceased to be European.

That the word 'Albania' was known at all to the English-speaking public in the early nineteenth century was largely down to Byron, who passed through on his first expedition to Greece, aged 21. After reaching Patras in September 1809, he made a detour lasting several weeks to Ioannina, which now lies in Greece but was then considered the de facto capital of southern Albania, the honour normally being accorded to Shkodra in the north. He also visited Tepelena, which, alongside Ioannina, was the headquarters of the notorious warlord, Ali Pasha. He then returned to Patras and continued to Athens.

Byron liked what little he saw of Albania, making much of the semi-feudal state of his entry into Tepelena, which reminded him of one of Walter Scott's Romantic novels. 'The Albanians,' he wrote to his mother in November 1809, were:

> in their dresses, (the most magnificent in the world, consisting of a long *white kilt*, gold worked cloak, crimson velvet gold-laced jacket and waistcoat, silver mounted pistols and daggers) [...] The Turks in their vast pelisses and turbans, the soldiers and black slaves with the horses [...] in an immense large open gallery in front of the palace.

> The kettle drums beating, boys calling the hour from the minaret of the mosque, altogether, with the singular appearance of the building itself, formed a new and delightful spectacle to a stranger.[8]

Byron declared that in spite of his reputation for 'roasting rebels, etc', Ali Pasha had been the soul of friendliness. The warlord was '60 years old, very fat & not tall, but with a fine face,' he recalled. During his stay in Tepelena, Ali Pasha showered him with gifts of almonds, fruit and sugared sherbet. The Albanians, Byron concluded, were 'brave, rigidly honest & faithful [...] cruel though not treacherous, & have several vices but no meanness. They are perhaps the most beautiful race in point of countenance in the world, their women are sometimes handsome also, but they are treated like slaves.'[9]

That Byron penetrated any part of Albania was remarkable, given the dismal state of communications. It had taken him nine days just to get from Ioannina to Tepelena. But even Byron never went near the less accessible mountainous north, the land that Durham later made her own. Instead, he and his companion, John Cam Hobhouse, stuck to the flatter lands of the south, around Ioannina, which was the centre of an Ottoman *vilayet*, and was home to a mixed population of Greeks and Albanians.

Hobhouse's account of their journey, published in 1813 – *A Journey through Albania and Other Provinces of Turkey in Europe and Asia* – was one of the first books to thrust the word Albania before the British public, and capitalised on the vogue for the Orient. 'All that we have, till very lately, known of modern Albania is that it is a province of European Turkey,' Hobhouse began promisingly.[10] In the event, he had little more to say, which was not surprising, as neither he nor Byron had seen much more than Ali Pasha's colourful court. Nor did they understand Albanian. The book covered much the same territory as Byron had done in his letter to his mother. It dwelled on exotic costumes and harems and contained a large illustration of an Albanian in full rig: long hair flowing down the back, a shaven front head, puffed-out pleated kilt or *fustanella*, and shoes embellished with pompons. Hobhouse informed his readers that 'all the Albanians strut very much when they walk', had small mouths and neat teeth, and treated their women like animals.[11] The title of the book was a misnomer; the bulk of the two volumes concerned his and Byron's true obsession, which was not Albania but Greece.

Hobhouse and Byron had prised open the door to Albania. But disappointingly few people from England followed them through it, in spite of the burgeoning interest in travel accounts about the Balkans and the cult of Byron. The young Benjamin Disraeli, conducting his own Byronic tour, was one of the few to include Albania, if only Hellenised Ioannina. Visiting in 1830, he declared himself enraptured: 'For a week I was in a scene equal to anything in the Arabian Nights,' he wrote. 'Such processions, such dresses, such corteges of horsemen, such caravans of camels,' he continued, adding frivolously: 'Then the delight of being made much of by a man [the Grand Vizier] who was daily decapitating half the province.'[12]

The Scotsman David Urquhart and the painter and poet Edward Lear followed in Byron's footsteps more self-consciously than Disraeli, and saw more of Albania. Urquhart was grievously disappointed with the state of Tepelena in the 1830s, having found it much decayed. Lear travelled a decade later, in 1848, from Ohrid westwards towards Elbasan and the port of Durrës, and then heading north up the coast as far as Shkodra. The result of the expedition was a book of beautiful watercolour landscapes but also full of dull, pedestrian observations about Albania – remarks about strange costumes, bad meals and difficulties with accommodation. The expedition to Tepelena proved a disappointment, as it had done with Urquhart. 'My curiosity had been raised to its very utmost to see this place [...] yet it seemed so strange, after all one had read of the "no common pomp" of the entertainer of Lord Byron and Sir J.C. Hobhouse, to find a dreary blank scene of desolation,' Lear wrote.[13] Whatever Byron and Hobhouse had seen, or had claimed to have seen, in the early nineteenth century clearly had not outlasted Ali Pasha's death in 1822.

The vogue for accounts of Balkan journeys expanded exponentially in the late 1870s, albeit for negative reasons, following the revolts in Bosnia and Bulgaria and after the Sultan had crushed both with bloodshed. The market changed promptly and radically in tone and outlook, thanks partly to one publication, William Gladstone's bestseller, *Bulgarian Horrors and the Question of the East*, which came out in September 1876. The Liberal leader rushed the booklet out on the back of the publication of sensational newspaper reports of Ottoman atrocities in Bulgaria, which included claims that fanatical units had massacred around 30,000 Christian peasants. Thrown together in only a few days at Gladstone's country house in Hawarden, North Wales, *Bulgarian Horrors* was not a scintillating read. But the tone of moral earnestness and outrage caught the public mood and it sold 200,000 copies within a month of publication.[14] Liberal England wanted a new cause and, in Gladstone's apocalyptic view of the situation in Bulgaria, believed it had found it. Gladstone turned the tradition of rhapsodising about the *Arabian Nights* culture of the Ottoman Empire on its head. According to him, the Ottomans were:

> upon the whole, from the black day when they first entered Europe the one great anti-human specimen of humanity. Wherever they went, a broad line of blood marked the track behind them; and, as far as their dominion reached, civilisation disappeared from view.

In a memorable phrase, he added:

> Let the Turks now carry away their abuses in the only possible manner, namely by carrying off themselves. Their Zaptiehs and their Mudirs, their Bimashis and their Yuzbachis, their Kaimakams and their Pashas, one and all, bag and baggage, shall, I hope clear out from the province they have desolated and profaned.[15]

The Conservatives, from Disraeli downwards, detested the tone of *Bulgarian Horrors*, seeing it as semi-revolutionary, and they were appalled by the book's extraordinary popularity and by what became known as 'the Bulgarian agitation' – a wave of tumultuous public meetings accompanied by a torrent of pamphlets and books on the subject of the Sultan's iniquities. The claims of insurgent peasants, Christian or otherwise, held no attractions for Conservatives, and reminded some of nationalist agitation in Ireland. Queen Victoria felt caught up in the first phase of the agitation over Bulgaria. She was 'horrified by the details of the massacres in Bulgaria [...] pray consider at once what can be done,' she told Disraeli in August 1876.[16] But after Disraeli had worked on her, she swung rapidly into the opposing camp, assuring him in September of that year that she understood 'his motive for *not* expressing "horror" at the "Bulgarian atrocities" [...] and she now leaves this entirely to Lord Beaconsfield's judgment'.[17] She now deplored Liberal sentimentality about the Balkan Christians and voiced the fear that the Liberals were inadvertently, or perhaps even deliberately, encouraging Russia to intervene. In February 1877, she urged the government to stand by 'our former faithful ally, Turkey', threatening to abdicate her 'thorny crown' if they didn't.[18]

This was a tall order, because the Gladstonian Liberals had public opinion behind them as well as the massed ranks of the churches and chattering classes. Gladstone was not unusual in using bellicose language about the Ottomans. Compared to some of his fellow Liberals, he was cautious. The historian Edward Freeman drew no distinction between Turk and Ottoman or between rulers and ordinary Muslims in his book, *Ottoman Power in Europe*, published in 1877; all were equally evil. The Ottoman Empire, he wrote, was:

> Europe's foulest wrong, its blackest shame [...] the common enemy of mankind [...] His [the Turk's] dominion is perhaps

the only case in history of a lasting and settled dominion, as distinguished from merely passing inroads, which has been purely evil, without any one redeeming feature.[19]

The suffering of the Christian Slavs in the Balkans and the beastliness of the Turks and most other Muslims appealed to a new generation of writers, poets and artists who took up the theme of the *Bulgarian Horrors*. The results of these endeavours were often execrable. Tennyson, following a conversation with Gladstone, put pen to paper on little Montenegro's heroic resistance to the Turks, in 'Montenegro'. 'They kept their faith, their freedom, on the height,' he wrote, 'Chaste, frugal, savage, arm'd by day and night / Against the Turk'.[20]

The young Oscar Wilde's contribution, 'On the massacre of the Christians in Bulgaria', was yet worse. Not of course acquainted with conditions in Bulgaria at the time of the alleged massacres, he continued:

For here the air is horrid with men's groans,
The priests who call upon thy name are slain,
[...]
Come down, O Son of Man! and show Thy might
Lest Mahomet be crowned instead of Thee![21]

At first thrown onto the defensive over Bulgaria by the Liberals, the poets and the clergy (except for the Catholics under Cardinal Manning), the Tories raised a counter-clamour of their own after Russia declared war on the Ottoman Empire in 1877. This opposing movement, more anti-Russian than pro-Turkish, grew in strength in the autumn of that year, after the Russian army crossed Romania and penetrated deep into the Balkans. For a while the Ottomans halted the juggernaut outside Plevna in Bulgaria but the outcry in Britain renewed when Plevna fell after a long siege in December, when the way to Constantinople appeared open.

The readiness of Tory Britain to go to war rather than see the Tsar stage a victory parade through Constantinople was the single most important fact that determined the outcome of the international congress held in Berlin the following year under the chairmanship of the German Chancellor, Bismarck. There, Disraeli faced down Russia, persuading it to agree to the return of most of Turkey-in-Europe to the Sultan. The Russians had to abandon the punitive peace treaty they had forced earlier on the Sultan at San Stefano, which would have consigned most of Turkey-in-Europe to a large new Bulgarian state.

'The old Jew', as Bismarck had called him – albeit affectionately – had come to Berlin in June 1878 with his mind made up and he settled everything in nine days. Theatrically, the Prime Minister let it be known that he had a special train waiting to take him back to Calais if the negotiations failed. Disraeli's assistant at Berlin, Montagu Corry, recalled that the crucial discussion only lasted 'about 7 minutes'. On that basis, Disraeli was able to telegraph Queen Victoria on Saturday 22 June 1878 at 10.30 a.m., with the triumphant words: 'Russia surrenders, and accepts the English scheme [...] B[ismarc]k says, There is again a Turkey-in-Europe.' 'All due to your energy and firmness,' Victoria responded, happily.[22]

Disraeli had appeared to turn back the clock in the Balkans through sheer force of will. But he could not turn back the clock entirely. After 1876 it became difficult in Britain to profess active sympathy, let alone admiration, for anything Ottoman, Turkish or, indeed, Muslim. Sympathetic literary accounts of the luxurious courts of Ottoman pashas and their fabulous processions, costumes, slaves and harems disappeared. Gladstone's blast against the Turks was not the sole cause of this change in fashion. The Evangelical Christian revival in nineteenth-century England, coupled with the growth of the High Church 'Oxford Movement', introduced a new, more earnest, more specifically Christian tone to discussions of the Near East, as the Balkans were also termed. When Byron and Hobhouse toured the Balkans, they had looked on Greek and Albanian with equanimity, not caring whether one group was Christian and the other Muslim. But the England of the 1870s was more self-consciously religious than the England of 1813 had been, and by then the churches had helped to make undisguised hatred for Islam respectable again. As Jews and Muslims were seen as mutually supportive in the Ottoman Empire, fashionable Islamophobia fed anti-Semitism. 'Dizzy's crypto-Judaism has had to do with his policy [of sympathy for the Ottomans],' Gladstone wrote conspiratorially, adding that what 'he hates is Christian liberty'.[23] While Gladstone made these poisonous asides in private, some Liberal Party supporters went further, publicly castigating Disraeli as an 'insolent Jew' for defending the interests of the Sultan.[24] The High Church party in the Church of England, which sympathised with the Orthodox Church for theological reasons and took a prominent role in the agitation over Bulgaria, made the same point. In its house organ, the *Church Times*, it lambasted Disraeli in 1876 as the 'Jew Premier'.[25] In this new discourse, both Jews and Muslims were openly described as enemies. The crusading language, and the way that Liberals made boasts of their special sympathy for the Sultan's Christian subjects and of their contempt for Muslims, would have astonished Byron.

This change of heart over Islam spilled over into discussions of the relative merits of the Balkan races, and the reputation of the Albanians suffered on account of their association with Islam. 'The Albanian Mahommedan represents a doubly conquered race,' Adeline Irby and Georgiana Mackenzie wrote in a much-praised book on the Balkans, *Travels in the Slavonic Provinces of Turkey-in-Europe*, meaning conquered by Islam as well as by Turkey. The Albanian was 'a European who has lost not only liberty but religion, whose past is barbarian, his present apostasy, and his future either a sneaking return to his former faith, or slavery to a despotic government,' they added.[26] First published in 1867, the book was reprinted in 1877, at the time of the 'agitation', containing an adulatory foreword by Gladstone.

Irby and Mackenzie reflected and helped direct the new way of thinking on Balkan questions, which drew a sharp line between Christians and Muslims. These two fervent champions of the Christian Slavs strongly disapproved of all Balkan Muslims and felt especially hostile to the Albanians, above all towards those they had encountered in the ethnically mixed *vilayet* of Kosovo. The fact that Albanians made up the majority of the population of Kosovo did not impress them. On the contrary, the number of these religious renegades made it more urgent that they be brought 'under civilization', which they defined as meaning the control of Christian Serbia. 'Were the southern frontier of the principality [of Serbia] extended so as to include Old Serbia [Kosovo], we should soon see brigandage put down and all clans and classes equal before the law,' they wrote.[27]

Turkey in Europe, a large volume by Lieutenant Colonel James Baker, also published in 1877, similarly had nothing good to say of the Albanians, who were:

> extremely dirty in their persons, seldom changing their clothes until they drop off and avoiding the external application of water as though it were poison.
>
> When not engaged in border forays, they are chiefly occupied in making firearms and gunpowder, herding and stealing large flocks of sheep and cattle, and collecting skins and furs.[28]

William Stillman's *Herzegovina and the Late Uprising*, again published in 1877, put the boot into Muslims generally. The moral qualities of the Bosnians, he opined, depended on their geographical location: 'The nearer the Montenegrin frontier the better the man; and in the lower country, where the predominance of the Mussulman [Muslim] element has been more complete, the character of the people is correspondingly debased.'[29] Like Gladstone, he advocated the expulsion of the Ottomans from Europe 'bag and baggage', and the installation of foreign, European governors. 'The Mussulman as a material for this purpose is mere dead bone, and must be eliminated,' he wrote, chillingly.

> Subordination of the governor to legislation never enters into the conception of one of his race, not even those who have the dubious advantage of European education. The absolute extirpation of Mussulman heads of administration – bag and baggage if needs be – is the essential basis of reorganization.[30]

The uniform hostility shown towards Islam in the books of the 1870s created a new consensus in Britain on the Balkans, alien to the spirit of the writers of an earlier generation. That tone had not altered by the time that Edith Durham arrived in Dalmatia. By then, Britain was under the hand of another Tory, Lord Salisbury, Disraeli's foreign secretary at the time of the Berlin Congress, and two decades of uneasy peace that had prevailed in the Balkans since the Congress were coming to an end. The failure of the powers to coordinate policy on the Balkans after Berlin meant that when tensions boiled over between the new Balkan states and the Ottoman Empire, nothing could restrain them. A new era of turbulence was beginning, which would climax with the assassination of the Archduke Franz Ferdinand in Sarajevo in June 1914.

Macedonia remained especially restless. Disraeli's great victory at the Berlin Congress had been to force Russia to agree to return it to the Sultan. But this arrangement could not last forever. The Slavs of Macedonia had been outraged to see the promise of union with Bulgaria, tendered by Russia in the Treaty of San Stefano, snatched away. Tired of waiting for matters to change in their favour, they turned to terrorism, forming the Internal Macedonian Revolutionary Organization, the IMRO. In theory dedicated to the creation of an independent or autonomous Macedonia, in practice the IMRO was largely a Bulgarian front, drawing almost exclusively on that element among the Slavic population that identified most with Sofia. The security situation in Macedonia deteriorated rapidly. As one recent history put it:

> Starting in 1900 the different groups began their campaigns, ravaging the countryside, slaughtering officials as well as Muslim and Christian subjects who refused to accept their points of view. Trains and postal carriages were intercepted, foreigners and wealthy natives kidnapped for ransom, churches blown up. Macedonia became a common expression of horror in the foreign press.[31]

In 1900, the year that Durham arrived in the Balkans, the IMRO concocted a plan to blow up the railway line carrying the Orient Express as it crossed through Thrace towards Constantinople. However, Macedonia was home to a medley of different peoples, all professing different loyalties, which impeded the possibility of joint action against the Ottomans. Slavs who identified with Serbia and Muslims who remained loyal to the Sultan did not wish to be catapulted into a big Bulgaria. The Albanians in the west and the Jews – very numerous in Thessaloniki – still looked to Constantinople for redress of their grievances; the Jews did not have many complaints in any case. As for those who considered themselves Greek, they would do nothing either without a nod from Athens, which never came. Greece, like Serbia, opposed the IMRO, seeing it as a tool of Bulgaria to force matters and make off with the Macedonian prize.

This was the complex world into which Durham, at first nothing more than a middle-aged tourist with a Baedeker guide and a set of paintbrushes, was to immerse herself. But she soon decided she had an aptitude for Balkan politics and an ability to decode the conflicting signals. As she wrote, much later, of her starting point in Montenegro: 'It was in Cetinje in August 1900 that I first picked up a thread of the Balkan tangle, little thinking how deeply emeshed I would later become.'[32]

CHAPTER 2

'The other end of nowhere'

O smallest among peoples! Rough rock-throne
Of Freedom! Warriors beating back the swarm
Of Turkish Islam for five hundred years,
Great Tsernagora!
                    (Alfred Lord Tennyson, 'Montenegro', 1877)[1]

EDITH DURHAM KNEW she had some form of vocation in the Balkans almost as soon as she stepped off the boat in Dalmatia. Exactly what form it would take was not clear. The agreement she had reached with her family in 1900 was only that she might take an extended spring or summer holiday every year, after which she would return to London to look after her mother.

It soon became obvious, to her and her family, that this first trip down the Adriatic would not be the last. Why she selected the Austrian province of Dalmatia for this initial foray is unclear. Given her evident determination to make up for lost time and explore, rather than merely sightsee, it is unsurprising that she preferred to start in this part of the world rather than follow the better-trodden tourist paths of Italy and southern France.

The choice was a good one. At once she felt convinced that she belonged here in a way that she had never belonged in England. The primary colours of Dalmatia were reviving, a welcome change from the dreary grey and pastel shades of her homeland. Leaving Trieste, she was struck by the contrast of the deep indigo of the Adriatic and the dazzling white of the shoreline and the bell towers of the Croatian churches spotted from the boat. Dalmatia was deliciously bright. However, she knew next to nothing of the region and its peoples and her initial observations were naive. The Croats, she wrote to her mother, 'have dark curly hair, ferocious black moustaches, clean cut aquiline features and 6 feet is quite a common height'. They also 'squat on their haunches just like savages'.[2]

After only a few days, however, the thrill of Dalmatia began to pall. On finding the centre of the city of Split under scaffolding – part of an Austrian plan to tidy it up by clearing the site around the cathedral of St Domnius – Durham could not stifle a feeling of disappointment. With its army of improving bureaucrats, Dalmatia was not the unknown aboriginal land she craved. Feeling restless, on 1 September she set off to Bosnia and Herzegovina for the market town of Trebinje, a few miles inland from Dubrovnik. Bosnia was not a separate country and had been under the control of Austria-Hungary since 1878. The same bureaucrats were busy taming the landscape and improving things here, too. But it still seemed a world away from the overly managed province of Dalmatia, which had been under Austria's thumb for far longer. Starting out from Dubrovnik at seven in the morning, Durham's spirits rose as she passed a large white stone reading 'Herzegovina' and entered Franz Joseph's newest acquisition. Passing a couple of Martello towers on which some soldiers sat dangling bandy legs, Durham found the town crammed on market day. This was more like it – peasants in archaic-looking costumes and sporting headdresses 'that begged description; the blaze of coin jewellery, scarlet caps and lace veils and embroidered clothes, both of the men and women'. It had all to 'be seen to be believed'. The profusion of earrings, necklaces, clasps and finger rings was such 'that you wonder how they got them all on'.[3]

Durham returned from Bosnia feeling that Dalmatia was too dull, and she was determined to venture deeper into lesser-known recesses of the Balkans. Little Trebinje had been a discovery but for all its oriental flavour it was still part of Austria and its sights, however colourful, could not satisfy her appetite for otherness, for lands beyond the reach of the solid, safe hands of Austria's dutiful bureaucrats.

A week later, having moved south down the coast of Dalmatia to the Bay of Kotor, she set out for the high peaks of the principality of Montenegro. As she began the long zigzagging climb 4,000 feet above the bay, catching dizzy-making views of the fjords, Durham felt excited by the stark scenery, so different from the gentle, domesticated world below. 'Such utter desolation and barren wilderness,' she mused. 'Such heaps and piled-up heaps of bare crags make one feel that one has arrived at the end of the world or the other end of nowhere.'[4] After that introduction, the capital, Cetinje, was a letdown: 'the ugliest, oddest toy capital conceivable,' she wrote. 'A straight street nearly as wide as Portland Place of one storeyed, red tiled cottages sat down in the middle of a plain encircled by mountains'. It was 'just like Ladysmith or Mafeking, barring the corrugated iron'.[5]

Most European visitors tended to react that way. When the Anglo-Irish travel writer Captain James Creagh visited Cetinje in 1875, he wrote, 'My first impulse on arriving in the main street [...] was to burst out laughing. It is the meanest capital in the whole civilized or uncivilized world; and the village of the most petty rajah, or chief, in India, is in every way superior to this small collection of Montenegrin cabins.'[6]

Durham initially dismissed Cetinje, and indeed all of Montenegro, as 'a Gilbert and Sullivan opera'.[7] Minute in size, the entire country had a population of only about 100,000. The tiny capital nevertheless boasted a two-storey royal palace, a stately mini-palace for the use of the heir to the throne, a theatre and an enormous Austro-Hungarian embassy, completed in 1899. A surprisingly large diplomatic corps had grown up in town since the Berlin Congress, when Montenegro's independence had been formally recognised, befitting its status as one of the powers' listening posts in the Balkans. For all that, most of the consuls still lived in cottages; the consulates of Russia, Italy, France, Germany, Britain and Greece were not completed until the end of the first decade of the twentieth century.[8] For lack of other options, the consuls dined at the same table on the upper floor of Cetinje's one decent hotel, the Grand, which had first opened back in the 1860s as the Lokanda.

Durham soon made herself at home in the Grand, mining the comic side of diplomatic life for the benefit of her family, jotting down the quarrels that regularly erupted between the diplomats over the dining room table. 'The Grand Hotel was in truth the centre of the life of the town,' she recalled later:

> Upstairs, where the Powers dined, the conversation was limited to more or less harmless topics. Downstairs, where there was a second-class dining room and a billiard table, Montenegrin officials and officers thronged and discussed heatedly and loudly the foreign politics of the day. For at Cetinje, as in other Balkan capitals, politics was almost a nervous disease.[9]

Beyond the welcome element of comedy, Montenegro had more of what Durham was seeking than Dalmatia or Bosnia. Montenegro really was a land apart from the enervating safety and predictability of Western Europe. Durham liked the lean look of people who 'preferred liberty in the wilderness to slavery in fat lands', their devil-may-care attitude, and even the fact that they smoked from morning till night, 'rolling up the next cigarette before the last is finished'. It amused her that several men had asked for her hand in marriage almost immediately.[10]

Montenegro, 'The Black Mountain', was not only intriguingly different from England, Germany and Austria-Hungary. It differed in one significant way from the other Christian states of the Balkans. Serbia, Greece and Bulgaria were new entities, very new in the case of Bulgaria, which had only emerged as an autonomous principality by courtesy of the Berlin Congress. Each traced its descent to an ancient kingdom or empire that the Ottoman Turks had extinguished in its prime. But, as modern states, none dated back more than decades. Montenegro was in a category of its own, having survived several centuries of Ottoman rule in the Balkans inviolate, a tiny island of Christian and Slavic freedom in a Muslim, Ottoman ocean.

This was partly because it was too small, barren and unimportant for the Ottomans to care about. Comprising no more than a range of mountains, it had no agriculture to speak of and no mines or industry of any kind. 'The manufactures of Montenegro,' Sir John Wilkinson wrote in 1848, 'if they can be so called [...] may be on a par with the manufactures of the Bedouins or Arabs of the desert', consisting mainly of a few items of furniture and coarse woollen garments.[11]

Montenegro might have carried on in this way, lively but forgotten, a quaint historical anomaly, like Liechtenstein, Andorra or San Marino. However, in 1715 the country's ruler, Bishop Danilo, had journeyed to Russia and presented himself to Tsar Peter I, who took the tiny Orthodox Christian enclave under Russia's giant wing. The alliance that Danilo forged with the Tsar had tremendous consequences for Montenegro, which found itself elevated from obscurity to the role of Russian protégé in the Balkans.

Montenegro's rulers were then a succession of Orthodox bishops, all of whom, from Danilo onwards, descended from the same Petrović family. But in 1852 the last of the prince-bishops, also named Danilo, secularised the dynasty, quit holy orders and married. His son, Nikola, came to the throne in 1860 and was still on it 40 years later, when Durham made his acquaintance.

Foreign visitors to Montenegro rhapsodised about Montenegro's Ruritanian flavour. 'Such is this strange and wonderful little state, the living relic of an age and order of things long since passed away,' Edson Clark wrote in an 1878 book, *The Races of European Turkey*, after an enthusiastic description of the strength, beauty and chastity of Montenegrin women, or, as he put it, 'the maidens of the Black Mountain'.[12] Writing almost 20 years later, William Miller felt charmed by the idea of Nikola as mini-despot. 'He can truly say, like the Grand Monarque, *L'état, c'est moi,*' he exulted. 'He is practically his own Premier, and both practically and theoretically his own Lord Chancellor and commander-in-chief. Whoever would see benevolent despotism in full working order had better go to Montenegro, whose ruler assured the present writer that there would be no parliamentary government there for a century.'[13]

Much of the Ruritanian flavour to which these writers, including Durham at one point, warmed was artifice. It was Nikola who had more or less designed the national costume and made wearing it practically obligatory. Both Nikola and his wife, the stately Milena, set an example in this regard, rarely appearing dressed like their counterparts in Europe. Milena scorned the bustles, tight corsets and hairpieces of contemporary European princesses, letting her abundant hair flow freely down her back and dressing in free-flowing peasant-like skirts. Nikola favoured a peasant-style white or cream jerkin and a round scarlet cap.

Behind the Gilbert and Sullivan touches that Durham remarked on, Nikola was a skilled political manipulator, well versed in the art of playing one power off another while remaining close to Russia, his chief ally and paymaster. His greatest asset in this diplomatic game was a squad of statuesque brunette daughters, most of whom he married off with an eye to Montenegro's strategic ambitions. Milica and Anastasia were dispatched to Russia to strengthen the all-important connection with the Tsar. The marriages of these striking but penniless women to Russian archdukes were a tremendous coup. But Nikola did not wager everything on the Russian connection.

With several other tall, marriageable daughters to play with, he sent a third, Jelena, to marry the Italian Crown Prince, Victor Emmanuel, who duly became King of Italy four years later, in 1900. The Italian marriage was another triumph for Nikola, who set great store by becoming grandfather to a future monarch. Durham, then staying in Cetinje, recalled with some amusement his disappointment when the couple's first child turned out to be a girl. 'Old King Nikola had a gun mounted ready to salute the arrival of his grandson,' she recalled:

> Orders went around that we were all to rejoice by putting candles in our windows. The hotel put a row ready in my room. We waited [...] at lunchtime in bounced a Perianik (Royal Guard) and saluted. The tutor was summoned to the palace. We waited breathlessly. Back came the tutor; he paused at the door, sighed and murmured sadly: *'Excellences – nous avons une fille!'* Poor Princess Yolanda [Jelena's daughter]! Cetinje tried to look as though nothing had happened. The gun was silent; the candles unlit.[14]

Nikola's disappointment over the birth of a princess did not last long. Following the birth of another daughter, Mafalda, Jelena and Victor Emmanuel produced the longed-for son, Umberto, in 1904, and he later became Italy's last and briefest monarch.[15]

Meanwhile Nikola had other daughters to sort out. Ana was sent north to Germany to marry into the house of Battenberg while his eldest son, Danilo, married Jutta of Mecklenberg-Strelitz. The German marriages did more than link the house of Petrović to that of a few German aristocrats. They 'brought his family into special favour with Queen Victoria, whom he visited at Windsor in 1898'.[16]

Zorka, meanwhile, married Petar Karadjordjević, then the exiled head of one of Serbia's two alternating dynasties. Had she not died young in 1890, she would have become the Queen of Serbia when her husband acceded to the throne in 1903.

Zorka's untimely demise was a diplomatic as well as a personal disaster for Nikola, wrecking his plans to have an ally at the centre of the royal household in Belgrade. The relationship between Montenegro and Serbia was complex and needed constant steering. Both saw themselves as Serbian states, which meant that they were rivals as well as allies.

Montenegro's claim to be the standard-bearer of Serbdom had gone unchallenged at the beginning of the nineteenth century when Serbia proper was still under Ottoman rule. But it was steadily undermined from the 1830s, once an autonomous principality of Serbia emerged.

At first, the new entity posed no competition to its older sister. Few foreigners visited the principality of Serbia in those years, which in theory remained a fiefdom of the Sultan's. Those that did usually returned with unfavourable reports. Sutherland Menzies, in *Turkey Old and New*, in 1880, wrote of the 'melancholy [...] sight of [...] here and there a heap of cabins dignified by the name of towns', complaining of 'the semi-savage inhabitants [...] careless, coarse mannered and unindustrious'.[17] The term 'melancholy' was also applied to the country's turbulent politics, which were characterised by coups, forced abdications and assassinations.

The reign of Milan, who took the throne in 1868, was one of several low points in Serbia's odyssey as an independent state. Often to be seen rowing in an undignified fashion in public with his wife, Natalije, he told one of his ministers that she had 'the face of a tigress'.[18] There was a shocking scene in the cathedral in Belgrade on Easter morning in 1888 when the King tried to force her to bestow a public Easter kiss on his mistress, which she refused to do, after which the royal couple began fighting with each other in front of a congregation of diplomats. An onlooker recalled that the King 'shook himself into a fury, rushed at the Queen and would have strangled her if several officers had not intervened and dragged him back'.[19]

Natalije got her own back, sending some of his most embarrassing private letters to the French press for publication.[20] The antics of Serbia's royal couple were the talk of Europe. The Serbian foreign minister, Čedomilj Mijatović, recalled that the pair 'hated each other, brought their quarrels to the market place of Europe and made them a public scandal of which even their most devoted subjects and friends were ashamed'.[21] After Milan launched, and lost, an almost inexplicable war with Bulgaria in 1885, he abdicated in 1889. At the time some observers described both Serbia and Greece as failed states.[22]

Over these decades, Montenegro maintained its ascendancy over Serbia. The throne of the Petrovićs' in Cetinje appeared stable and august compared to the rickety throne in Belgrade. But, in spite of Milan's erratic behaviour, the differences in the two countries' respective demographic assets began to tell. The austere beauty of Montenegro that delighted the casual visitor was a beauty born of poverty and barrenness. As one sympathetic British visitor reported of Montenegro in 1849:

> With a population of little more than one hundred and ten thousand souls, her part must ever remain a subordinate one [...] without either fertile plains or access to the sea, the humanising influences of commerce and agriculture must remain dormant and inoperative.[23]

The poverty and daily hunger of many ordinary Montenegrins appalled the more perceptive observers, some of whom compared the conditions to those in the worst parts of Ireland and Scotland.[24]

Serbia, on the other hand, was loamy and fertile, a land overflowing with food. A London clergyman, William Denton, noted that:

> the forests of Servia abound with such game as is usually met with in England – hares, stags and foxes [...] wild fowl

abound in the islands and on the low grounds which border on the Danube; the ortolan, the quail and the snipe are common [...] the rivers are equally prolific, and the sturgeon of the Danube is a dainty and common dish.[25]

Although Serbia remained undeveloped and had few towns, it still had a population of 1.25 million, even by the 1860s, which was more than ten times the population of Montenegro. Moreover, possession of the city of Belgrade gave the Serbs a large, strategically important capital, especially after 1862, when they expelled the last Ottoman garrison from the fortress in the middle of the city. No such claim could be made for Cetinje. The European powers gradually came to acknowledge the growing disparity between the two Serbian states. At the Berlin Congress they had rewarded both Montenegro and Serbia with slices of territory at the expense of the Ottomans. Nikola obtained the towns of Podgorica and Nikšić in the interior as well as a long-sought port on the Adriatic at Bar. The population increased from around 196,000 to around 280,000. But Serbia obtained much more territory and many more people than Montenegro in 1878, including the towns of Niš, Leskovac, Pirot and Vranje, and as a result of these gains and natural increase Serbia's population now rose to almost 1.7 million. It was becoming clear to everyone that the future of the pan-Serbian movement lay in Belgrade, not in Cetinje.

By the time that Durham arrived in the Balkans in 1900 Nikola's authority in Montenegro was being challenged. As part of his campaign to keep the more undesirable democratic aspects of the modern world at bay, he had neglected to found any institution of higher education. He was not hostile to education per se, and primary schools multiplied during his reign. He had also founded a seminary school and, in 1869, a girls' academy in Cetinje, the Montenegrin Institute, though the money for this came from the Russian royal family. But there was no university, and as a result, after the Serbs established a university in Belgrade in 1863, the better-off Montenegrin families began sending their sons there. Many of these young men then returned with ardently pro-Serbian views. As the Croatian historian Ivo Banac put it:

> Montenegrin expatriates, who constituted almost half the country's population by the eve of the First World War, especially the fair number of students who attended Serbian high schools and the University of Belgrade, had a great deal to do with the lessening of Montenegro's reputation and the spread of the sentiment that only a reactionary could be a loyal Montenegrin.[26]

The advantageous marriages that Nikola's daughters had contracted gained him the nickname 'the uncle of Europe'. But the marriages alone did not provide a sufficient counterweight to the other forces eroding his prestige in relation to Serbia. By the 1900s, Nikola knew he had to bolster his status more forcefully if matters were not to deteriorate, which meant acquiring more territory. With Montenegro hemmed in on two sides by the Adriatic Sea and by Austria-Hungary, this could only come from the Albanian lands to the south, inside the Ottoman Empire. This ambition would lead to a total breach with Durham, once the Prince's admirer and confidante.

This, however, lay in the future. Durham at first was content to luxuriate in the sheer oddness of Montenegro, a piece of granite that came complete with a court, princesses and ambassadors. Her priority was not to become an intimate of the royal family in any case but to explore those parts of the Balkans that few others had seen.

One of her first expeditions in Montenegro took her to the remote, seventeenth-century monastery of Ostrog, which was perched on a crag above the Bjelopavlići plain, several hours' ride from Cetinje. Few of the foreign diplomats based in Montenegro had ventured there. That a well-born foreign woman was even thinking of going, alone, struck them as incredible. Durham set out regardless. The ascent was memorable. In spite of her facility with languages and rapid progress in Serbian, she could not communicate effectively with her teenage girl guide, who resorted to snorting like a pig each time she wanted Durham to turn this way or that. On reaching the summit, after hours of these snorts, a shattered Durham was informed that, as a mere woman, she would not be allowed to enter. Thankfully the archimandrite of the monastery appeared, showed her round the church and gave her dinner, enabling her to return to Cetinje in triumph.

The journey to Ostrog earned Durham a reputation, at first confined to the diplomats in Cetinje, as a highly unusual woman who was prepared to undertake expeditions that no foreign woman and very few men had ever considered. She followed up the conquest of Ostrog with journeys to other destinations in Montenegro, including the port of Bar, which Nikola had obtained from the Ottomans at Berlin, and the port of Ulcinj, which he subsequently obtained in 1880. Both were sleepy, mainly Muslim, towns and the sight of a foreign woman travelling unaccompanied by a husband or some other suitable male escort created much the same sensation there that the journey to Ostrog had done. Ulcinj, or Dulcigno, as it was known, was one of the most ancient ports on the Adriatic, but was now so rarely visited that it had only one inn, which had neither windows nor furniture. Durham sat on the floor cross-legged, staring at the blazing open fire, reflecting on the probability that even Anglo-Saxon inns in England had boasted tables of some sort. The innkeeper and his wife were astonished when she pulled out two hitherto unseen items, a bar of soap and some toothpaste, after which they begged her to remain with them forever. As word of the remarkable Englishwoman spread throughout Ulcinj, people came to stare through the doorway of the inn at their visitor, including a man who stood there, solemnly declaiming to her in English the only words he knew: 'dog', 'cat', 'horse' and 'man'.[27]

Expeditions to remote parts of Montenegro awakened a desire in Durham to go further. In the distance beckoned the bluish-tinted mountains of northern Albania, a land into which scarcely anyone from the West had penetrated, except some hardy Catholic clergy. The main city in northern Albania, Shkodra – Scutari, as it was then known, or Skadar, as the Serbs called it – lay on the far side of a large lake on the border of Montenegro to which it had given its name.

Shkodra was practically the only place in northern Albania that anyone from Europe had visited. A sizable trading town, several great powers maintained consuls there. For all that, Shkodra had only recently opened up to the world, and only partially. When Creagh visited in 1875, he maintained that only a few years had passed since 'the population was so fanatical that no European dared walk the streets in his native dress; and the French consul, who happened to be the first political agent sent there, was threatened with death unless he wore the fez'.[28] Even in Creagh's time, the women, Christian or Muslim, all wore veils outdoors, and the town appeared a world away from its neighbours to the north in Austrian Dalmatia. It was a mysterious place to him. 'Surrounded by walls more than twenty feet high and generally placed in the centre of pretty flower gardens, the houses can hardly be seen,' he wrote:

> Streams of water purl gently in the centre of the lanes or streets, and single arched bridges [...] about a yard high, enable foot passengers to go across [...] when the gates of these pleasant residences are shut, Scutari appears like a labyrinth of stone; and the lanes, the running and limpid streams, the quaint bridges and fords, present such uniformity of appearance that it is difficult for a stranger to find his way.[29]

Durham did not make it to Albania during her first expedition to the Balkans in the summer of 1900. The opportunity to reach Shkodra did not arise until her second summer visit to Cetinje, in June 1901, when she encountered a group of Frenchmen, 'French swells', as she called them, who were on their way to visit the French consul in Shkodra. After deciding to accompany them, Durham boarded a steamer that took them over the lake into the Ottoman Empire. In a dreamlike state, she felt entranced as the boat gently ploughed through beds of water lilies and forests of reeds. Spoonbills and herons, disturbed from their frog and fish hunts, flapped past her as the hazy mountains drew closer and as the skyline of the city revealed itself in the mist. The Frenchmen disappeared with their consul, who had ridden out to their steamer in high state, complete with six rowers and flags flying, and Durham found herself alone on the quay and not a little frightened, surrounded by mobs of screaming children until the kindly Montenegrin captain of the steamer appeared and 'whacked the little boys off us and selected a clean one' to take her to a hotel.[30] At once, her fears vanished, giving way to a sensation of having crossed a threshold into the unknown. The boy guide, she recalled, 'set off like a hare and plunged into the depths of the bazaar, dim dark passages crowded with Albanians, dazzling sun spots through the broken roof, dashes of brilliant colour, shouts, cries, donkeys, stenches'. Durham hurried after him, trying not to slip on slimy cobbles drenched in donkey manure. 'The boy whirled round corners and over puddles and dodged packs of people' before they emerged beyond the bazaar, at which point Durham was hurled into a fly that galloped off to a hotel run by a portly Greek. The next day, accompanied by the hotel gofer, whose knowledge of English consisted of one phrase, 'This is Scutari Albanese' ('This is Albanian Shkodra'), Durham returned to the bazaar to find out whether it would have the same magical effect, which it did. 'The swarming seething mass of savages I can give you no idea of,'[31] she wrote breathlessly to her family on her return to Cetinje.

'The wild men of the mountains [were] clad in striped legs and sheep's skins, heavily armed with magnificent silver weapons,' she noted, 'and girdled with cartridges, the handsome Christian Albanian women from the mountains in more clothes than you can imagine [...] then there were the Christian women of the town in white and scarlet, masses of coins, silver buttons and embroidery.' Durham felt dizzy, assailed by 'the unutterable rags, the squalor and the gorgeousness, the heaps of newly flayed hides sizzling in the sun, the clatter and slither of pack animals, the goats, the cattle, the oxcarts and the dust'.[32]

Among the Albanians, Durham felt as if she were stretching her wings. She no longer felt strange and out of place as the only woman, the only Briton and the only non-diplomat, seated at the dining table of the self-important consuls stationed in the hotel in Cetinje, listening to squabbles over which consulate flew the largest flag.

By the spring of 1902, on her third expedition to the Balkans, she had already fashioned a role for herself as a kind of semi-permanent part of the scene in Cetinje. She felt increasingly intrigued by the royal family, whom she glimpsed from time to time in the distance. A chance to see the family *en fête* arose soon after her arrival back in Cetinje that year, when flags went up all over town in honour of Princess Milena's saint's name day, or *slava*. Bands blasted away in the park, illuminations lit up the town in the evening and from her hotel bedroom Durham observed candles flickering in every window in honour of the Princess. Later, she hurried to the theatre where the royal family was due to attend the premiere of a play on the theme of heroic Montenegrin battles with the Turks. The following day, she saw them all again, filing out of a service in the monastery church, followed by a procession of diplomats in cocked hats. By now, she felt the time was right to establish some contact with the royal family, who she was certain must have heard of her activities. The problem was that of all the great powers, her own, Britain, was at that point the least interested in Balkan affairs and, as a result, no British diplomat was stationed in Cetinje. Durham was unwilling to solicit an audience without direct diplomatic mediation. She would not meet the Prince just yet.

Having exhausted the possibilities of Montenegro, that year she decided to branch out and undertake a grand tour of Serbia, starting in Belgrade and working her way south to the border with Bulgaria and the Ottoman Empire. Later in life, by which point anger at what the Serbs had done to the Albanians had consumed her, she rarely referred to her travels in Serbia. This is not surprising. The book she compiled at the end of her tour, *Through the Lands of the Serb*, was a glowing portrait of the country's achievements and prospects.

Physically, the Serbs did not attract Durham. Short, dark, slow and abstemious, they were not like the 'long legged giants who strode tirelessly over the crags' in Montenegro and who shot back glasses of *rakija* when not endlessly rolling their cigarettes. The Serbs were not a people about whom it was easy to entertain romantic feelings. The inhabitants of Belgrade, Durham noted at the beginning of her expedition, walked slowly and cautiously along their streets, almost continually drank glasses of water and appeared devoted to dull pursuits such as card games and chess. Each town in Serbia looked like the last: the same wide street lined with red-tiled houses; the same unlovely, modern Orthodox church; and the same large, functional schoolhouse. The Serbs appeared to be puritans and disciplinarians, tolerating neither prostitutes nor beggars. Their idea of entertainment could also be morbid. When Durham left Belgrade for Čačak, a little to the south, the local notables laid on a treat for their visitor – a front-row seat at a public execution. They were disappointed and surprised when she declined to attend.

The country people of Serbia turned out to be as cautious and unexciting as the townsmen. Travelling round rural Serbia with a peasant guide was torture. The men insisted on starting every journey excruciatingly early, at around 5 a.m., but did not accomplish much from these dawn starts because they moved at a snail's pace. To Durham's frustration, a journey of a few miles could take up to around 15 hours, several hours of which her peasant guide would spend 'tootling wooden pipes under beech trees' while Durham seethed nearby. She began to dread arriving in those same-looking villages, each centred on a bare, whitewashed inn whose walls were lined with flyblown portraits of Serbian royals and a few copper pots dangling from nails.

For all that, Serbia's air of industry and manifest destiny marked it out from Montenegro, and Durham was alert to the difference. Serbia was not picturesque, nor were the Serbs – but the country was developing at a tremendous rate. Railway lines had been laid down, several towns now had electric lighting, some had army barracks and all had schools. Durham regularly encountered children marching in crocodile fashion to school. Serbia, she declared, was 'an amazing land'.[33]

Just as it had done in Ulcinj, the arrival of the Englishwoman in the remote towns of provincial Serbia caused a sensation. Delegations of teachers, policemen and mayors trooped to her hotel in the hope of an introduction, or just came to stare. 'I made a sort of triumphant progress,' she recalled, 'and was passed from town to town.'[34]

Durham finished her progress on a high note. Not satisfied with seeing only the existing kingdom of Serbia within the borders settled at the Berlin Congress, she risked an additional trip to the *terra irredenta* of Kosovo, crossing Serbia's southern border into the Ottoman *vilayet* and heading into what Serbs called 'Old Serbia', in homage to its former role, at the heart of the medieval Serbian Empire.

The goal was to reach the ancient headquarters of the Serbian Orthodox Church at Peć (Peje in Albanian), where for several centuries the Patriarchs of Serbia were enthroned and buried, until the Ottomans had the see suppressed in the mid-eighteenth century.[35] This was a far riskier journey than the short trip to Shkodra. Few westerners had attempted to cross Kosovo in recent years. Of all the Ottoman *vilayets* in Europe, Kosovo was reckoned the most lawless and dangerous. The Serbs regarded Kosovo with longing as their ancestral homeland, and the feeling of longing was increased by the fact that Kosovo was out of reach, and under the thumb of the Ottomans. They wanted it back. As Durham wrote to her mother, more in admiration than anything else at this point, the Serbs were 'extraordinarily visionary and dream dreams of the Great Servia that is to be [though...] they have not the faintest idea of how to set about it'.[36] As Noel Malcolm remarks, the fact that the Patriarchate lay in Peć was one of the principal justifications for Serbia's claim to Kosovo as a whole.[37]

However, the Serbs were now only a small minority there, their depleted villages having long since filled up with Albanians who had drifted east over the mountains of Albania proper and resettled the Kosovo plain. The splendid monasteries at Peć and at Dečani had become small pools of Serbdom in a none-too-friendly sea of Muslim Albanians.

The Ottomans regarded this demographic shift with approval. Britain had saved Turkey-in-Europe from shipwreck in 1878 but the Ottomans had still been forced to cede significant slices of land to Serbia and Montenegro at Berlin, and resented the losses. If they didn't actively encourage the Albanian incomers to harass the dwindling Serbian communities in Kosovo, they did nothing to stop them. Durham, at the height of her pro-Serbian phase, observed everything through Serbian spectacles. What the Ottoman tax collector did not take from the Serb, the Albanian looted, she remarked.

The province also appeared to swarm with brigands and highwaymen, and the roads on which they operated seemed to have disintegrated. Durham was unconcerned by the danger. Later she declared that this was because the ten months of each year that she still had to spend in England, until her mother's death in 1906, were so grim that the prospect of an untimely death in the Balkans seemed positively inviting. 'My two months' liberty each year [...] made the endless vista of grey imprisonment at home the more intolerable,' she wrote in her book, *Twenty Years of Balkan Tangle*. 'And a bullet would have been a short way out.'[38]

It took Edith almost 17 hours to ride from the Ottoman border to Peć, starting just before 5 a.m. The seat of the Serbian Orthodox Church she found 'filthy and awful', full of dogs and hovels. To her dismay, the monks in the monastery church were so amazed to see her that they would not let her go to bed but forced her to sit in a chair in the moonlight, answering endless questions before finally handing her a dish of meatballs and a glass of *rakija*. She collapsed exhausted. From Peć she rode the next day to the other great monument to Serbia's vanished glory in Kosovo, the fourteenth-century monastery of Dečani, founded by King Stefan and also his mausoleum. She was the first English person to make it there in 15 years, the impressed monks told her. She then returned to Peć by nightfall. Peć was one of the few places in the Balkans where Durham ever confessed to having felt afraid, but as she tucked herself into bed she comforted herself by telling herself: 'Savage as are the Albanians, I have been told repeatedly that they never assault women.'[39]

After a second difficult night, spent in a hovel in a village in Montenegro, where she shared her bed with 'the most alarming insects', some of which she pondered capturing and sending to her scientist brother, Herbert, Edith returned to Montenegro to even greater acclaim. Scaling a mountain to Ostrog monastery had already impressed the fastidious diplomats of Cetinje. Crossing the lawless province of Kosovo all the way to Peć and Dečani in order to gain a more complete picture of Serbian life was a feat of a different order. Most Serbs and Montenegrins would not have dreamt of undertaking such a perilous trip across these badlands. As word of Durham's adventures spread, she found herself treated as a living legend in Montenegro – a *dobar junak* (great hero) in the eyes of the people, 'which has its inconvenience', she told her mother, 'as it means that the other *dobar junaks*, of which there are many, all stand one drinks'.[40] Her unmarried state – and who would have the privilege of altering this unheard-of state of affairs for a woman in her late thirties – was the talk of the Montenegrin countryside, as was her pedigree. To her amusement Durham learned that she was rumoured to be a noblewoman who had fled to Montenegro following a scandalous engagement to a man of low rank of whom her family disapproved. Word of her expedition to Kosovo also reached the ears of Prince Nikola, who was curious to see this strange, foreign woman who had seen the shrines of the Serbs in Kosovo – and had lived to tell the tale.

Durham's decision to publish a book on her travels in Serbia and Kosovo marked a milestone on her odyssey. From now on she wished it understood that she was not just another lady traveller with an easel and a private income. In her own mind at least, her journeys round Montenegro and Serbia placed her in a different league, and entitled her to be considered an authority on Balkan questions. The timing of her first book's publication was fortuitous. Had she written *Through the Lands of the Serb* a year earlier, she might have struggled to get a publisher, or got one only to find her book subsequently ignored.

Instead, the book appeared shortly after the murder in Belgrade, on the night of 11 June 1903, of King Aleksandar and Queen Draga, and the dramatic overthrow of the house of Obrenović, a revolution that brought the question of the Near East sharply back into focus. The murder of the King and Queen by a group of pro-Russian nationalist officers was a disquieting reminder that the arrangements made for the Balkans at the Berlin Congress were breaking down. Durham found herself being talked about in London as one of a handful of people – and the only Englishwoman – who understood what was going on.

It was almost a routine matter for anarchists and lunatics to take pot shots at kings and queens, and occasionally they succeeded, as Tsar Alexander II of Russia and Elisabeth of Austria-Hungary had found to their cost. What was shocking and unprecedented about the events in Belgrade was the nature of the crime – both the King and Queen were butchered and their bodies thrown over the palace balcony – and the fact that it was an inside job. The Serbian regicides were not revolutionaries in the commonly understood sense of the word, but army officers. The chief organiser of the conspiracy, Colonel Dragutin Dimitrijević, also known as 'Apis', had been a guest at the King's own wedding.

Outrage over the events in Belgrade was felt across Europe, with the exception of republican France, Italy and, of course, Russia, which had an interest in the fall of the Obrenovićs. Several powers recalled their ministers from Serbia in protest. The ill feeling was strongest in England and Holland, which not only withdrew ministers but broke off relations – in Britain's case for three years. Edward VII felt that 'there was no need for England to recognise a Government of assassins'.[41] No British representative attended the new King's coronation in September 1904, and that October, when Ferdinand of Bulgaria invited King Petar to Sofia, Edward insisted on the British minister in Sofia absenting himself from public events while the Serbian monarch was in the city. It was only in 1906, by which time Serbia had put the principal regicide officers on the retired list, that Edward VII agreed to Sir James Whitehead going to Belgrade as British representative.

Hostility in Britain to the regicides in Serbia was not confined to court circles and parliament. It was a popular phenomenon, fed by lurid articles published in mass-circulation newspapers that reconstructed the royal murders in fine detail, and came complete with fanciful artistic illustrations, mostly dwelling on the death of the Queen, whose only crime in the eyes of most editors, it seemed, was that she had been 12 years older than her husband. Memories of the deed were kept bright for another year or two by the publication of follow-up books, some of which played on the word Belgrade – 'Beograd' in Serbian, meaning 'white city'. *Belgrade, the White City of Death*, by Flora Northesk Wilson, included an imaginary dialogue between the King and Queen in which they courageously confronted their assassins and declared their undying love for one another for the last time. 'Never again could Belgrade be called the White City. It was the City of Death,' Mrs Wilson wrote. 'The throne which a new King ascends is still slippery with blood.'[42] Herbert Vivian's *Servian Tragedy* was yet more condemnatory, fulminating against the regicides as 'dastardly butchers who have trailed the name of Servia in the mire'.[43]

Durham's own book on Serbia had little to say on the subject of the monarchy, as she had written it on the basis of information compiled on a tour that had almost come to an end before the assassination took place. She was not as moved as Mrs Wilson purported to be by the royal couple's death in any case. Unsentimental about royalty in general, she had become very aware of the unpopularity of the house of Obrenović. But her work still filled a niche, providing the only recent all-round account in English of a country and people that were suddenly in the news, even if for all the wrong reasons.

Through the Lands of the Serb appeared amid further signs that the Berlin 'system' in the Balkans was falling apart. In August 1903, a little band of Macedonian fighters hoisted the rebel flag over the hilltop town of Kruševo in what became known as the *Ilinden* rising. In the event, the powers hesitated to do anything to assist the rebellion and the Ottoman army felt it had a licence to move in and crush the revolt. The reprisals, especially the torching of dozens of villages, created a major refugee problem. Tens of thousands of people fled, or were driven from, their homes to the hills, where they began to run out of food and fall ill within weeks. As in 1876–7, at the height of the Bulgarian 'agitation', Liberal opinion in England shuddered with a collective sense of disgust at the behaviour of the Turks. A Liberal Party pamphlet, *Macedonia and Great*

Britain's Responsibility, set the tone, describing in detail 'a land whose snow-capped mountains are being dyed red with the blood of the innocent, whose fertile valleys are being made desolate by the devouring Turk. Cannot we hear the crackling of the flames and smell the smell of burning wood, of human flesh?' it inquired.[44]

However, as in the 1870s, the Liberals were out of office and condemned to play the roles of spectators, well aware that a Tory government, this time under Arthur Balfour, was no more likely than Disraeli's had been to intervene, whether or not the land was being dyed red with human blood. Once again they had to be content with holding meetings in church halls and signing angry petitions.

The Liberals were, however, able to pressurise the British government into getting the Ottomans to agree to allow a British relief mission to operate in Macedonia. Thanks to Durham's burgeoning reputation as a Balkan expert, and the publication of her book, just after Christmas 1903 the newly formed British Relief Fund asked her to go to Macedonia and supervise distribution of relief in the town of Resen and then take over management of the hospital they were setting up for victims of the uprising in the lakeside town of Ohrid.

Only a few years before, the prospect of spending the rest of her mother's life as her nurse had stretched out before her as a kind of nightmare. Now her belated dash for freedom started to pay off, as the great and the good solicited her opinions and sought her involvement in the Balkans. Durham had definitively ceased to be a tourist and had reconfigured herself as a writer and journalist. 'I wanted to go more than words could express,' she recalled much later in *Twenty Years of Balkan Tangle*. 'I was now forty and this might be my last chance.'[45]

Quite what she intended to get done in Macedonia was still unclear. *Through the Lands of the Serb* had been the work of a Gladstonian Liberal, breathing optimism about the region's prospects if only the Balkan peoples could be left to work out their separate but complementary destinies. It was a doctrine to which she would cling for several years before deciding that it was, in fact, unworkable and inappropriate.

Meanwhile, back in London, Durham skipped Christmas with her family and took a train to Vienna immediately. She had already seen Montenegro, Serbia, Kosovo and a fragment of northern Albania. Now she had the opportunity to explore Macedonia, the land at the epicentre of the worsening crisis in the Balkans.

CHAPTER 3

'My golden sisters of Macedonia'

I sometimes wonder whether I belong to the same genus, let alone species.
                    (Edith Durham on the Macedonians, 1904)[1]

AS HER TRAIN thundered over the iron bridge across the Danube into Belgrade in January 1904, Durham was reminded of the capacity of minor events in one part of the Balkans to send shock waves throughout the rest of the region. She found the Serbian capital in mourning. Far away in Ottoman Macedonia the Orthodox bishop of Skopje, Firmilian Dražić, had just died, but he was a Serb and Durham plunged into a wailing, black-clad crowd, awaiting the arrival of the bishop's funeral train.[2]

At the time, the train bearing Firmilian's corpse[3] was still steaming northwards from Skopje through Serbia, the railway track lined by weeping Serbs. Durham, now more expert on the politics of such events than she had been a few years earlier, was alert to the political significance of the prelate's death. Sultan Abdulhamid had succumbed to Russian pressure to appoint Firmilian in 1901, and the bishop had been installed in Skopje for one purpose: to build up a pro-Serbian party in the north of Macedonia, which both the Russians and the Ottomans, operating with different agendas, hoped to exploit in order to counter the growing threat of expansionist Bulgarian nationalism.

Back in the early 1870s, the Ottomans had encouraged the Bulgarian revival in Macedonia as a means to counter what was then seen as a more imminent Greek threat to Ottoman rule. With that in mind, in 1870, the Sultan had promulgated a *firman*, or decree, establishing a separate Bulgarian Orthodox Church, known as the Exarchate, as its leader was styled the Exarch. In theory, the Exarch was ecclesiastically subordinate to the (Greek) Patriarch in Constantinople. According to the *firman*, the Exarch was obliged to 'make mention in the liturgy of the name of the Patriarch of Constantinople', defer to him in matters of faith and, among other things, apply to him for holy oils for use in services.[4] In practice, apart from these minor constraints, the Exarchate was an entirely independent organisation that acted in competition with, and even in opposition to, the Patriarchate. The Ottomans made no secret of hoping to use the Exarchate to exacerbate divisions between the Orthodox Christians throughout the Balkans, Macedonia especially. According to the Russian ambassador in Constantinople, Count Nicholas Ignatiev, 'speculating solely on the rivalry which the bitter struggle had (already) sown between the Greeks and Bulgarians [the Ottomans] calculated that it would be worth while [...] to recognize the Bulgarians [...] and by doing so break the unity of the Christian nationalities of Turkey'.[5]

They succeeded in doing that. After the belated appointment of the first Exarch, Anthymos, in February 1872, the Patriarch responded in September by excommunicating him and his followers as schismatic. The excommunication had no effect on the Exarchate, but sealed a division between Greek and Slavic Orthodox Christians in the Balkans. The Sultan's advisers could congratulate themselves. But a few years later the Ottomans began to wonder if the Exarchate had not been more successful than they had intended.

'My golden sisters of Macedonia' 59

Under the terms of the *firman*, an Orthodox diocese could remove itself from the jurisdiction of the Patriarchate of Constantinople and place itself under the Exarchate if two-thirds of the local Orthodox Christian population voted to do so. Several dioceses then proceeded to do just that. The outbreak of the Russo-Turkish War in 1877, which resulted in the formation of a semi-independent Bulgarian principality, then interrupted the process. For a decade after the war and the formation of autonomous Bulgaria, the Ottomans felt too disappointed with the Bulgarians to assist their schemes against the Greeks. But the expansion of the Exarchate resumed, very rapidly in the 1890s, by which time the Sultan had reconciled himself to the existence of a free Bulgaria. That year, the Sultan made a number of key appointments, approving Bulgarian candidates for the bishoprics of Ohrid and Skopje. By the end of the decade, Exarchate bishops governed two-thirds of the parishes in Macedonia.

The state of the religious parties in Macedonia by the time that Durham arrived revealed the growing force of the Bulgarian 'idea' there. Durham's base of Ohrid, to the north, had by then become a fortress of pro-Bulgarian sentiment, where exarchists outnumbered followers of the Patriarch by over three to one in the diocese.[6] The 8,000 inhabitants of the town of Ohrid itself were pro-Bulgarian almost to the last man. The position of the religious parties was also reflected in the educational system. By 1895, the Serbs controlled only 77 schools in Macedonia. By contrast, the Bulgarians controlled 843.[7] The Bulgarian Exarchate had succeeded in creating a state-within-a-state in Macedonia.

By the late 1890s, the Ottomans were keen to check the assertiveness of the Bulgarians but did not want to hand Macedonian churches back to the distrusted and unpopular Greeks. This lay behind the decision to hand the important see of Skopje over to a third party, namely the Serbs. But, Firmilian ruined everyone's plans by dying shortly after his arrival, leaving Serbia's hopes for the further penetration of Macedonia in disarray. 'A bitter blow to the Serbs,' Durham mused. 'From every soldier-guarded station rose the harsh and penetrating Serbian wail; a black-robed crowd lamented Firmilian and burned candles for his soul's salvation.'[8]

Durham did not have much time to dwell on the Serbs' disappointment over the death of their ecclesiastical agent in northern Macedonia. She had work to do further south, distributing relief for the refugees in Resen, nearer the heartland of the recent revolt.

The *Ilinden* rising had lasted only weeks. The rebels had hoisted their flag on 2 August 1903, the feast day of the Transfiguration of St Elijah. But the revolt had been doomed because it was too obviously the work of a pro-Bulgarian party, as a result of which the Greeks and Serbs had either held aloof, or actively supported the Ottoman troops. Their hope was that the Ottomans would crush the revolt and, by doing so, annihilate Bulgaria's prestige in the region.

Nor could Bulgaria count any longer on the automatic support of Russia. Russia had insisted on the creation of a Bulgarian state after the Russo-Turkish War with a view to having a client state in the Balkans. But the Tsar became disappointed in his protégé, which turned out to have a mind of its own. Enraged by Bulgaria's determination to act independently, the Tsar ordered its first sovereign, Alexander of Battenberg, his own nephew, to abdicate. Alexander obeyed in 1886. But his successor, Ferdinand of Coburg, proved no better from a Russian standpoint. 'Foxy' Ferdinand, as he was nicknamed, incurred a certain amount of ridicule for his eccentric and effeminate mannerisms and obsession with protocol. But he turned out to be nobody's cat's-paw. Disraeli's great fear, which was that Bulgaria would act as an extension of Russia – the fear that had dictated British policy at the Berlin Congress – turned out to have been based on a false assumption. As one historian of Bulgaria noted, while Bulgaria was created to serve Russia, it 'in fact proved detrimental to Russian interests'.⁹ It was not until the end of World War II that Russia was able to remould Bulgaria to its liking.

Apart from Bulgaria's own wayward behaviour, the change in dynasty in Belgrade had also affected Russia's calculations in the Balkans. Ordinary Serbs had always been Russophiles. In the 1880s, a Serbian minister told Lord Salisbury that, 'beyond a dozen or so of exceptionally well-educated and far-seeing Serbians, there is scarcely a native of this country [...] who at heart is not Russian'.[10] But the house of Obrenović, which had held power since 1858, had frustrated the desire of most Serbs to work with Russia. Autocratic, conservative and distrustful of populism, the Obrenovićs normally preferred to lean on Austria-Hungary. The expulsion of the Obrenovićs in 1903 and the return of the Karadjordevićs changed everything, transferring power to a regime that was both more democratic and more pro-Russian. Russia now began to consider Serbia, not Bulgaria, or tiny Montenegro, its principal partner in the Balkans, and no longer championed the idea of a greater Bulgaria including all of Macedonia.

None of the other great powers had any interest in helping the Macedonian rebels in 1903. Austria-Hungary and Britain, then under a Conservative government, did not want to disturb the status quo. As a result, the Ottomans believed that they had a free hand to suppress the rebellion, burning down the rebel capital of Kruševo and torching another 200 villages, mostly in the *vilayet* of Bitola. Many other villages were not burned but stripped of everything they contained.

By the time Durham reached Resen, the fighting had been over for months. What most concerned the sympathetic English Liberals who sponsored her expedition to Macedonia was not the number of fatalities, which was relatively small at around 5,000,[11] but the plight of tens of thousands of refugees. 'It was the non-combatants who bore the full weight of their masters' wrath,' Henry Brailsford, founder of the British Relief Fund, recalled later. 'Each village which joined the revolt did so in the knowledge that it might be burned to the ground, pillaged to the last blanket and the last chicken.'[12]

Durham's immediate task was to manage the distribution and delivery of relief to the 70,000 or so Macedonians who had been left homeless as a result of the uprising, either because the Ottomans had destroyed their homes, or because they had fled to the hills in anticipation of being raped or killed. At first these refugees remained in a fairly good condition in forest or mountain retreats. The Macedonian summer is long and warm and they had taken food and livestock along with them. But by late September in 1903 they were getting hungry and bands of Ottoman troops were harrying them in the hills, determined to flush them out.

By November the nights were getting cold and family groups were breaking up. Some of the women were returning to their burned-down villages, camping in improvised lean-tos with nothing to eat, no seed to sow in spring, no ploughs or tools of any kind, or livestock, not even chickens. Other women headed for the towns, where they roamed the streets and begged from door to door. The men stayed in the hills, not trusting in a vaguely worded amnesty that the powers had compelled Abdulhamid to issue in the late autumn. Some of the men had wounds incurred in the fighting in the summer that had not been treated for three months and were gangrenous.

Durham's sponsors in the British Relief Fund were all Liberals of a radical hue, the same people or kind of people who had rallied to Gladstone's call in 1876 for civilised Europe to expel the Ottomans, 'bag and baggage'. The moving spirit behind the fund, Brailsford, was a radical journalist, and his wife, Jane, a militant suffragette. They were a slightly bizarre couple, as it was widely known that Jane found her husband physically repulsive and had only agreed to marry him as long as the marriage remained unconsummated.[13] But they came together, as Liberal couples often did, over their love of progressive causes. Using their many connections on the left of the Liberal Party and within the churches, the Brailsfords set up a fund that gathered substantial sums for a relief operation, tasked with two aims: distribution of money, seed, clothes and food to villages from an operational centre in Resen, and the establishment of a hospital in the lakeside town of Ohrid to treat the sick and wounded.

The Relief Fund functioned as an offshoot of a larger, more permanent, body – the Balkan Committee, founded earlier in 1903 by another left-wing Liberal, Noel Buxton, who would shortly enter parliament in the Liberal landslide of 1905 as the MP for Whitby. Buxton's Committee mustered a number of prominent Liberals and Church of England dignitaries, united in furious disapproval of what they saw as the Tories' pro-Ottoman, pro-Muslim policy in the Balkans. The Committee's vice-presidents included such Liberal royalty as Herbert Gladstone, son of William Gladstone, and the earl of Aberdeen. Four other MPs, all Liberal Party stalwarts, sat on the executive board.[14] Another prominent supporter of both the Committee and the Relief Fund was the left-wing journalist and 'great genial champion of freedom', Henry Nevinson.[15]

In Macedonia, Durham found herself thrust into the high-octane world of Liberals like the Buxtons, the Brailsfords and Nevinson. She had no option but to work with them because they were the only people in England who seemed interested in the Balkans. Most of them detested the memory of Disraeli's 'victory' at the Congress of Berlin, seeing it as a Tory-inspired betrayal of the Balkan Christians. As one recent historian put it, their passionate interest in the Balkans was not only motivated by altruism but by 'an overwhelming sense of guilt'.[16]

Forced to choose, Durham was more on the side of the do-something Liberals than the do-nothing Tories when it came to the Balkans, but it was never a happy, easy partnership. The Liberal temperament was alien to hers. Noel and Lucy Buxton, Henry and Jane Brailsford, Henry Nevinson and the rest were archetypal Liberals in that they passionately espoused a long list of causes of which the liberation of the Balkans was only one. They were just as emphatic and just as angry about women's suffrage, home rule for Ireland, independence for India, the liberation of Armenia and the downfall of the Tsar. Durham, the practical daughter of a London surgeon, child of a family that worshipped science, distrusted what she saw as their windy religiosity and emotionalism. Their eagerness to embrace multiple causes in the abstract struck her as insincere as well as unscientific. Temperamentally, she was averse to linking a whole raft of problems from Ireland to India via Armenia, and assuming common causes and solutions. In secret, she despised, or just didn't care, about many of the Liberals' top obsessions, starting with Ireland and votes for women. Nevinson and the Brailsfords were naturally ardent on both subjects; Jane Brailsford had refused even to wear a wedding ring, considering it a sign of female bondage. Durham thought the suffragettes were 'ninnies' at best, dangerous fanatics at worst.[17] Their window-smashing activities showed they had no right to aspire to any public role in the management of the Empire. She once confided to one of her sisters that she wished the government would deport them all to Australia.[18]

Durham also recoiled from the Liberals' extreme language about their enemies – the frequent use of words like 'fiends' to describe the Ottomans – and their habit of posing as the party of God, as if it could be taken for granted that he, too, was a paid-up Liberal. Many stalwarts of the Balkan Committee came from Evangelical Christian backgrounds. In most cases, as with Nevinson and Brailsford, they rejected the religious dogmas of their parents but, without being conscious of the fact, transferred their parents' general approach to life from the heavenly sphere to secular politics. They were every bit as idealistic, dogmatic and denunciatory as their parents, and just as inclined to divide the world into two opposing camps: angels and the forces of Satan. In the Balkans they saw only two forces at work; loathsome Turks and heroic Christian peasants.

Durham did not come from an Evangelical background and felt dubious about dividing the world into black and white. She did not prize passionate intensity as a virtue in its own right or see it as a substitute for informed, empirically gathered, knowledge. From the start, though she opposed Ottoman rule in the Balkans, she was not comfortable with the demonisation of the Turks that the Liberals had inherited from Gladstone. She was even less comfortable with their assumption that the worst Balkan Christians were, as Christians, automatically superior to the best Muslims. In time, these divisions would become apparent. But in the spring of 1904 Durham could not afford to quarrel openly with the Liberals. They were paying for her passage to Macedonia. It was thanks to them that for the first time in her life she had a real job.

Passing hurriedly through Skopje, where she found more wailing crowds and black-clad ecclesiastics, Durham got to Bitola before arriving in Resen just after New Year 1904. After settling into her digs she got to work almost immediately, checking and investigating the claims contained in lists compiled from each of 115 or so devastated villages in the *vilayet*.

Running the refugee operation in Macedonia was complicated. Even a professed friend to the Macedonians like Brailsford admitted that they were often difficult to deal with, or even like. 'First impressions are rarely favourable,' he recalled. 'It is a race with few external attractions [...] neither hospitable nor articulate [...] even the women are unprepossessing.'[19] Moreover, 'the peasant has no conception of a frank relationship with any superior'.[20]

It did not help that Durham could not understand much that any of them were saying and had to rely on a local interpreter who spoke to her in French. The weather now was vile, making visits to outlying villages an ordeal. When she encountered refugees, as Brailsford had experienced, she found it hard to decide whether they were telling the truth or were just making up things as they went along.

At first, Durham was too shocked by the state of the refugees to worry about the absolute veracity of their accounts. She came across people who had been living for months solely on flour distributed by the Brailsfords. Others had ghastly wounds, the consequence of savage beatings endured at the hands of the Ottoman soldiery. In one village she found 24 people huddling in a windowless cell.

Life in Resen was not easy. It was not a particularly attractive town, lined with wooden shops and badly paved alleyways, and Durham had no occasion here to regret not packing her box of paints. Her eccentric landlady seemed agreeable on her arrival, sending up bowls of milk in the evening. But she soon interfered and got on Durham's nerves, creating a fuss when she decided that she needed a wash and took a bowl of water up to her room. The Macedonians observed this with suspicion. They rarely washed, and when they did so, conducted the ritual outdoors and with solemn ceremony, one woman pouring a little trickle of water over the hands and face of the other. The women of Macedonia did not remove any of their heavy and elaborate garments for this infrequent event and were alarmed by reports of the action involving bowls of water that was said to be going on in Durham's bedroom. An even bigger scandal followed when her landlady discovered that she slept in a nightgown. Macedonian women slept in the same gear that they wore all day and that they had probably worn all year. The idea of lying in bed, semi-naked, in a flimsy shift, horrified them. While her landlady buzzed around like a wasp, spreading rumours, Durham had to cope with the annoyance of Ottoman officialdom. As a garrison town, Resen swarmed with soldiers as well as refugees and, irritatingly, none of the Europeans was permitted to travel around freely without a police escort. Durham tried to make a joke out of this. Brailsford, she wrote, was 'not allowed to move without an officer and five cavalry', while the

Relief Fund's aristocratic benefactress, Lady Thompson, 'owing to her title, has a major and 20 cavalry'.[21] Fortunately, as a 'nobody', Durham was considered less worth guarding and had nothing more bothersome than a few low-ranking *zaptehs*, or police, whom she discovered she could intimidate, which was not the case with the 'high and mighty' officers. But even the humble and cowed *zaptehs* were a constraint. She had come to the Balkans to be free; being followed around all the time went against the grain. She longed to get away from Resen and its spies and go on tour, especially now that she had discovered she could ride well on horseback. Out and about on her horse, having shaken off the *zaptehs*, she could breathe and take in the landscape of snow-covered mountains.

The temporary lift that she derived from these rural rides faded each time that she reached a village. Once there she would find herself climbing ladders to visit families roosting in the lofts of other people's houses, while on descending she had to avoid the packs of wild dogs that roamed everywhere, attacked strangers and fought till 4 a.m. every night. The refugees were difficult to warm to – 'a crushed and ignorant lot and in a state either of pitiable terror or of sullen ferocity'.[22] When she did bond with them she sometimes found she had nothing left to give. In one village she encountered a family of 12, sleeping in the freezing winter nights under three miserable rags. Durham felt devastated on realising that she had only one blanket to hand them. Some of the children won her heart. A little refugee girl of four impressed her when she told Durham that she would not go back to her burned village because she was convinced that the Turks would come and steal her earrings. At such times, the thought of the Turks filled her with rage. They were a 'densely, crassly, hopelessly stupid people,' she wrote. 'They are so stupid and so incapable [...] that at times one is sorry for them. Then one comes across the results of their inability to control things and one wants to chase the lot out of Europe. They have messed up things past all cure.'[23]

After a few weeks in Resen, Durham was dismayed to find out that no sooner did she hand out relief money or corn to returning refugees than the Ottoman tax collectors turned up and tried to pocket it. It was an absurd, vicious circle. As the tax collectors went around the villages, 'all the remaining store of corn that people possess has to go to pay [for] it. The government sells it, and we buy it.'[24] The relief fund then handed it out again.

But by the end of the first month in Macedonia, she was finding the refugees every bit as frustrating as the Ottoman officals. For the first time in the Balkans Durham had to confront the fact that people who wore fascinating, antique-looking costumes – the same women who looked charming in photographs and in water colours, leaning against wells and holding pitchers of water – could be infuriating to deal with. On closer inspection she found that those same interesting-looking costumes were often crawling with lice and that the women who wore them were reluctant to take them off, even to receive a much-needed injection. Durham found peasant amulets fascinating. She felt less enamoured with them once she discovered that the Macedonians placed more faith in the healing power of their amulets than they did in her western medicines.

The Macedonians' passive resistance to learning or trying almost anything new got on her nerves. When Durham decided to vaccinate as many of the refugees as possible against smallpox, the refugees wanted nothing to do with it. As she had found out earlier with the affair of the indoor washing bowl, Macedonian women considered it indecent to remove any of their cumbersome drapes, and would not even bare their arms for any inducement.

While trying in vain to get the women to roll up their sleeves for injections, Durham ran up against a broader ingrained fatalism, a superstitious fear of modern medicine in general. 'The peasants consider smallpox a great black spirit or bogey and they are afraid of being vaccinated lest it should be angry with them,' she noted, crossly.[25] What the peasant refugees did want was money, food and clothes. After an exhausting, nine-day tour of villages Durham returned to Resen to find a huge, excitable crowd practically laying siege to her headquarters and shouting at once. As her local hired helps roared back at them, Durham tried to escape to her room, only for the crowd to follow her up the stairs.

When the Relief Fund told her to move on to Ohrid to take over management of the hospital from Jane Brailsford, who had fallen ill, her spirits rose. Ohrid sounded more interesting: more oriental and cut-off, and altogether less European than Resen. Today, Ohrid is scrubbed and sanitised, a tourist resort in the Republic of Macedonia brimming with hotels and gift shops. In 1904 it was more squalid and at the same time more mysterious.

Ohrid is one of the great religious centres of the Balkans, long a place of pilgrimage for Slavic scholars as the last resting place of the ninth-century Orthodox missionary, St Cyril. In the early Middle Ages it had developed into an ecclesiastical centre of learning before the Ottoman conquest in the fifteenth century brought this golden age to an abrupt end. Since then, most of the numerous chapels and churches had crumbled into dust while the venerable cathedral of St Sophia had been converted into a mosque. But, unlike the case in so many cities in the Balkans, the past in Ohrid had not been totally extinguished. Enough remained of the ancient architecture to offer tantalising hints of old glories.

Henry Brailsford recalled his feeling of fascination on first catching sight of the town. Ohrid was 'built on the shores of a great lake and the white mountains that enclose it shut out the modern world and banish civilisation,' he wrote:

> Fishermen put out upon it in prehistoric boats...The peasants come and go under crumbling medieval gateways in costumes which can hardly have varied since the first Slavs

invaded the Balkans [...] one walks among them as one walks along avenues of gods and mummies in some great museum.[26]

The melancholy charm of the ancient town beside the vast, trout-filled lake, which vaguely reminded Durham of parts of the English Lake District, stirred her imagination and made her regret not having brought her paint box after all. Soon after her arrival she chanced on one of those peasant ceremonies that never ceased to appeal, however disenchanted she became with other Balkan traditions. Visiting a village on the feast of St John the Baptist, she came across a column of women in fantastic-looking headgear, each bearing an intricately woven piece of straw. Processing from a church they headed up a valley towards a stream headed by a splendidly robed priest for the blessing of the waters. Durham hurried after them, relieved that she had brought her camera and snapping away from the sidelines as the priest, glittering in his brilliant blue and gold silk vestments chanted away, dipping his cross into the freezing waters. This then became the signal for a mad rush into the stream on the part of all the men and boys while the women knelt on the banks, dipping their plaited straws into the waters and solemnly blessing one another.

Durham was also excited to be working in the hospital. As the daughter of a surgeon, blood, gore and even amputations held no terrors for her and she was pleased to be working with a doctor she respected. From time to time the stoicism of her patients tore at her heart. One 'poor devil', she noted, had arrived at death's door. He had heard that Durham was touring villages near Resen and had ridden to the town for seven hours in agony only to find out that she had already left for Ohrid. Her interpreter in Resen had sent the dying man on another six-hour ride to Ohrid. 'He was shot through the chest at the beginning of August [1903] and had had no medical aid of any kind,' Durham recorded. 'We took him of course into our hospital but he is, I fear, a hopeless case.'[27] She grieved again when a little boy died of typhoid in the hospital. His only surviving relative and mourner was his sixteen-year-old sister. Durham was so upset that she paid for an Orthodox funeral feast, although she usually disapproved of the custom of spending money on laying out food for the dead.

But, as in Resen, she found that working with, and trying to cure, people who looked as if they had stepped out of an ethnographical museum was a different experience from drawing and painting them. By the end of her stay in Ohrid Durham was just as irritated as she had ever been in Resen, railing at the medieval-looking Macedonians as stupid, base and 'degraded' – a favourite expression. Her disillusion with the Macedonians, which in time became close to hatred, was a factor in her steady conversion to the cause of Albania.

As in Resen, the addiction of the people of Ohrid to time-honoured traditions got on her nerves. Processing in a mysterious fashion from churches to streams was one thing. Their eating and drinking habits, along with the virtual prohibition on washing, was another. In Ohrid Durham began to question whether the Ottoman Turks were solely to blame for the degraded condition of the Christian peasantry in the Balkans. She felt it was also a result of drinking too much. The Macedonians were 'tubercular to an unusual degree and are sodden with alcohol,' she complained. 'The amount they give to children is extraordinary. They give it in large quantities to children that are still being suckled.'[28] Durham believed that the combination of brandy and pickled cabbage – and the refusal of most people to eat meat unless it was covered in spicy red pepper – was responsible for their often poor health and constant stomach aches.

The Macedonians' rigid observance of Church fasts, which Durham saw as superstitious nonsense, was another stumbling block. To her dismay, Durham found that some of her patients preferred to die rather than break one of the many fasts listed on the Orthodox Church calendar. When she tried to do something about this she immediately became locked in a power struggle with Methodius, the Exarchist Bishop of Ohrid,[29] and his allies among the nurses in the hospital, whom she rightly suspected were working with the bishop to enforce the observance of Church fasts even on the sickest patients. Unfortunately for Durham, the patients, their relatives, the nurses and the bishop combined forces to undermine her regime at the hospital. Various witches and wise women joined in, lurking around the doorway of the hospital, and prophesying a horrible death for all who entered. The bishop flatly refused to lift any of the Church fasts. Faith was far better than food, he told Durham ('He looks extremely well fed'), she observed grimly, later.[30] Meanwhile, mothers slipped into the hospital when she was not around and threw out the nourishing meals that she had ordered to be prepared for their children. When they did so, the nurses looked the other way, or helped them throw the dishes away.

Durham began to lose confidence. Sitting in her room one night, going through a consignment of nightgowns that had arrived from abroad – all useless, of course, to Macedonian women – she was seized with the idea of turning them into soft pillows, to replace the hospital's rock-hard traditional bolsters. She soon abandoned the idea, miserably convinced that the patients would shun her comfortable pillows and holler for their rock-like bolsters. In her letters home she poured out her frustration. The Macedonians were 'a singularly stupid breed of people,' she grumbled to her mother. 'The peasantry are the lowest type anywhere. I am quite decided that the Serb peoples are infinitely superior in all ways.'[31] She was losing sympathy for the 1903 rebellion as well, now judging it 'wrong and foolish or marvellously ill-advised. I would not want to hand over much territory to Bulgaria after what I have seen.'[32]

The more she grew to despise the Macedonians, the more they clustered round her. As in Resen, women who heard that she was distributing relief targeted her and spent the entire day milling around the hospital door, or around the entrance to her apartment. She came to dread 'the howling [...] females who call me "their golden sister"'. It was impossible, she told her mother, to sort out deserving cases from the rest, 'as they all shout at once. I sometimes try bellowing in English with effect.' Each woman wanted exactly what all the others were getting, whether or not they needed a particular item. 'A certain set cannot bear anyone to have more than themselves,' she noted. 'If you give a woman in absolute rags a length of linen for a shirt, they loudly demand the same [...] they persist until I feel inclined to smack them.'

'My golden sisters are extraordinary,' she mused to herself one evening in her room, referring to the supplicants who gathered round her doorway. 'I sometimes wonder whether I belong to the same genus, let alone species.'[33] Durham began exploring new ways of avoiding physical contact with them, shoving her hands deep into her pockets and hunching her shoulders forward to make it more difficult for them to hug her. It made no difference. Ignoring her attempt at *froideur* they flung their arms round her neck.

While Durham raged against the Macedonians in private, she must have behaved quite differently in public because at the end of February, when the Brailsfords left Ohrid, they gave her sole control of the hospital. With his strong sympathy for Macedonians and Bulgarians, Henry Brailsford had been a restraining force on Durham. With him out of the way, her fury with the Macedonians increased. She identified the head nurse, Vasilica, as especially 'maddeningly stupid', but the rest were no better, possessing 'the brains of tortoises,' she said. She saw Vasilica as a kind of zombie, or automaton. 'I vow I believe if Vasilica's brains were extracted she would go on boiling onions by reflex action,' she wrote venomously after one bruising encounter. The Macedonians were now ugly as well as stupid, the 'women with faces like Dutch cheeses'.[34] The nurses, she joked maliciously, could not even master a novelty as simple as turning on and off a tap. When Durham tried to introduce them to the rubber hose that led from a tank, containing a cleansing solution that Durham used to wash down wounds, they had no idea how to turn it off and let it gush all over the hospital floor.

Clashes between Durham and the nurses over the business of food peaked after the start of the most important Church fast, the Great Easter Fast. The nurses now dug their heels in well and truly, and when Durham ordered them to feed a sick girl with warm milk laced mildly with brandy every two hours, they threw it away, consumption of dairy products being prohibited during this time. She had another battle with Vasilica over consumption of meat during the fast, which the Church also prohibited. She and the other nurses were determined not to let any of the patients in the hospital touch so much as a morsel, while Durham was equally determined that they should. After Vasilica slyly informed her that meat was no longer available at any of the Christian butchers in Ohrid, Durham stormed off to the market herself and bought a consignment from the town's Muslim butchers.

Behind the evasive figure of Vasilica, the fawning golden sisters, and the Cassandra-like crones who prowled round the hospital doorway muttering curses, Durham detected the sinister influence of the bishop of Ohrid. All the black threads, she concluded, led back to the bishop, via him to the headquarters of the Exarchate and thence to the Bulgarian government in Sofia. Never a friend to the bishop, whose piety she found 'unctuous',[35] and whose demeanour had offended her from the start – she deemed him inappropriately sleek and self-assured – by the end of her stay in Ohrid she had come to detest him as 'a swindling humbug'.[36] After several interviews that developed into arguments, relations between the proud Englishwoman and the implacable Bulgarian froze into place. Durham got nowhere with him. The bishop continued to bat aside her pleas for him to lift the Church fasts on her patients and, according to her, said it did not matter if many more people died in another uprising in Macedonia. All that mattered, apparently, was that if carnage was to occur, it should attract the intervention of the great powers.

The final showdown occurred shortly before she left Ohrid, with a conversation that started on hospital topics but soon broadened out into a bad-tempered exchange about the IMRO, the merits of Bulgaria, the future prospects of the British Empire in India – dire, according to the bishop – and the likely outcome of a Russo-Japanese war. Durham and the bishop took diametrically opposing positions on each point, with Durham claiming that the bishop had insisted that England would be 'wiped out by Holy Russia, the sooner the better'. He had also threatened to have her killed. 'You kill me,' she had responded, dramatically, 'and there is the end to your Bulgaria.'[37]

Durham began winding up the hospital in Ohrid in mid-March 1904, determined to leave before the end of the month. She did so in a mood of foreboding, having heard reports that the men of the IMRO were indeed plotting another uprising. Given the outcome of the last revolt, Durham considered this madness. She now believed that Bulgaria's grandiose regional ambitions, not Ottoman misrule, were responsible for much of the trouble in Macedonia. She did not trust 'the wire-pullers in Sofia' who were trying to persuade European opinion that 'there is no one here but Bulgarians,' she wrote.[38]

Never intended as a permanent operation, the Relief Fund had fulfilled its mandate efficiently and successfully. The experience that Durham gained in running a significant aid operation and a hospital would later prove invaluable, when the 'grand finale', as she put it, occurred, and the Ottoman Empire collapsed.

Before she left Macedonia, an early blast of warm weather inspired her to organise a group picnic to the nearby church of St Naum. As a special treat she lifted the ban that the puritanical

Brailsfords had imposed on the male staff's favourite pastime – taking pot shots at local birds. Durham concealed her smirks as the men blasted away ineffectually with their rifles, hour after hour. 'Net result, a coot, a greenfinch and a sort of grebe,' she snickered.[39] As the men peppered the reed beds beside the lake with gunshot, Durham sat with her nose in a book, absorbed in trying to make sense of Albanian. In the shade of the dreamy, ancient church she experienced a sort of epiphany. From the moment that she had first set foot in the Balkans in the summer of 1900, she had been puzzling over her destiny. Now the pieces of the jigsaw fell into place, and she realised that her real vocation in this land was not to roam mindlessly, paint picturesque scenes, hang around with the diplomats in Cetinje or run aid operations. It was to redraw the borders of the Balkans and sort nation from nation. 'When I delimit the frontiers, I shall draw them close by [St Naum],' she told herself. 'I remain faithful to the Montenegrins and the Albanians,' she added grandly, 'and when the grand finale comes, shall back them.'[40]

Her experience in Macedonia had transformed her perspective. It was not simply that Durham now saw herself as much more than an observer in the Balkans and was already drawing frontiers in her own imagination. She had realised that her views on the Balkans no longer matched those of most Gladstonian Liberals. In fact, her standpoint did not match that of either the Tories or the Liberals, but was evolving in a third direction – supportive of western intervention in the Balkans, but not of intervention conducted in the service of the Christians. In the meantime, she would not return to Ohrid for many years. The mysterious land that had intrigued her from the start of her Balkan odyssey four years earlier beckoned beyond the mountains to the east. Durham packed not for England, but for Albania.

CHAPTER 4

'God has sent you to save us'

> People have been praying me and calling one in God's name to help them.
>
> (Edith Durham, April 1904)[1]

Durham had so far only scratched the surface of Albania. It remained for her almost a mirage – an object of intense curiosity and longing, but far in the distance. That first, all too brief, expedition to Shkodra had been a revelation, but the northern city was not quite the real Albania. With its foreign consuls and large Catholic population, Shkodra was more connected to the outside world than the rest of the country, which remained *terra incognita*.

Durham was now about to set off on a prolonged expedition that would take her to remote towns and villages: places that hardly anyone from the West, and certainly no woman, had ever visited. She did not go alone. She had a guide and companion, Constantine Sinas, an Albanian distributor of devotional literature, or colporteur, from the British and Foreign Bible Society, which had obtained permission from the Ottoman authorities to sell a cargo of translated Bibles in Albania. Abdulhamid, the 'Red Sultan', so named for the amount of blood he had shed in Armenia, did not welcome Christian missionaries. But he had no option but to let them in occasionally, now that his European empire remained in existence only by consent of the European great powers. For its part, the Bible Society had kept an eye on Albania for decades. 'The furnishing of the Albanians with a New Testament, at least, in their own language is an object highly worthy of the attention of the British and Foreign Bible Society,' a report for the society from Vienna in 1816, covering the situation in Central and South-Eastern Europe, declared. The author of the report, the Revd R. Pinkerton, recommended that the work of translating the scriptures be entrusted to Albanians living on the Ionian Islands, and he lamented that such Christians as remained in Albania had to listen to services 'performed in the Greek language, which is quite unintelligible to the people, and even to most of their priests'.[2]

While the Bible Society continued to prod and push at the door of Albania, Ottoman officials fell back on the tried and trusted tactics of passive resistance, trying to tie up the business with bureaucratic obstacles. Each book destined for sale had to pass through the creaking machinery of the ministry of education in Constantinople and bear a government-issued watery pink seal on the inside cover.

There was something ironic about someone as sceptical about religion as Durham accompanying a hard-line Protestant missionary around Albania ahead of a fleet of mules and donkeys, all loaded up with copies of the scriptures. But Durham admired her doughty guide even if she could not share his faith. She approved of Constantine personally as a man of integrity; a serious person herself, she credited seriousness in others. She also approved of the fact that, by translating the Bible into Albanian, the Bible Society had placed an important educational tool into the hands of ordinary Albanians that was not otherwise available to them.

Writing things in Albanian was a sensitive matter as far as the Ottomans were concerned. After losing so many other provinces in the Balkans, they were determined to stall the rise of a national movement among the Albanians and, with that goal in mind, virtually prohibited use of Albanian in print. In 1885, the Sultan expressly forbade the publication of books and newspapers in Albanian, ordering the local Muslim clergy to issue a *fatwa* condemning them.[3] A handful of Albanian-medium schools opened, but only with great difficulty and under foreign protection. They included an Austrian school for Catholics, which opened in Prizren in Kosovo in 1889, and two American Protestant schools in Korça: one for boys, which opened in 1887, and another for girls, which opened a few years later. But the schools in Korça had a hard time, as local Ottoman officials put pressure on local Muslims not to let their children attend. In the absence of much else in Albanian, the Bible filled an important gap.

Durham and her guide left Ohrid at the end of March 1904, accompanied by a posse of Ottoman gendarmes, passing through Bitola and Resen and then skirting round Lake Prespa before heading west into deep Albania, towards Korça. The ride was a harsh lesson about how undeveloped the country was. After leaving Bitola at around 2.30 a.m. so as not to get caught in the middle of nowhere on the following day, they pulled in for lunch at the only known inn for miles around, only to find that it had burned down. Some Albanians camped in the blackened ruins. The party had to go on, but the frozen ruts in the road made the journey atrocious. Durham recalled feeling like a dried pea being hurled round its shell. Always willing to put aside physical discomfort when the surroundings were sufficiently interesting, she absorbed herself in the sight of lush grassland dotted with fine stone houses, owned by Muslim *begs*, or landlords, and Albanian men striding along the road with their peculiarly long, swinging gait, dressed in white gaiters and cloak, their shoes adorned with tassels.

After a brief halt in Korça, where Durham visited and commiserated with the heroic teachers at the Protestant schools, she went on to the old market town of Debar (Dibra in Albanian) to buy a saddle and a bridle. By now the bush wire was humming, and word had begun to travel from village to village that an important foreigner was in their midst. A large crowd gathered by the roadside as she and Constantine pulled into the village of Kolonja and a larger one still was waiting for them when they reached the next two destinations, Leskovik and Postenani, 'no foreigner having been here lately and never a woman,' Durham crowed.[4]

It was the start of her rise to fame in Albania. At Postenani, Durham received local dignitaries in high state, the women filing ceremonially into her lodging to kiss her and place their hands solemnly on her forehead. They then presented gifts and walked out backwards. It was not simply the fact that she was the first foreign woman to reach their remote villages that intrigued them. A rumour had begun to course through the countryside that Durham 'had come to help them,' she noted in her diary, and for her part Durham was now determined to be much more than a smiling tourist. She wanted to help – in what way was not clear to her. But it would be difficult to knock into shape such a backward, divided people as the Albanians. They 'were a fine race but have no external friends and the savage part of the nation is very difficult to organize,' she told her mother.[5]

The country remained murderously difficult to cross. On the way to their next stop, the fortress town of Tepelena, where Byron and Hobhouse had stayed in the company of Ali Pasha, she and Constantine met driving rain and she got her first real taste of the rough, upcountry life that would become very familiar to her in the years to come. Unable to reach Tepelena before nightfall they pulled in at a hovel-like inn that reeked of petrol and where Durham was shown into a windowless room containing no furniture, only some straw and a few lumps of coal burning in a brazier in the middle. After politely spurning an invitation from a local *beg*, who turned up in the rain to offer her a bed in his harem, she camped in the barn, which was almost full to the ceiling with onions but was at least dry.

The next morning, the road to Tepelena was even worse. Dense sleet and rain had turned the track into a mass of mud and sludge, and the mules were suffering horribly with their heavy loads of books, stumbling into hidden potholes and sometimes collapsing onto their knees. On the descents Durham had no choice but to dismount and try and wade though the deep, freezing slime as the mules slithered around helplessly, at times rolling down the slopes on their sides. After a long day on the road, soaked and covered from head to foot in mud, Durham staggered into the next inn, which boasted the luxury of a room containing both a fire and a window. But there was no chimney, so Durham drifted off to sleep amid clouds of smoke, covering her face with a wet towel to keep from inhaling the fumes. The following day, it seemed as if things would be no better. Again, the mules slithered all over the place and Constantine kept tumbling off his horse into the icy sludge. Finally, after ascending a hill that Durham likened to a wall of mud, the battered party, Bibles and all, reached dry pasture and, as if from nowhere, the blue waters of the Adriatic Sea and the port of Vlora came suddenly into view.

The gruelling nature of the journey from Ohrid to Vlora gave Durham some idea of the challenges awaiting anyone who had ambitions to unite the Albanians. The odds looked stacked against such a people ever coming together. Overwhelmingly illiterate, possessing only a handful of schools, without roads that anyone could use in winter, the Albanians were divided along almost every conceivable line. For one thing, they belonged to three faiths, Muslim, Catholic and Orthodox.[6] They were also spread over four different Ottoman *vilayets*: Shkodra in the north, Ioannina in the south, and Bitola and Kosovo to the west. But they were only an overwhelming majority in the Shkodra *vilayet*. The city of Ioannina was still generally thought of as part of Albania. Byron had taken it as such in the 1800s, and a century later a British encyclopedia also took that fact for granted when it described Shkodra, Ioannina and Prizren as the three principal cities of Ottoman Albania.[7] But by the 1900s the Greeks were making headway in Ioannina, funding new churches and schools. The Greek merchant class now dominated the city itself while the surrounding *vilayet* remained evenly split between Greeks and Albanians.[8] In the Kosovo *vilayet*, which then included large parts of modern Macedonia, Albanians outnumbered all the others by a ratio of at least two to one in the 1890s.[9] But they still had to compete with the Serbs in the east and with the Bulgarians in the south.

In the Bitola *vilayet*, Albanians dominated the western parts, around the town of Elbasan, but Bulgarians dominated the east, around Ohrid. According to the historian George Gawrych, the ethnic composition of the *vilayet* was 'much more complicated than in the other three provinces. No one ethnic community dominated provincial life there. Turks, Albanians, Bulgarians, Greeks, Vlachs, Armenians and Jews all played a role in shaping the province's internal pulse.'[10]

Scattered over these four *vilayets*, Albania had no obvious centre, and remained an ill-defined linguistic notion. Albania was presumably where speakers of Albanian lived. But the language was divided as well. Albanian speakers split into two groups, those who spoke the northern Geg dialect, or its southern Tosk counterpart. Albanians in the northern *vilayets* of Kosovo and Shkodra spoke Geg. In Ioannina and Bitola, the majority spoke Tosk.

Divided by faith and language, the Albanians were also, Durham realised, without foreign backers. The Ottomans had kept the Albanians unschooled, undeveloped and divided, so that the brightest and the best would leave their homeland and go to Constantinople, from which they would never return, becoming deracinated servants of the Ottomans.

Constantinople was full of such people, for Abdulhamid's partiality towards Albanian servants was well known. As one recent historian noted:

> Observers confirmed the favoritism Abdulhamid accorded the Albanians in the palace guard. No one in the palace could speak disparagingly of them [...] those fortunate Albanians and their families back in Albania, in deference to their benefactor, often referred to Abdulhamid as 'father-king'.[11]

While the Sultan pampered a select group of Albanian pets, Catholic Austria cast a benevolent eye on its coreligionists in the north of Albania. The treaty between Austria and the Ottoman Empire in 1699 had given the Austrian emperors vague protective rights over Catholics in the Balkans. The Austrians had not made much use of those rights with respect to the Albanians in the eighteenth century, but as great power rivalry increased in the Balkans, the Austrians became more involved. In the 1860s they had established a small seminary in Shkodra, and it was Austrian money and protection that enabled the Franciscans and other Catholic orders to set up a small network of schools and hospitals in the city. According to Gawrych, these 'helped train a small native clergy and run schools using the Albanian language, thus permitting the development of an Albanian literature'.[12] The Austrians also established a chair in Albanian in Vienna in 1889, as well as opening the Albanian-medium school in Prizren in Kosovo referred to earlier. But this activism affected only a small minority of Albanians, as Catholics made up no more than 10 per cent of the population. Muslims made up at least 75 per cent, and the Habsburg government took no interest in this huge non-Catholic majority. It had no interest in the fate of Albania as a whole, to the disappointment of Bismarck, who thought it was more important than most people realised, and who told the British diplomat, Lord Goschen, that he had 'tried in vain [...] to get the Austrians to make friends with them'.¹³ The Austrian foreign minister, Alois Aehrenthal, summed up the monarchy's position in August 1908 to the British diplomat, Charles Hardinge, when 'he alluded to the situation in Albania, remarking that the Austrian Government would under no circumstances put their hands into that hornet's nest'.¹⁴

The other powers behaved as if the Albanians did not exist. At the Congress of Berlin, Disraeli and Bismarck had parcelled out Albanian lands both to Serbia and to Montenegro. Serbia received the Toplica region while Montenegro obtained the town of Podgorica and the port of Bar, to which a second port, Ulcinj, was added in 1880. When the Serbs expelled thousands of Albanians from the Toplica and Vranje area in 1878 to make way for colonists, the British Resident in Serbia, Gerald Francis Gould, complained to Lord Salisbury of Serbian brutality. 'The peaceful and industrious inhabitants of over 100 Albanian villages in the Toplitza and Vranja Valley were ruthlessly driven forth from their homesteads by the Servians [sic] in the early part of this year. These wretched people have ever since been wandering about in a starving condition,' he wrote. Nothing happened to Serbia as a result of these complaints, and the Serbs quickly and efficiently resettled the area.

The Montenegrins were less harsh with the territorial gains they made at the expense of the Albanians in 1878, mainly because they had far fewer potential colonists. As a result, Ulcinj – first a Montenegrin, then a Yugoslav, now again a Montenegrin town – remains overwhelmingly Albanian in terms of ethnicity. Nevertheless, the casual decision of the powers to hand an ancient and important town that was almost entirely Albanian to Montenegro was a sign of how little Albanian wishes counted in European capitals. It was not as if the town passed docilely into the hands of Montenegro. The Albanians of Ulcinj resisted the Montenegrin army for months in 1880, after which the powers hypocritically prevailed on the Ottomans to send a warship to enforce its surrender. Such bullying made some British politicians and diplomats uneasy. Lord Goschen, the British ambassador in Constantinople, told the new Liberal Foreign Secretary, Lord Granville, in 1880 that it was wrong to neglect the Albanians' legitimate interests in the Balkans. Albanian nationalism, he wrote, could 'be utilized with much advantage to general interests, and I should deprecate any partial measures which would be likely to impede the formation of one large Albanian province [...] A united Albania,' he continued, 'would bar the remaining entrances to the North, and the Balkan peninsula would remain in the hands and under the sway of the races who now inhabit it.'[15]

Lord Goschen's was an unusual voice, and his words were wasted on Granville, who was serving under Gladstone, Montenegro's great admirer. In July 1880, Granville told British ambassadors to ignore Albanian complaints concerning the loss of Ulcinj. Opposition to the cession of the town, he wrote, 'proceeds only from the Turkish government, and [...] the objections of the Albanians will become merely nominal once the will of Great Powers is clearly expressed'.[16]

As the Christian states in the Balkans, with the aid of the powers, chipped away at Albanian lands, Abdulhamid fitfully toyed with the idea of encouraging the Albanians to organise a modest national movement of their own – whose purpose would be restricted to stating the case for the right of the Albanians to remain in the Ottoman Empire. In June 1878 the Ottomans allowed a congress to meet in Prizren in Kosovo and draw up a memorandum of protest, which was dispatched to the powers meeting in Berlin. Among Albanians today, the formation of the League of Prizren is seen as a milestone in national history, the start of a genuine movement of self-determination. But the case made for the League is often exaggerated. In reality, the League stood for Muslim rather than Albanian solidarity: its principal demands were for the retention of *sharia* law and the preservation of the integrity of the Empire. The only sop to Albanian feeling was the demand for the creation of a single Albanian *vilayet* in the Ottoman Empire. In any case, Abdulhamid soon tired of it, and after fighters loyal to the League attempted to stop the surrender of Ulcinj to Montenegro, the Sultan sent a large force to Kosovo to suppress it. He officially disbanded the League once again in 1897 and had its president executed in 1902.

It was that feeling of encirclement and abandonment by the world – a feeling that had begun to penetrate even the remotest corners of Albania – that caused so many people to invest such hopes in Durham's arrival. In the villages and towns through which she passed, they hailed her as the ambassador or princess of an unknown but hopefully important and benign power.

Her official reception in Vlora was, however, quite different, and the interview with the local Ottoman governor was uncomfortable. Durham suspected that he knew very well that she had worked for the British Relief Fund in Macedonia, and saw her as a revolutionary troublemaker, bent on encouraging the Albanians to rise against the Sultan. She was being 'watched as a mouse by a cat,' she wrote home angrily, after visiting the Austro-Hungarian consulate.[17]

Her encounter with the Italian consul in Vlora, on the other hand, surprised her. The Italians were widely and usually correctly seen in Albania as potential predators with designs on the whole eastern seaboard of the Adriatic, the acquisition of which would fulfil the Italian nationalist dream of turning the Adriatic Sea into an Italian lake. But the consul in Vlora was sympathetic to the Albanians and gave Durham a useful pep talk on the workings of the *vilayet* of Ioannina, whose governor, she learned, was deeply hostile to all reform of the empire and 'opposes all schools, and says the people are better off if not able to read and write'.[18]

Durham had further cause to feel ill-disposed towards the Ottomans when she returned from the Italian consulate to town to find the police harassing Constantine about his Bibles. They had encountered no problems in the country villages with their cargo but the authorities in Vlora insisted on going through each book to check whether it contained the correct pink seal of approval from Constantinople on the inside leaf. Durham stormed into the police station, determined to unnerve the police as they interrogated her guide, and made it clear she was ready 'to scare off these wretches,' as she reported back to England.[19]

The battle of the Bibles took several days to clear up because they could not reclaim their books until the governor of the *vilayet* had wired to confirm that the expedition had an official imprimatur. In the meantime, Durham remained ensconced in talks with the Austro-Hungarian and Italian consuls, feeling more hostile to the Ottoman Empire each day. She didn't need much persuading from the consuls about this. The hovel-like inns, impassable roads, ruined towns and shocking lack of schools had already persuaded her of the rotten consequences of Ottoman government.

Her short stay in Tepelena had already prompted rueful reflections on Albania's dismal decline. After Byron and Hobhouse visited, Hobhouse had described a magnificent court full of marble, splashing fountains and splendid-looking Albanians dressed in long white cloaks. Almost a century on, Ali Pasha's palace was 'a heap of ruins', inhabited only by 'gypsies of a low and most villainous type'.[20] The bridge that the chieftain had built over the river had fallen into the water and the old merchants' houses lay deserted.[21] The comparison between Albania and Serbia, which had liberated itself from the Ottomans in the 1830s, spoke for itself. While the two peoples both lived under the Ottomans, the Muslim Albanians had been in the ascendant, favoured for their religion. In the seven decades that had passed since the Serbs had freed themselves, Serbia had developed at a tremendous pace, as Durham had noted in her book, *Through the Lands of the Serb*. Serbian towns now had electric lighting, decent roads and trams, and were linked by railways, while everywhere phalanxes of uniformed children were to be seen marching off to school. Albania had slid backwards, rotting from the inside, its energy and lifeblood sucked out in the service of a diseased and dying Empire. Durham despised the way that so many Ottoman officials seemed to think they could win over foreign visitors with a few honeyed words. Whiling away the time in Vlora she sometimes passed the governor of the town on horseback. The two of them would awkwardly salute one another, the governor inquiring in a syrupy tone about whether she felt '*contente*' with her stay. 'Silly fool,' Durham mused to herself afterwards. 'He thinks he prevented my having any chance for my imaginary propaganda, whereas he is really giving himself and the Turkish administration away in the most hopeless manner, and providing me with "copy" of a kind he would not appreciate.'[22]

Finally the wire arrived from Ioannina, giving Durham and her guide permission to carry on distributing their Bibles. The expedition could continue. Before pulling out of Vlora, she left Constantine selling some more Bibles in town while she observed the Good Friday service in the local Orthodox church. The service, conducted, of course, in Greek, reminded her again of the almost insane situation in Albania, where it appeared that everything had to be carried out in a language that almost no one understood, be it Turkish, Arabic or Greek. No wonder the Albanians seemed so bored and listless attending even the most solemn ceremonies. Their 'ceaseless shuffling and chattering' in the church reminded her of a parrot house.[23]

At last they set out with their mules, planning a wide circuit of southern and central Albania that would take in the towns of Berat and Elbasan and the port of Dürres. From there, Durham planned to head back north to Shkodra via Tirana, and ponder her options.

The next leg of the journey was far less horrifying than the cross-country trek from Ohrid to Vlora. Spring was taking hold and the countryside was drying out. On leaving Vlora Durham found herself in flat, grassy pastureland, passing Christian villages from which plumes of smoke arose from the roasting of Easter lambs. They passed a mysterious village of Vlachs in which she observed people 'dancing and singing weird songs',[24] and then passed the lost Roman city of Apollonia whose extant remains consisted of little more than a lonely fluted column standing in a grass meadow. As they jogged along on horseback in the grasslands beside the desolate column, a distant scene caught her eye: a column of Albanians processing in exotic-looking clothes, the men dressed in white *fustanellas* and blue leggings, towards what looked like a monastery church. To the dismay of her guide, Durham insisted on making a diversion to follow the procession towards the church where she found that the processing Albanians had been watching her just as intently as she had been observing them. 'We are ignorant Albanians,' their leader told her, humbly, on approaching her after the service. 'We would like to see what you are doing for we have never seen such a thing before. But if it troubles you, we will go.'[25] Deeply touched, Durham accepted their invitation to return to their village for a feast.

As a great, albeit unknown, personage, she found the Albanians were not willing to communicate further with her. She found herself having to walk a fair way to the village in solitary grandeur, followed at some distance behind by a whispering column. She tried to forget her feeling of embarrassment, concentrating on a landscape that was coming alive with the advent of warm weather, the copses already in full leaf, primroses bursting from ditches and butterflies emerging from the fields in multicoloured clouds. Durham delighted in counting them as the sun slowly descended: great swallowtails, fritillaries, red admirals, clouded yellows, brimstones, large and small tortoiseshells, red coppers, and many more. Judas trees and wild plums were in full blossom. 'All most beautiful,' she marvelled. It was dusk when the party reached the village, and she was starving, but the preparations for the feast had only just begun. Exhausted and drunk on tots of brandy, she was almost comatose by the time the men came into the room where she had been deposited alone, and wordlessly placed a gigantic platter before her. A lamb's head stared back. Beside it was an enormous loaf of bread. After consuming what she could of this 'fleshy and barbaric meal', she returned to the monastery.[26]

Durham's dreamlike encounter with the villagers near Apollonia intensified a conviction that she had come to this unknown land for good reason. This feeling of destiny was strengthened when she reached her next destination, the town of Berat. 'I am the first Englishwoman here in the memory of man,' she exclaimed triumphantly, 'where very few strangers of any kind have been.' The experience in Berat was as weird and wonderful as it had been in Apollonia. Reports of Durham's perilous journey across Albania created a tremendous excitement in the town and she found herself being hustled to a secret location, far from the eyes of the police, where an assembly of the local notables presented her with a strangely worded address. 'Honoured mademoiselle, we cannot express to you the joy that your journey gives us,' it began. 'We know that you cannot have gone though such suffering on the road except for some good purpose. God has sent you to save us.' It added: 'The Slavs have Russia to help them, we have no one.'[27] Durham gazed around the room, impressed by the Albanians' humility, and by the magnitude of the task that she felt was being handed to her. Other nations were old and tired but the Albanians, like their country, in her eyes, had a childlike, untouched quality.

She moved on to Elbasan, where she was again pleased to learn that she was one of the first English people and certainly the first Englishwoman to visit the town. From a local Catholic priest she also learned more of the Hellenising activities of the local Greek Orthodox clergy in the south of Albania, and their active connivance with the Ottoman government in blocking the use of Albanian in the country's handful of schools.[28] It was deeply confusing. In general, Greeks and Turks were enemies, and had been since the Greek revolt against the Ottoman Empire in the 1820s. The overwhelmingly Muslim Albanians had remained loyal to the Sultan. Yet the Ottomans had rewarded the loyal Albanians with dull oppression and with policies designed to divide them and keep them in a state of perpetual ignorance. It appeared that they would rather see them become rebellious Greeks than educated Albanians. Durham was a fast learner when it came to navigating the treacherous waters of Balkan politics, but even she had trouble making sense of matters as they were explained to her in Elbasan. 'The propaganda of the Balkan peninsula makes one's head turn round,' she wrote.[29]

It was a relief to saddle up on the grey stallion she had just hired and to ride out. Again, the intoxicating beauty of the Albanian countryside assaulted her senses. The hills blazed with blossom, fields were full of flowers and bees, and emerald green lizards darted from the pathways as Durham and a couple of hired outriders galloped past, heading uphill, until Elbasan was no more than a twinkling mass of minarets on the plain below. As the Albanian guards began to sing to one another in high falsetto voices, Durham again felt herself falling into a sort of trance. Halting in a village, and shouting '*mik*' ('friend') they came across a grizzled old patriarch who laid on a great feast in her honour, of lambs, fowls, scrambled eggs and bowls of milk and bread, which the men then devoured like wolves. The scene charmed her on one level, though she was not taken in by it. She felt that its picturesque qualities reflected the degrading nature of Ottoman rule. No one in the village even knew their age, for example. The old man told her this was because 'We are wild ignorant men here and do not know how to write.' Most local men were, in fact, absent from the village because they had taken part in various affrays, outrages, feuds and revolts, and in consequence were wanted by the Ottoman police and were in hiding. The few men still lurking there were afraid to show themselves to strangers, though while Durham was eating she spotted one from the corner of her eye, crouching behind a bush. The children seemed free, but for how long, she wondered? They were 'bright-eyed little chaps who looked as keen as terriers,' she reflected, 'but will grow up perfect savages. At the age of 15 they would be given weapons and told to keep up the honour of the house.'[30] Of course there was no school to attend; the nearest was miles away. Durham visited it on her way back to Elbasan and found the experience predictably depressing. It boasted three pupils, all struggling along hopelessly in Greek.

After their expedition finished in the port of Dürres, Durham journeyed northwards up the Adriatic coast towards Shkodra. From there, she had decided, she would try to penetrate the even more remote and unexplored mountains on the border with Montenegro, after which she would continue into Montenegro. The journey north was uneventful, the coastal road being one of the few decent routes in the country. She halted in Tirana, today the brash and very modern capital of Albania but then a small, conservative Muslim backwater of about 12,000 people. From there she reached the relative civilisation of Shkodra at the beginning of May. Staring into a mirror in her hotel, the first mirror she had seen in weeks, she observed a changed woman looking back at her: hardy, tanned from the weeks on horseback, a little rough-looking.

The Catholic Mirdita tribe of the northern mountains now claimed her attention. No Englishwoman had ever been into their redoubt but by now Durham had visited any number of towns and villages into which no English person of either sex had penetrated, so this latest challenge filled her with no trepidation. Her fame had continued to spread among the Albanians and, back in Shkodra, she learned that the aged princess of the Mirdita tribe, Marjella Bib Doda, who had come down from the mountains to pray in the Catholic cathedral, had forwarded a message. She was not well enough to meet Durham in person, the message ran, but she wished her to know that her safety was guaranteed, should she wish to travel into her domains. Durham was ready to saddle up and ride off.

The lands of the Mirditi had suffered badly at the hands of the Ottomans in the late 1870s, when they had refused an order to support an Ottoman attack on Montenegro. Now they were effectively leaderless. Their hereditary captain, or prince, Prenk Bib Doda, or Prenk Pasha as he was also known, had been banished to Anatolia in 1881 – one of the many casualties of the Red Sultan's clampdown on the League of Prizren. The princess was ailing. The only man of significance left in the area was the captain's right-hand man, the abbot of Orosh, Prenk Doçi, a remarkable man who had not only studied in Rome but had spent a year in New Brunswick, in Canada. Not many Albanian notables had had such a broad education. Durham set off escorted by a single outrider, a remarkable non-smoker 'in a land where every male wears a cigarette in his mouth from the age of ten upwards'. When she got to the great pilgrimage church at Orosh, the abbot received her with afternoon tea, complete with Marie biscuits. Durham's delight was complete. She had come to 'the wildest part of the Balkans,' she noted, 'and found the greatest luxury'.[31]

She had seen more of Albania than any English person alive, more than any Englishman since Byron's time, and he had never seen the mountains of the north. Byron had impressed the British public with his travels in the Balkans, but had left no impression on the local Albanians. By contrast, Edith Durham's fame would continue to spread among the Albanians, and would prove enduring. Knowledge of her growing celebrity filled her with elation, but she had no intention of continuing to explore remote villages solely in order to impress the crowds.

Durham was torn between a desire to explore the wilderness and, at the same time, be at the heart of political action. After spending months in Macedonia and Albania, she wanted to get back to Montenegro, the cockpit of the Balkans. Throughout her journey she had tried to keep abreast of events in the world. Dürres had been one of the few stops on her journey that boasted a post office, and while she has there, she had gone through a number of letters sent from her family, informing her of developments in England. The most significant news had been of a big protest rally that the Liberals had organised in London, demanding that the Conservative government put more pressure on the Ottomans over Macedonia. The news infuriated Durham, widening the mental breach between her and her Liberal patrons in the Relief Fund. Having seen both Macedonia and Albania at close quarters, she was in no doubt which of these two was worse off, by far. The only result of the London meeting, she suspected, would be pressure on the Ottomans to spend more money on relief in Macedonia that would be deducted in taxes from peasants elsewhere in the region. The people attending the meeting, Durham wrote back, were 'ignorant' people and, however unintentionally, cruel. 'People have been praying me and calling one in God's name to help them,' she told her mother, majestically. Countless Albanians had 'waited and waited, trying to get me to promise to personally interview [Prime Minister Arthur] Balfour [...] now that Europe is forcing the [Ottoman] government to spend money in Macedonia, the state of the others will be worse'.[32]

Durham's store of sympathy for the Macedonians and their Bulgarian patrons, never large, was evaporating further. But she drew comfort from one important international development. In February 1904, war had broken out between the empires of Japan and Russia. The Russian Tsar, Nicholas II, was disillusioned of the anticipated easy victory over a despised Asiatic race as the Japanese crushed the ill-prepared Russian forces. Tsarism was humiliated before the world. While the Tsar's discontented subjects plotted revolution, Russophiles and pan-Slav enthusiasts outside the country felt appalled. Durham was delighted. Her strong and growing suspicion of Russia was another aspect of her growing estrangement from the Liberal tribe. Left-wing Liberals hated the Tsar but the bulk of the party still saw Russia as a potential ally, and as a liberating force in the Balkans, as Gladstone had done. But Durham no longer subscribed to the Liberal narrative on Macedonia, feeling the situation there was more complicated than they realised, and she could not subscribe to their general enthusiasm for Russia, with or without the Tsar. Were Russia to 'free' Turkey-in-Europe from Ottoman rule, she felt, that could not possibly benefit the Albanians. As a non-Slavic, mainly Muslim people, they could expect nothing from that corner. The destiny of the Albanians started to weigh more heavily on her mind. Everything she had seen in Albania convinced her that these people were in no position to articulate their interests or defend themselves from their better-positioned neighbours. Durham was not becoming a Tory on foreign policy. They wanted the status quo to stay as it was. She considered the Tory position unsustainable. The Ottoman Empire was too decrepit to revive or be reformed, and the Tories were wrong to think a corpse could be made to breathe again. But the Liberals were also wrong to concentrate exclusively on the Balkan Christians and feed the raging ambitions of Bulgaria and, more distantly, Russia.

Durham was finding life in the Balkans more stimulating than ever. The further she journeyed, the more fresh possibilities opened up. She had arrived in Dalmatia as an artist. The expedition around Serbia had turned her into a published author and a Balkan expert – it was at this point that she also started writing articles for British newspapers.

In Macedonia, she had reinvented herself once more, as a relief worker among refugees while continuing to build up a literary and journalistic career. Along with a flurry of articles for the papers, a new book emerged in 1905, *The Burden of the Balkans*, in which she tried to explain the conundrum of Macedonia.

Now, the Albanians – or some of them, at any rate – were pressing on her a far more exalted role, as an advocate of their national interests to the great powers. The prospect was daunting, but with no hesitation Durham, at some level, had already responded to this overture, although she did not yet know where it would lead her.

CHAPTER 5

'A fine old specimen'

I hope old Nikola's reign won't end in fiasco. Without him Europe would never have heard of Montenegro.
(Edith Durham, June 1908)[1]

DURHAM MADE HER way back to Montenegro in the spring of 1905 a celebrity, and she knew it. Everyone was talking about the unusual Englishwoman who lived on and off in a hotel in Cetinje, dining with consuls and scaling mountains in her spare time, who had crossed the wild and unknown land of Albania and reached the Serbian holy places of Kosovo – off limits to all but the bravest.

Among those filled with curiosity was Montenegro's autocratic ruler, Prince Nikola. Durham had by now been roaming his domains for the best part of five years. For her part she no longer felt shy about encountering the Prince, seeing herself now as a person of consequence in the Balkans, not a long-stay tourist. As for Nikola, he had been anxious to meet Durham since she returned from Kosovo. A friend of her latter years, Harry Hodgkinson, recalled the *'King-and-I'* air of their relationship.[2] 'As well as being intrigued by his pretensions, and wishing to keep an eye on his intrigues towards her beloved Albanian mountaineers, she was flattered when a crowned head, passing her on the road, would stop and ask her to step up into his barouche and talk politics,' he recalled.

> As to her motivation, he could hardly think, as the country folk did, that she was the sister of the King of England, sent out by him to redress their wrongs. But he knew she was a correspondent for the *Times* and the *Manchester Guardian* and his Balkan mind would tell him that even if she did not have a direct remit from the British government, it was more than likely that her observations and conclusions would find their way onto the desks of the Foreign office clerks.[3]

Their long-delayed encounter had a typically odd Balkan quality to it. The day was arranged but the Prince was no longer young, had been up since dawn attending an Easter service, and was fast asleep by the time Durham hurried through the front gate, as a result of which she had to retrace her steps and wait in a little house near the royal residence. By the time Nikola was up and ready to receive her, a clutch of government ministers was waiting to do the same, and Durham had to pass a long row of officials, all seated on a long bench placed outside the palace door. As she passed, they raised their hats to her, one by one. Once inside, the Prince was solicitous, but he planted her in an armchair that was far too small and presented her with an unappetising meal of boiled eggs dyed red for Easter, lumps of ham, cups of weak tea and glasses of Madeira. While Durham alternately sipped tea and Madeira, her backside straining against the tiny armchair, the Prince prattled away about the great battles that he had fought with the Turks in his youth. Durham half-listened, much more interested in his person than in his tales of derring-do. 'A fine old specimen of an almost extinct type,' she mused to herself as the whiskery monarch burbled on. 'He speaks of his people as if they were his own children.'[4]

At 63, Nikola appeared to be at the height of his powers, 45 years into a reign that had brought Montenegro unparalleled growth, prosperity and prestige. Evidence of Montenegro's international reputation was visible in the streets of the tiny capital, where several grand embassies had recently been built or were under construction. The bulky consulates of Austria-Hungary, Russia, Italy and France – outlandish-looking structures in a capital of one-storey cottages – bore witness to Montenegro's new status as the listening post of the Balkans. A few days after her interview Durham watched the Prince depart on a splendid foreign expedition, soldiers drawn up around the palace, the ministers clustered round the door. As the band struck up the national anthem, the Prince in full dress walked down a line of soldiers before entering his carriage to wild shouts of '*Zivio!*' ('Long life!'), followed by two carriages of escorts. Durham thought it a splendid sight.

In reality, behind the air of patriarchal grandeur and bonhomie, Nikola was struggling. As Durham was soon to find out, in spite of his many achievements the people of Montenegro, the younger generation especially, were becoming disaffected with the Petrović dynasty. The Prince's failure to set up a university was one of several strategic errors. A handful of the wealthiest families sent their sons straight to Italy and France for higher education but the mass of Montenegrins of the ambitious middling sort ended up sending their sons to study in Belgrade. There, they contrasted the semi-feudal conditions of their own country with the bustle of fast-changing Serbia.

The change of dynasty in 1903 in Serbia had, in fact, changed everything for Montenegro as well. Serbia's new monarch, Petar Karadjordjević, was little more than a cipher of the Radical Party, the real force behind the 1903 coup. A middle-class party with republican roots, after 1903 the Radicals became the political establishment. But the atmosphere in Serbia after the coup remained much more egalitarian and democratic than it had been before. In Serbia, unlike

Montenegro, an elected parliament was the active partner of the Crown in government and everyone knew that it was the Prime Minister, Nikola Pašić, who set policy, and not the King. Even before 1903, while Serbia languished under the unpopular rule of the Obrenovićs, Serbia had been encroaching slowly on Montenegro's claim to lead the pan-Serbian movement. After the Karadjordjević restoration, Serbia's ascendancy over its smaller rival became unassailable.

As Nikola tried vainly to keep up, Durham found herself drawn into his complicated plans to promote Montenegro on the world stage. As a result, when the idea arose to hold a Balkan States Exhibition in London in 1907, Montenegro eagerly subscribed, and Durham found herself unwillingly placed in charge of running the Montenegrin stand.

Meanwhile, the Prince continued with his schemes to expand his country in size, hoping that the acquisition of more territory and people would reduce the yawning imbalance in the respective power, population and size of Montenegro and Serbia. He also made a few political concessions at home. In October 1905, shaken by the convulsions that followed the disastrous war with Japan, Nikola's Russian patron, the Tsar, issued a manifesto promising elections to a Russian parliament. A few weeks later, Nikola took a few steps of his own towards a form of constitutional government. Without warning, he proclaimed a new constitution, as well as liberty of the press, and announced that elections to an assembly would take place, in theory divesting himself of his absolute powers. Unconvincingly, the Prince said he was only putting into practice the liberal ideas he now claimed to have absorbed during his youthful stay in Paris.[5] Durham was unconvinced. She told a correspondent that she remembered an earlier discussion she had held with Nikola who, 'after expressing boundless admiration for Mr Gladstone and Liberal principles, stated emphatically that he had not the least intention of introducing parliamentarism into Montenegro'.[6]

According to Durham, Nikola,

> one of the astutest of Balkan rulers, was perfectly well aware that he was living in what Metternich called that most unpleasant of all ages – a transition period; he recognized that the human state of society which he found still existing in the Black Mountain at his accession in 1860, could not withstand the encroachments of Western Europe.[7]

Whatever the reasoning behind them, his belated and half-hearted reforms whetted an appetite for change among Nikola's democratic opponents but did not appease them. Montenegro's new constitution borrowed heavily from the old Obrenović constitution in Serbia,[8] which left a good deal of discretionary power in the hands of the sovereign. Of the 62 new deputies in parliament, 14 were royal nominees – three of them clerics – and all of these were seen as placemen of the Prince, who also retained absolute control of foreign policy. Durham observed the ageing Prince's unconvincing attempts to keep up with the times with a mixture of understanding and regret. The rationalist surgeon's daughter accepted that change was inevitable and even necessary. But she could not help but regret the death of a political order that appealed to her at some level precisely because it was so archaic. The Balkan states 'were the happiest which had the fewest newspapers. Montenegro will now be less happy,' she predicted.[9]

Durham enjoyed her new celebrity status in the country: she had 'risen many degrees in the eyes of Montenegro'.[10] Her reputation, she told her family with satisfaction, was tremendous as a result of having returned alive from Kosovo. After observing her valour, she wrote, the Montenegrins nodded to one another and told her that they now understood why Britain was a great power. 'They agree here that it is not surprising that the British Empire is the largest.'[11] On her latest expeditions to different mountains, she sent her Montenegrin guide, Krsto

Pejović, up into the high meadows to gather flowers. Pejović was an expert at this activity. Now in his early forties, he had been selecting herbs and flowers for visiting botanists, mainly Italians and Czechs, since his teenage years. His habit of introducing her to all the Montenegrins they met as an unmarried foreigner with a vast fortune disconcerted her. But she found him good company, so much so that she spent an entertaining Christmas in his cottage with his family in their home village, Njegusi.

Seeing the flower meadows, and being stood endless rounds of drinks in remote *hans*, or inns, was all very well. At the same time she was starting to find Montenegro confining and at times depressing. A journey to the remote monastery at Kosijerevo lowered her spirits, leaving her shocked at the sheer 'blank desolation on the land [...] all around, a grey wilderness of rock towering up to the sky'.[12] As a result, she decided to move further afield and spend part of the following year in Bosnia and Herzegovina. So far, all she had seen of the Habsburgs' newest acquisition was the border town of Trebinje, which she had visited on market day during her first trip to Dalmatia in 1900. It was surprising Durham had not explored the rest of Bosnia before. No one could claim to understand what was going on in the Balkans without trying to grasp what was happening in the 'dark *vilayet*' that Austria-Hungary had snatched from the Ottomans in 1878.

Bosnia's ethnic and confessional breakdown was almost as complex as Macedonia's. Orthodox Serbs were by far the largest of the three main communities, numbering around 850,000. Another 650,000 were Muslim Slavs, descendants of converts rather than settlers, who made up the majority of the population in most towns. The dry and largely barren south-west and a few fertile pockets in the centre were home to about 400,000 Catholics. Besides them, there was a Jewish community of about 10,000, mainly Ladino-speaking descendants of refugees from the Spain of Ferdinand and Isabella, who had arrived in the sixteenth century when the Ottoman Empire was a haven of tolerance compared to Counter-Reformation Europe. Most of the Jews lived in Sarajevo.

As in Macedonia, the communities faced in different directions, precluding the development of a specific identity. Serbs chafed for union with the Kingdom of Serbia, outside the Habsburg Empire. Most Catholics dreamt of union inside the Empire with the Croats of Dalmatia and Slavonia. The Muslims pined for the days of the Sultan and cherished the forlorn hope of a restoration of the *status quo ante*. Alone among the other communities, the Muslims continued to acknowledge the Sultan's theoretical lordship over Bosnia, which Austria had been obliged to concede when the Congress of Berlin had sanctioned Austria's occupation of Bosnia but not its annexation.

By the time Durham got to Bosnia, while the Sultan's ghost still hovered over the province, everyone else had more or less forgotten about him. Austria-Hungary, in control since 1878, had been ensconced now for a quarter of a century, building schools, barracks, government buildings and railways. The Austrians had brought with them their methodical and honest bureaucracy. But, as Durham noted, their plodding efforts to rule the country justly had won them few favours. The Serbs were not reconciled to Habsburg rule, preferring to be ruled badly from Belgrade than ruled well from Vienna and Budapest. The ultra-conservative Muslims could never develop any real loyalty to an Emperor they saw as an infidel and an imposter. Only the less numerous Catholics were enthusiastic about the Habsburg connection. They had done well since 1878. Religiously and politically marginalised under the Ottomans – who treated them far worse than they had done the Serbs – they were now fellow Catholics in a predominantly Catholic Empire. An influx of civil servants from other parts of the Empire had markedly increased the number of the Catholics in Bosnia, and the community demonstrated its new self-confidence by building a new cathedral and archbishop's residence in the centre of Sarajevo.[13] For all that, most Bosnian Croats cared little for the person of Franz Joseph or for Austria; they supported the occupation and future annexation of Bosnia as a stepping stone towards the goal of pan-Croatian union. Durham judged the Habsburg occupation a failure on every level. An unstable province had been added to an unstable Empire, which already suffered from a surfeit of national disputes.

For Durham, personally, the visit was also a failure. For the first time she found her growing fame in the region a hindrance. The Austro-Hungarian bureaucrats appeared to know a fair amount about her travels in Albania, Serbia, Kosovo and Montenegro, and smothered her with unwanted attention. To her annoyance, she found herself being coerced into undertaking guided tours around factories where she was expected to admire Austria-Hungary's civilising mission. 'I missed the long evenings in Albanian and Montenegrin huts around the fire,' she recalled wistfully.[14] She took her revenge on her hosts by teasing them with her superior knowledge of the Balkans.

The new railway stations and factories did not impress her. It was obvious that the Emperor was not loved in Bosnia, or in Dalmatia, for that matter. She picked up on that on the first day of her journey, in Dubrovnik, where she observed the cold dislike with which the townspeople greeted the heir to the throne, the Archduke Franz Ferdinand, there overseeing naval manoeuvres. To the embarrassment of the Archduke, the crowd fell silent when he appeared, breaking into cheers only when his Montenegrin guest, Nikola's son, Danilo, appeared at his side. The air of hostility, even hatred, towards the monarchy startled Durham. 'It was the most extraordinary display of political feeling I have ever seen. The street was packed with people and they stood as dumb as the stones they stood on,' she recorded.[15]

The anti-Habsburg atmosphere of the crowd in Dubrovnik was a sobering reminder of the Emperor's diminished appeal to his Slavic subjects in general. Dubrovnik was a fortress of

Croatian sentiment in Dalmatia, and the Croats had once been one of the great props of the Habsburg dynasty, almost as reliable as the ethnic Germans. In the revolutionary year of 1848 the Croats had proven more loyal to the Emperor than the Germans of Vienna. Six decades on, that sentiment appeared dead in Dalmatia. Dynastic loyalty counted for nothing, it appeared, and was easily trumped by the appeal of a prince from Montenegro who, unlike Franz Ferdinand, was, all importantly, a Slav.

In Bosnia and Herzegovina Durham felt unable to connect to the Muslim Slavs, whom she found more conservative, more narrowly Turkish in their outlook and generally less lively than the Muslims of Albania. 'One feels very much the numbing influence of the harem system,' she complained. 'The men ask about Queen Victoria, King Edward and the outside world in general. The women have no conversation beyond asking how much one's clothes cost, and the same old questions about marriage.'[16] Durham wanted to fall asleep as the Bosnian Muslim women droned away, badgering her about why she wasn't married and how many children her various sisters had.

There were a few interesting sights. She visited the remote eastern town of Srebrenica, which at the end of the twentieth century would become infamous as the site of a massacre perpetrated by the Bosnian Serbs – Europe's worst single atrocity since the end of World War II. There was, of course, no hint of the horrors to come when Durham went there. She noted only 'pretty wooden houses in a valley of trees, wooden hills all around' and some 'funny old watermills'.[17] There were a handful of other charming scenes. She saw some whirling dervishes. She alternately amused and shocked the people of Sarajevo by winding up and playing her new phonograph in the cafes. It was not all miserable, but it was far less appealing than weird and wonderful Albania, land of the living past. Durham left Bosnia full of foreboding, convinced that this land, even more than Macedonia, was the proverbial Balkan powder keg, waiting to explode. 'The Austrian occupation seems to me a great failure,' she wrote home:

> Austria has had the place for 30 years and has exploited it [but] the wretched natives are poorer than they were before. Many Austrian officials admit quite frankly that it isn't a success for the people...
> The peasant in Serbia is certainly much better off. He has a voice in his government and muddle-headed though that government is, it suits his nature far better than the foreign and despotic military rule here does.[18]

Eight years before the assassination in Sarajevo of the archduke she had seen in Dubrovnik, Durham sensed that war clouds were circling over Bosnia. With Russia weakened by its defeat in the war with Japan, she wondered presciently whether Austria-Hungary might not feel emboldened to start a short, sharp war in the Balkans, in the hope of silencing its own internal disputes. 'Russia's misfortunes are to be Austria's opportunity,' she wrote to her uncle. 'I expect they [the Austrians] think that a successful external war would turn people's attention away from their internal difficulties.'[19]

Durham had no more time to speculate on the prospects of the Austro-Hungarian regime in Bosnia because she had work to do in London. After her *tête-à-tête* with Prince Nikola, her stock had risen further in Montenegro, so that when the subject of the forthcoming Balkan States Exhibition in London arose, the Prince earmarked Durham as the best person to manage it. A formal invitation followed, an honour for a foreigner that she could not refuse, and all the more so as this was to be Montenegro's first major foreign exposition. After leaving troubled Bosnia a few days after Christmas 1906, she had time only for a quick stopover back in Montenegro, spending Orthodox Christmas in the agreeable surroundings of the mountain home of her Montenegrin guide, Pejović, before returning to London to start work on the exhibition. Before she left Cetinje for London she tried to winkle more precise information from the Montenegrins about what she was supposed to do. It was not as if she had ever managed an international exhibition and she was aware of the importance that Montenegro invested in the success of the event.

More than ever that Christmas, Durham sensed that power was shifting away from the Prince in Cetinje to the more powerful court of his son-in-law, Petar of Serbia. Trouble was coming also from the direction of America, from where many Montenegrin emigrants were returning bearing tales of the unheard-of prosperity of the New World. 'America was a republic and in America there were jobs,' the talk went, 'Therefore, if you had a republic, you would have jobs.'[20] The success of the London exhibition had become vital to the royal family in Cetinje as a means of restoring the dynasty's prestige.

Durham was content to play her part in such a project. She was still not much of a monarchist and had felt only scorn on reading reports of the pageantry surrounding Edward VII's coronation in England. What moved her about Nikola's plight was the thought of the stag at bay, the old warrior stumbling, and thrashing around with his sword at invisible enemies. She hated to think of Nikola and Milena ending up as laughing stocks, or worse. But how was she to help? Each morning, the Montenegrin interior minister, Petar Plamenac, assured her that he would present her with the relevant facts and figures that she was to highlight in the pavilion at Earls Court, along with some idea of how to showcase the country's achievements. Each day, nothing happened. Durham ended up writing the programme and choosing all the exhibits herself. Having been given precious little advice about what to display she decided to showcase the kinds of things she was interested in herself, which were 'a lot of wooden models of ploughs, etc, and a case of amulets and ornaments'.[21] Once she was in London, the

Montenegrin government assigned her five assistants to help prepare the stand, but as far as Durham was concerned they only got in the way. Plamenac came to London but almost failed to attend the opening of the exhibition after complaining that he didn't have the right kind of shirt. As a result, Durham had to rush out and buy one for him herself.

In the end, it didn't matter that much what went on in the pavilion in London. The opening of the Balkan States Exhibition was overshadowed by dramatic news from Montenegro where a terrorist plot had been discovered against Nikola. Plamenac had to hurry home, leaving Durham wondering whether what she was doing in London had any point. It was months before she could wrap up the stand at the exhibition and return to Cetinje, her role in the pavilion forgotten and the country embroiled in treason trials. Once she was back in Montenegro, Durham concluded that the discovery of the plot against Nikola was even more serious than she had originally believed. Now she saw it as a great turning point, a moment when Montenegro and its ruling house finally lost hope of winning the race against Serbia to lead the pan-Serbian movement.

The truth about the conspiracy was hard to disentangle from the heated accusations flying in all directions. The Montenegrin police claimed that they had discovered a number of bombs that had been smuggled into the country for the purpose of carrying out high-level assassinations. The bombs had apparently been manufactured in Kragujevac, an armaments town in central Serbia, and the Montenegrin government suspected that the new regime in Belgrade was behind the whole business, having resolved to get rid of the Petrović dynasty by force. Whether or not this was true, Durham saw that the dynasty was in deep trouble, battling an incoming tide of radical, democratic and pro-Serbian sentiment that had captured a large proportion of the nation's youth.

In the meantime the government seized on discovery of the plot to launch a crackdown on all known enemies of the court, over 130 of whom soon found themselves on trial for treason. Pro-Serbian, anti-dynastic circles in the country were outraged, seeing the crackdown as a crudely concocted excuse to restore autocracy. But Durham felt sorry for the embattled Prince. 'I hope poor old Nikola will come out with flying colours and that the end of his reign won't be a fiasco,' she wrote. 'Without him Europe would never have heard of Montenegro and the country would still be in the state of roadless desolation that Albania is in now.'[22]

For all her affection for Nikola, she was irritated when officials started quizzing her over what the government should do next. After that heady trip through Albania, where she had been acclaimed as the potential saviour of an entire nation, Durham was more than ever convinced she had an important role to play in the Balkans. But the role to which she aspired was that of remote queen, above the fray and the hurly-burly of politics. She felt uncomfortable being dragged into the minutiae of day-to-day policy, especially when that might involve people being put on trial and put to death. She resolved to get out of Cetinje until the political temperature in Montenegro had cooled down, having decided 'it was anthropology I wanted, not plots'.[23] Durham followed the treason trials in Cetinje from a safe distance, over the Ottoman border in Shkodra. She was there in May when three of the chief alleged conspirators were executed. She was glad she was not in the country. A few years earlier, as an innocent abroad in the Balkans, she had seen Montenegro as a Shangri-La. Now she left a country that was 'in a very bad way,' she wrote home. 'The political state of affairs is awful. Cetinje is said to be full of spies and no one knows who will be denounced next. The prisons are full... Some hope for a universal amnesty – others are in favour of slaughter. What it's all about, God knows.'[24] Either way, she felt Nikola's image was fast declining in the eyes of the world and of his own countrymen. He was no longer 'the father of his flock'.[25]

Durham had been predicting the collapse of the Ottoman Empire in the Balkans ever since she first stepped off a boat in Dalmatia in 1900. Her expedition through Serbia in 1902 had revealed that Serbia was not the squalid, oriental land of British imagination but a rapidly modernising country whose people had enormous regional ambitions. In Macedonia and Albania she had seen the hopelessness of the position of the Ottomans, their European empire an exhausted, hollowed-out shell, the subject peoples all anticipating an imminent change of ownership. The visit to Bosnia and Herzegovina had convinced her that Austria-Hungary was not up to the challenge of managing the Ottoman Empire's imminent dissolution either.

The great question was which country, or countries, were to benefit from the coming earthquake? As Durham had noted, the initiative was passing from the fumbling hand of Montenegro, whose ruling house now had a full-blown crisis of legitimacy on its hands. Bulgaria seemed best placed to profit from the collapse of Turkey-in-Europe, because it had secured the allegiance of the bulk of the Christian population of Macedonia through the joint activities of the Bulgarian Exarchate and the IMRO. But Durham had no great faith in Bulgaria, or in the pro-Bulgarians of Macedonia, whose allegiances she thought were on sale to the highest bidder. The Albanians she increasingly considered the most deserving cause. 'The more I saw of the Albanians, and of the Slav intrigues for their destruction, the more I thought Albania worthy of help,' she wrote.[26] But, however worthy, the Albanians were in no position to achieve their national aims. That left Serbia, increasingly alienated from Montenegro but now operating in tandem with Russia. Serbia's weakness was its relatively small support base in Macedonia and in Kosovo, where the majority of the population was Muslim and Albanian.

In the summer and autumn of 1908, Durham's predictions of a great Balkan shake-up began to be borne out. The tectonic plates shifted and the region lurched suddenly and dramatically closer to war. The touchstone was an event far from the Balkans. On 10 June in the Russian port of Reval, now Tallinn in Estonia, Edward VII held a splendid and widely publicised meeting with his Russian opposite, Nicholas II. The meeting of the sovereigns was rightly interpreted in Europe as confirmation of Britain's commitment to a Russian alliance and its final departure from the policy of splendid isolation that had been associated with Lord Salisbury's Tory government. Throughout the Balkans, the news from Reval put everyone on alert. The extension of the Anglo-French *entente cordiale* to include France's alliance with Russia held implications for all of them. It brought Serbia, via Russia, into the Anglo-French camp, ending the diplomatic isolation into which the royal assassination had earlier cast it. Britain had already restored diplomatic ties with Serbia in 1906. Serbia's apparent elevation made Bulgaria nervous, prompting Sofia to consider a diplomatic coup of its own. But the most immediate result of the Anglo-Russian meeting was not felt in Serbia or Bulgaria but in the Ottoman Empire, where discontent among the army officers over the state of the Empire reached boiling point, aggravated by the inability of the Ottoman authorities to pay their soldiers on time. Important elements in the army had lost patience with what they saw as Abdulhamid's counter-productive obscurantism. As reports swept the Empire of plans being hatched in the Baltic for the dismemberment of the Sultan's European possessions, the military conspirators brought forward their own plans to reform the Empire before the Europeans forced reform on them. On 3 July, Ottoman officers raised the standard of revolt in Resen, Durham's former base camp in Macedonia, demanding the restoration of a short-lived constitution that Abdulhamid had been forced to accept at the beginning of his reign in 1876, and that he had scrapped as soon as he felt able to do so in February 1878.

The rebellion spread like wildfire and by the end of July had embraced the whole of the Third Army in Macedonia, from where it spread into other Ottoman provinces. Abdulhamid was outraged but, cornered by hostile crowds in Constantinople, was obliged to concede. By the end of the summer he was still on the throne – although not for much longer – but having to work with the Committee of Union and Progress, as the rebels called themselves. They were more generally known in the world as the Young Turks. In theory, the Ottoman Empire was about to turn itself into a representative constitutional monarchy on the European model.

The revolution in the Ottoman Empire and the proclamation of the restoration of the constitution were the beginning of a long and turbulent summer in the Balkans. Next off was Bulgaria. The ructions inside Turkey now encouraged Bulgaria's ruler, Ferdinand of Coburg, to try to upgrade his status and dispense with the fiction of ruling an autonomous principality within the Ottoman Empire – those being the terms handed to Bulgaria at the Congress of Berlin. Citing a minor diplomatic insult at a dinner in Constantinople, Ferdinand took himself off to the thirteenth-century Church of the Forty Martyrs in Trnovo, the ancient capital of the Bulgars, and on 5 October solemnly proclaimed Bulgaria's formal independence from the Ottoman Empire, before 'accepting' the title of Tsar.[27] The grandiose title was something of a joke. The Bulgarians might have ruled an empire in the early Middle Ages but had no empire now. By claiming the ancient title of Tsar and proclaiming his parity with the emperors of Russia, Austria and Germany, not to mention the Sultan, Ferdinand exposed himself to ridicule. According to Nicholas II, it was the 'act of a megalomaniac'.[28] Nevertheless, for all its comic aspect, the proclamation was more than an attempt to resolve all those arguments about precedence in royal processions that preoccupied the sensitive Ferdinand on his foreign trips. It was a sign of Bulgaria's imperial pretensions in the Balkans, towards Macedonia in particular.

Two days later, Austria-Hungary unveiled its own, more important, thunderbolt. Worried by the more assertive tone of the Serbian government and by growing pan-Serbian agitation in Bosnia, the Dual Monarchy decided to teach Pašić's Radicals in Belgrade a lesson. It had already tried economic pressure in vain, imposing a blockade in 1906 on Serbian livestock, the country's main export. But Austria-Hungary had come off worst in what became known as the 'pig war', as Serbia merely diverted part of its livestock trade down the new railway line to Thessaloniki and exported the rest through neighbouring Bulgaria. Humiliated by its failure to bring Serbia to heel in the 'pig war', Austria-Hungary resolved on stronger measures. As the foreign minister, Alois Aehrenthal, confided to a German diplomat, the aim behind the annexation of Bosnia had little or nothing to do with Bosnia per se. The goal was 'the complete elimination of the Serbian revolutionary nest', and was also to involve the donation of parts of Serbia to Bulgaria.[29]

On 7 October 1908, the Emperor Franz Joseph proclaimed the annexation of Bosnia and Herzegovina. Proclamations were posted throughout the province, informing the inhabitants that integration into the Empire would bring numerous benefits, starting with the introduction of limited representative government. Loyal deputations were encouraged to come to Vienna to thank the Emperor in person. The Serbs and Muslims held aloof. But the Catholics of Bosnia, who felt they could only gain from annexation, came in some numbers, led by their redoubtable leader, Archbishop Stadler.[30]

Annexation only altered matters superficially. None of the great powers gave serious consideration to the fact that the Sultan might have serious objections to the loss of his ghostly sovereignty over Bosnia, though in fact he was very angry, and the Ottoman Empire launched a boycott of Austrian produce, forcing Austria to pay a considerable indemnity. The outraged feelings of Serbia were another matter. While the province remained under Austrian military government, Serbia continued to cherish the far-fetched idea that it might receive Bosnia in some future dispensation, when the province's final status was put to another conference of the powers. Serbia did not see Bosnia as just another item on a long territorial wish list. According to the Serbian academician, Jovan Cvijić, the relationship between Serbia and Bosnia could not be compared even to that of France and Alsace-Lorraine, or to that of Italy and Trieste. Bosnia was to Serbia what Moscow was to Russia – the heart of the matter, Cvijić said.[31] Now Austria-Hungary had declared that even the dream of unification was off the agenda and that it was swallowing Bosnia for good.

For the next six months, while loyalist delegations trundled between Sarajevo and Vienna by train, the Serbian government did its best to keep the Bosnian crisis on the boil. The parliament in Belgrade voted war credits and mobilised 120,000 reservists, hoping a display of fighting spirit would force Serbia's Russian ally to do the same.[32] This did not happen. The annexation caught Russia as much by surprise as everyone else. Aehrenthal and his Russian opposite, Alexander Izvolsky, had for some time in 1908 been exchanging ideas on a two-pronged assault on the terms of the Congress of Berlin. The plan involved Austria-Hungary annexing Bosnia while Russia secured the opening of the Straits of Constantinople to Russian warships, which Russia hoped would pave the way to the seizure of the city. But nothing had been finalised, and the news that Austria-Hungary was unilaterally going ahead with the annexation wrong-footed the Russians. Public opinion, by now a real factor in Russian foreign policy, was outraged on Serbia's behalf.[33] But, as Izvolsky regretfully informed the Serbian minister in Paris, Germany had declared its support for Austria-Hungary and the Tsar was not prepared for an all-out war over Bosnia with Germany as well as Austria-Hungary.[34] Both Russia and Serbia were forced to back down. Serbia felt humiliated, Russia double-crossed.

Austria emerged victorious, but at a cost. The annexation broke the rules of international diplomacy and tore a hole through the terms of the Congress of Berlin. Austria-Hungary gained a new reputation for deviousness and unpredictability. The French leader, Georges Clemenceau, described the annexation as 'a gross breach of a treaty arrangement'.[35] The British, from Edward VII downwards, felt baffled. Until now they had regarded Austria as by far the most benign of the three great Continental empires, less aggressive than Germany and less brutal than Russia. Edward VII, whose dislike for his bumptious German nephew, the Kaiser, was well known, cherished his ties with Franz Joseph. When Wickham Steed of *The Times* met the King on one of his spa cures in Bohemia on 15 August and warned him that Austria-Hungary was planning to annex Bosnia, Edward had dismissed the report. 'I cannot believe that,' he retorted. 'It would upset the whole of Europe. Surely the Emperor would have said something to me.'[36]

The annexation of 1908 did not restore Austria-Hungary's prestige as a great power. Nor did it cow the Serbian nationalists. On the contrary, the Serbs had received public confirmation that Austria-Hungary was their connatural foe. Previously they had worked covertly for the break-up of the Habsburg Empire. Now they openly expressed hatred. Speaking of Austria, Professor Cvijić wrote in 1909: 'The more manifest her desire for further conquest of Serb lands, as in the case of Bosnia and Herzegovina, the stronger detestation does she inspire.'[37] As a historian put it much later, 'even the ordinary peasant population of Serbia was now hopelessly embittered against the Monarchy'.[38]

The clamour for revenge had one result. Two days after Franz Joseph proclaimed the annexation, a group of Serbian nationalists met in the city hall of Belgrade and launched a new society, the Narodna Odbrana (National Defence). Committed to the unification of all Serbs in one state, the new organisation made it clear that Serbia was not going to take the annexation in a spirit of submission. From this group there emerged a more militant offshoot in 1911, known as Ujedinjenje ili Smrt

(Union or Death), and in English as the 'Black Hand'. Article 1 of the Black Hand's constitution noted that the movement existed for the purpose of 'realising the national ideals – the unification of Serbdom'. Article 2 stated that the organisation 'gives priority to the revolutionary struggle rather than relies on cultural striving'.[39] The Black Hand had an ancillary in Bosnia, Mlada Bosna (Young Bosnia). The two groups – they were more or less interchangeable – worked hand in hand with the highest authorities in Serbia. The King's son, Crown Prince Aleksandar, let it be known that he was a generous contributor to the Black Hand's organ, *Piemont*, whose name suggested that Serbia aimed to play the same role in the Balkans that the kingdom of Piedmont had played in the unification of the Italian peninsula. The leader of the Black Hand was not some obscure teacher, journalist or junior army officer but Colonel Dragutin Dimitrijević, 'Apis': a key figure in the palace coup of 1903 and now head of the Serbian intelligence service. Apis held open court at the heart of the Serbian establishment. As a contemporary recalled:

> The ante-chamber of his offices in the headquarters of the Serbian Grand General Staff was one big beehive of callers: army officers of all ranks [...] diplomats and domestic servants, bishops in disguise and actresses in deep veils, highly placed government officials and nondescript persons of no fixed abode.[40]

The same writer observed Apis at his usual table in the restaurant Kolorac in Belgrade, seated 'with his permanent smile and ever burning cigarette', presiding over a fawning assembly of 'army officers, diplomats, merchants, bankers, journalists and other classes of the intelligentsia'.[41]

Exactly how much the Serbian government and court knew of Apis's violent plans in Bosnia was to become the subject of Durham's penultimate book, *The Serajevo Crime*, published in

1925. Seven years after the end of World War I, it remained a highly divisive topic. This was, of course, because the Black Hand, with Apis at its head, had by then triggered a European war, after one of its agents, Gavrilo Princip, assassinated the Archduke Franz Ferdinand in Sarajevo in 1914.

CHAPTER 6

The Great Mountain Land

For folk in such lands, time has almost stood still. The wanderer from the West stands awestruck among them.
(Edith Durham, *High Albania*, 1909)[1]

NORMALLY SO AWARE of the most minute tugs and vibrations on the Balkan spider web, Durham was largely oblivious to the seismic events shaking the Balkans in the summer of 1908, as she was far away in the mountains of northern Albania. One of the few benefits she had incurred from the otherwise thankless task of managing the Montenegrin pavilion at the Balkan States Exhibition in London had been the chance to meet distinguished anthropologists. The idea behind the Balkan exhibition had been to attract businessmen and investors to the region. In the event, too few turned up to make much of a difference, but several leading anthropologists had taken their places, drawn by reports of the interesting amulets and folk ornaments that Durham had put on display, and by the chance to meet the woman herself. She was a name in London as a result of her newspaper articles on the Balkans and two published books, *Through the Lands of the Serb* and *The Burden of the Balkans*. One visitor to the exhibition was the Cambridge archaeology professor Sir William Ridgeway. He was about to become director of the Royal

Anthropological Institute in 1908 and it was he who invited her to give a lecture on the Balkans at Fitzwilliam College in Cambridge and become a fellow of the Institute, starting a connection that she maintained to the end of her life. Intrigued by her collection of amulets on display at the Montenegrin stand, Ridgeway suggested that she undertake an extensive tour of the northern mountains of Albania, an idea that Durham was keen to follow up. It provided the material for her third book, *High Albania*.

Durham stole out of Shkodra on a May morning at 5 a.m. in the company of an Albanian guide, Marko Shantoya, at the start of three separate expeditions to the mountains. They lasted a total of eight months and during that time she did her best to explore every facet of the 'land of the living past'. *High Albania*'s occasionally gruesome details of Albanian blood feuds and Durham's insistence on recounting some of them in detail drew complaints from reviewers that she was bloodthirsty. But this was the cavil of a squeamish minority. The book won Durham a more solid intellectual reputation than its two predecessors and is the only one of her books that has been reprinted regularly. Much of its success was down to the simple fact that Durham had gone where no one else had gone before. She probably was the first Briton ever to venture into these parts, and, if others had preceded her, they left no account of their journeys. She was certainly the first woman from Britain to explore the northern mountains.

High Albania was a new type of book in other ways. Earlier accounts of encounters between Britons and Albanians had centred on splendid powwows with Ottoman governors and warlords with walk-on parts for the odd faithful guide or interpreter. Like Disraeli, they romanticised both people and landscape in order to accentuate an image of 'barbaric splendour'.[2] Durham spurned that approach. There were no turbaned governors or splendid palaces in her description of the *Maltsia e madhe*, the Great Mountain Land, and *High Albania* contained no accounts of lavish dinners. The only people of any rank that she met were the odd Italian or German priest.

Among the five tribes of the *Maltsia e madhe*, the Hoti, Gruda, Kastrati, Shkreli and Kelmendi, Durham found an enclosed, self-referential society that operated on codes of conduct and value systems that appeared to have established themselves long before the advent of Islam or Christianity, and encountering these people she felt she was getting a taste of what most of Europe might have been like 1,000 or even 2,000 years ago, long before the rise of nations, governments, cities or moralistic deities. The thought of being the first person to shine a torch into this hidden corner of Europe excited her. 'The wanderer from the West stands awestruck,' she wrote. It seemed as if the great currents of European civilisation, the age of faith, Reformation, Counter-Reformation and Enlightenment, had all flowed round this land, lapping around the edges but never passing through it or exercising any kind of transforming influence. The people had remained granite-like in their resistance to the outside world and, at least in Durham's mind, had involuntarily preserved a kind of prelapsarian innocence that had been lost elsewhere. She had no idea at this point how brittle this ancient way of life was. After the foundation of an Albanian state in 1912, and following World War I, the tribal society of northern Albania decomposed. Less than 40 years after Durham's expeditions, Albania became a communist state, run by people committed to obliterating what remained of the past. Durham discovered her lost world just in time, not knowing that she was writing its obituary.

For now, however, everything appeared to continue as it had had done since time immemorial. Islam and Catholic Christianity were more or less equally represented among the tribes of the Great Mountain Land but neither religion had much impact on the mores of the population. 'For all their habits, laws and customs, the people as a rule have one explanation,' Durham wrote in the second chapter of *High Albania*.

'"It is in the Canon of Lek", – the law that is said to have been laid down by the chieftain Lek Dukaghin.'[3] It was because Lek had said so, she continued, that men walked exactly the length of a gun barrel apart from one another, that women walked behind men, that children were betrothed at birth and that convicted thieves had to repay their victims with goods that were twice the value of those they had stolen. Above all, the Canon of Lek regulated the code of revenge – the law of blood vengeance – to which Durham decided all else was subservient. 'Blood can be wiped out only with blood,' she explained:

> A blow also demands blood, so do insulting words. One of the worst insults is the marrying of a girl betrothed to one man to another. Nothing but blood can cleanse it. Abduction of a girl demands blood, as does of course adultery.[4]

In her lengthy examination of the rules governing the code of blood vengeance among the Albanians of the northern mountains, Durham was careful to distinguish between vengeance and murder, which was what started blood feuds in the first place:

> In blood vengeance the rules of the game are strictly observed. A man may not be shot for vengeance when he is with a woman, nor with a child, nor when he is met in company, nor when *besa* (an oath of peace) has been given [...] there are men who on account of blood have never been out alone for years.[5]

'When the avenger has slain his victim,' she continued, 'he first reaches a place of safety, and then proclaims that he has done the deed. He wishes all to know that his honour is clean. That he is now liable to be shot [...] is of minor moment to him.'[6]

Any house to which the *ghaksur*, or taker of blood, flees, is bound to take him in and provide shelter, food and protection.

Women were not subject to blood vengeance. Even in the rare instances of women rendering themselves liable to vengeance, 'there seems to be a feeling that it would be very bad form to shoot her,' Durham noted.[7] The inhabitants of the Great Mountain Land were horrified when Durham told them that when women in England were found guilty of murder they faced the same penalties as men. However, women still suffered the consequences of blood vengeance. They could not be shot dead but they and their families could be burned out of their houses. House burnings and crop burnings were included in the carefully graded hierarchy of punishments that the Canon prescribed.

The most damaging aspect of the blood code was the way that its provisions extended to the entire male extended family of the accused, which meant that they were all liable to pay for the sins not only of brothers and father but even of distant cousins. Long after the taker of blood had fled the scene and sought sanctuary, these relatives remained in constant danger. Time was not a healer in northern Albania. Debts could be passed from one generation to another and even children could be shot dead for a father's crime. Whether or not a man named Lek had actually authored the Canon, or whether the name had simply become attached to an inherited body of traditions, Durham believed that the original intention had been benign. In carefully codifying the nature of feuds, the aim had been to regulate and limit them. But the consequences had still been disastrous. Society in Albania, especially though not only in the north, had become infested with vendettas passed from one generation to another. Extended families had become caught up in cycles of tit-for-tat killings, which had not only resulted in the deaths of many innocent people; Durham maintained that the feuds had gravely undermined the ability of the Albanians as a whole to unite against a common enemy. It was while gathering information for *High Albania* that she felt that she understood the paradox of Albanian history. Now she knew why, in spite of their tremendous vitality, the Albanians had so easily been subjugated by a succession of outsiders, from the Ottomans to the Serbs and Montenegrins. Albania was a house divided on multiple lines.

Visiting the Kastrati tribe, Durham encountered two young men fleeing blood vengeance:

> One was but fifteen, from the Skreli [sic], and had just killed his first man. He was a big, dark boy who did not look his age. I think his first blood lay heavy on him – not as a crime, but as a momentous act that had brought him up suddenly against the raw facts of life. He sat silent. The first flush of victory had worn off... He had been to school in Scutari [Shkodra]. Now he could return there no more. An outcast, dependent on charity for his bread, his steps were dogged by the avenger of blood.[8]

The other man took no pleasure in his crime either. 'You must kill the man who injures you yourself by the Old Law,' he told Durham. As the family sheltering these two was also 'in blood', only the women could venture out of doors with any safety. Durham left the 'dreary, blood-stricken house'[9] downhearted. She felt more despondent still when she later reached a village in which a boy aged eight had just been shot dead. The child had wandered too far from home, tending sheep on a hillside. He had offended no one but his father had committed a grave insult when he had thrown a burning brand plucked from the hearth at a member of another tribe. The offended man had demanded blood and had refused to swear *besa*. When the father of the boy fled to Shkodra, he left his family exposed. The offended man 'had now washed his honour in the blood of a helpless victim whose only crime was that he belonged to the same tribe as the offender.'[10] Durham was shocked to discover that not everyone believed it was wrong to kill a boy aged eight in such circumstances. Feeling was on the whole against it, she noted, but this sentiment was far from universal. Others held that 'male blood of the tribe is what is required, and in whose veins it runs is a matter of no moment – it is the tribe that must be punished. Even an infant in the cradle has been sacrificed in obedience to the primitive law.' She was told: 'It is a pity, but it is the law.'[11]

The northern mountains and the city of Shkodra were the last bastion of the Catholic religion in Albania and Durham devoted considerable attention to the subject of belief. In the Middle Ages the whole of Albania had been at least nominally Christian, the people of the north following the Latin rite, and those of the south the Byzantine rite. However nominal or shot through with pagan traditions, an awareness of being Christian was one of the factors that had inspired Albanians to join Skanderbeg in resisting the Ottoman invasions of the fifteenth century. And it was also a factor in the flight of thousands of Albanians to southern Italy after the Ottoman conquest.

But, following the Ottoman conquest, Catholicism especially had steadily lost ground. The mass of the population in the central belt and in Kosovo went over to Islam. Only in the mountains of the north and in Shkodra did around half of the population remain faithful to Rome. But organised religion had only a tenuous grip on this society, Durham observed. Even in the remote mountain parishes the Catholic clergy now knew how to preach – a far cry from the days when some of them had not known so much as how to make the sign of the cross. But their sermons had little effect on their hearers because the mountain people did not appear to believe in God, and certainly not in the personal, loving God of the Christians. If they had a God, Durham noted, it was the semi-pagan God of their ancestors, an impersonal force, or fate, that they respected rather than worshipped. They did not believe in the immortality of the soul either, in spite of the clergy's best efforts to promote the concept. When the priests told them that they had souls, which needed looking after, they answered that they had not asked for such a thing and felt no responsibility for it. Sometimes, they laughed and flapped their hands on hearing talk about souls. Inasmuch as they understood what the clergy were driving at, they assumed that the soul was a physical object, like a bird, which flew out from the body when the host died. What happened to it from then on was of no interest to them. One man argued ingeniously, Durham recorded. 'He denied all responsibility about his soul. The Padre said God had given him his soul. "Very well then, it is God's business to look after it. I never asked Him to give me a soul."'

> To Marko's [Shantoya's] suggestion of eternal torture, he replied that the torture of his soul would not affect him after he himself was dead [...] they all seemed to regard the soul as something quite apart from their own identity – possibly as the sort of bird that flies from the mouth of the dying in cheap religious prints. 'When *I* am dead it does not matter to me what becomes of my soul,' was the general idea. Two things only did they consider important – to keep the fasts and to be buried in consecrated ground.[12]

This keen interest in being buried in a churchyard was not connected to any real interest in the concept of an afterlife or to a belief in resurrection. No pious phrases about trusting in eternity marked the graves of the people of the mountains, just roughly carved crescent moons and suns. The mountain people wanted to be buried in churchyards because 'the churchyard was theirs and they had a right to be buried where they pleased,' Durham heard.[13]

Churches in the mountains were well attended on feast days, or when the bishop came, but this appeared to Durham to be no more than an occasion to muster the clan. An anecdote that she heard illustrated the Albanians' indifference to the sublime mysteries supposedly taking place in religious services. 'One woman actually came into the church when the Franciscan was serving mass, walked straight up to the altar and said "Padre,

I want you to write a letter for me,"' Durham recorded. 'He took no notice of her, so, as he was raising the chalice, she caught hold of his arm and repeated her request much louder. His servant then, to her surprise, led her out.'[14]

Having failed to make much headway with the idea of God or the soul, it wasn't surprising that the people of the mountains did not have much idea of sin. Right and wrong they understood, but to do right was to obey tradition, to follow the eye-for-an-eye code of justice in the Canon of Lek. To do wrong was to neglect the Canon by not taking vengeance when it was due. The clergy, Durham understood, accepted their circumscribed position, which involved them acting as local peacemakers where circumstances made it possible. The other great task was to keep their flocks from turning Muslim, but this was now less of a problem than it had been a generation or two back, when whole villages had been known to go over at the slightest pretext. Catholics were more steadfast in their allegiance now. The opening of a seminary and a Catholic printing press in Shkodra, and the creation of an archbishopric there in 1886, had pumped new blood into the withered veins of Albanian Catholicism. But however devoted and reformed the new generation of clergy, those serving in mountain parishes had to work with the material in hand. They could not afford to alienate people just because they had someone's blood on their hands. In one of her tribal encounters Durham met an altar boy who boasted openly of the number of people that he had killed. At the same time he served his local Franciscan priest with devotion and, during mass, Durham thought he looked quite the part as he assisted the priest at the altar. But even elementary Catholic doctrines had not rubbed off on him. As far as Durham could grasp, he too found the ideas of souls and sin more comic than threatening.

The further that Durham journeyed into the high mountains, the more attenuated and bastardised she found the Catholic faith. Among the Nikaj tribe, who comprised about

300 houses, Durham found men who each took several wives, dropped their Christian baptismal names and adopted Muslim names as adults because they preferred the sound of them, and who sold their daughters to Muslims. The Nikaj:

> shot one another, stole within the tribe (which they admitted with grins), never came to church [...but] persisted that they were [Christians], and chorussed that they shot Moslems whenever a decent chance occurred.

Even Durham allowed herself a rare moralising comment on this group. The life of the Nikaj clan she pronounced 'degraded'. In nature, she added, 'nothing stands still; it either develops or atrophies'.[15] The Nikaj had relapsed, in her view.

The irreligious Albanians that Durham encountered in the mountains were not atheists in any modern sense. Their belief system was not post-Christian but pre-Christian, which is why Durham found it so absorbing. They had no time for 'the devil', understood in the Christian sense as the personification of evil, but believed wholeheartedly in devils in the plural; in the evil eye; and in charms, amulets, dragons, vampires and witches. Most tribes appeared to suffer from infestations of vampires and witches who were blamed for the terrifically high death rate of infants and other unexplained catastrophes, such as droughts and sick livestock. Witches and vampires were nearly always women, naturally, but were not regarded with the same revulsion as their counterparts in Western Europe. They were not 'servants of the devil', because there was no devil to serve, just a nuisance whose confessions of ill deeds had to be beaten out of them. There was no question of the Albanians killing their witches. There were far too many of them for one thing. In some villages that Durham visited, people told her that at least a third of their womenfolk were witches or vampires. These mountain people were more interested in devising ingenious methods to track down, outwit and neutralise the witch, or *shtriga*, than in devising excruciating punishments for those that they found. Dipping a coin into a *shtriga*'s regurgitated vomit was seen as a particularly useful talisman. Anyone getting hold of that was safe from the whole lot of them. As for punishments, most of the stories that Durham heard involved nothing more than slapping, beating or pointing a gun at the head of the *shtriga* until she agreed to undo her curse. After that she might be flung out of the house. But quite often, whether or not her spells had been recognised, the Albanians left the village witch alone. Durham's travelling companion, Marko Shantoya, lived very close to a notorious witch whose malicious acts he preferred to ignore rather than confront. Durham had been alerted to this witch's proximity while staying at his home in Shkodra, where she noticed an extraordinarily large number of rodents, so many that they scampered over her bed at night, keeping her awake. Durham begged her friend to buy some traps in vain. She soon found out why.

> Teresi, his wife, came to me and said: 'Please do not ask Marko to buy a trap; he does not want to.' 'But why?' She hesitated. 'Marko thinks the mice are sent.' 'Sent?' I asked. 'But who can send them?' 'Marko thinks that woman – the *shtriga* – has sent them.' I was delighted and asked: 'How do people send mice?' 'Marko says that with Beelzebub all things are possible.' 'But why should we not kill the mice?' 'Because she would be angry and send something worse. Perhaps rats! Who knows?'[16]

The vast number of women believed to be witches was only one of many indications of the low regard in which women were held in Albania. Another was the absence of romantic love. The mountain people appeared oblivious to love between the sexes. As they had missed out on so many other chapters in European history, it was no surprise to Durham that the notion of romantic courtship had passed them by. She learned that in the mountains women existed to be sold, keep house and bear children. Beyond that, women 'were very disobedient and you had to beat them a great deal'.[17] There was a fixed code about such punishments, as there was about most matters. 'A man must order his wife three times before he may beat her and then if, for example, she still refuses to go and fetch water, what can he do but beat her?' When Durham suggested that the woman in question might just be tired, the men shook their heads: '"Oh no [...] they are quite used to it." Also, if a man tells his wife not to answer him, and she does, he must beat her, or she would go on talking.' When Durham replied that men could be punished in England for beating their wives, 'this staggered everyone – even the Padre'.[18] The mountain men discussed buying and selling women in the same way that they discussed buying and selling livestock. When Durham met the master of one household among the Kastrati, she asked the price of a woman in those parts. 'Twenty Napoleons for one from my house,' he told her.

> 'Some will take as low as sixteen. I call that giving a girl away. You don't get one from me at that price. This one here,' he pointed to an infant eight months, tightly swaddled in a large wooden cradle, 'is already sold. I've had fifty florins down, the balance to follow when I send her to her husband.'[19]

Girls were dispatched to their husbands when they reached sixteen. The Kastrati man saw nothing wrong in this trade even though the Catholic Church, to which he belonged, forbade it. 'He regarded his women as chattels, and would allow them no opinion. Only if a woman were sworn to virginity did he allow her equal rights to a man.' He knew of one aged forty, who dressed like a man, had a good deal of land, bore a gun like any of the men and ate with the men, too. That kind of liberty was unthinkable for the rest of womankind. Ordinarily, women did not eat with men but stood and served their husbands, snatching whatever they could find later on.

Durham was intrigued by these reports of 'sworn virgins' – women who had taken oaths of life-long celibacy and who in some cases had adopted male clothing and almost changed sex. As a single, unmarried woman she may have felt something in common with these land-owning, gun-slinging women, rather more than she did with the veiled women of the towns or the mass of other women in the mountains – beasts of burden, breeding, cleaning, cooking, sewing, and staggering to and from wells with buckets of water.

She finally came across one of these fabled creatures while halting to water the horses.

> Then she came up, a lean, wiry, active woman of forty-seven, clad in very ragged garments, breaches and coat. She was highly amused at being photographed [...] had dressed as a boy, she said, ever since she was quite a child because she had wanted to, and her father had let her. Of matrimony she was very derisive – all her sisters had married, but she had known better... She treated me with the contempt she appeared to think all petticoats deserved – turned her back on me and exchanged cigarettes with the men, with whom she was hail-fellow-well-met.[20]

Durham went on to meet a total of four virgins who wore men's clothes and heard of three more, including one who had apparently served, and passed undetected, in the Ottoman army.[21] She met other sworn virgins who wore women's clothes.

The bulk of *High Albania* was an account of the laws, tribes and customs of the highlands of northern Albania. But she completed the book with a return visit to Kosovo, which she had last visited years earlier, when writing *Through the Lands of the Serb*. She did not return to Peć, or the monastery at Dečani, but headed for the town of Gjakova, the Serbian Orthodox monastery at Devič, and the towns of Prizren, Pristina and Mitrovica.

On her first visit to Kosovo she had viewed the *vilayet* through Serbian eyes, seeing it as the Serbs did, as an unredeemed part of the national patrimony that was labouring under the temporary joint tyranny of the Albanians and the Ottomans. By the time she wrote *High Albania* her opinions about Kosovo had evolved, reflecting a more sophisticated understanding of the ethnic realities of the Balkans and a new sympathy for the Albanian cause. Durham had not become anti-Serbian – yet. She spoke better Serbian than Albanian, so that travel among the Serbs remained congenial to her. In any case, the Serbs of Kosovo still had much in common with their Albanian neighbours, perhaps more than they did with the Serbs of Serbia proper. Not for them politics, western clothes, trams and train journeys. Most Serbs in Kosovo spoke Albanian as well as Serbian and their lives and imaginations were every bit as circumscribed as those of their Albanian neighbours. Many of them assumed that England, wherever it was, was just another Ottoman *vilayet*. They were as fascinated as were the Albanians with Durham's unmarried state – and with her straw hat. The Albanians in the mountains had forced her to take it off, saying it was just foolish to put a confection of dried wheat on one's head rather than wear what everyone wore, which was a long piece of cloth wound around the head and then under the face. The Kosovo Serbs did not force her to remove her hat but looked at it with amazement. What kind of *vilayet* did she live in where people wore wheat on their heads, they wondered? Was she forced to wear it by some decree? As with the Albanians, Durham found that there was a failsafe way to halt such a discussion, which was to declare that wearing a circle of wheat on her head was an old custom in her parts. That terminated the debate because for the Kosovo Serbs, like the Albanians, that was the end of the matter. Better a whole village should die than a custom should fall into neglect, they nodded.

The great difference between Durham's later description of Kosovo in *High Albania* and her earlier one in *Through the*

Lands of the Serb lay in her estimation of which nation had the better claim in the event of the Ottoman Empire's dissolution. On her earlier expedition, all she had really known about the Albanians was that they were dangerous people who fleeced the Serbian peasantry with the assent of the Ottoman authorities. This time she looked more closely at the demographic question, and noted that the Serbs were only a small proportion of the population of Kosovo, a quarter at best. However, she still had some sympathy for Serbia's claim.

'The Kosovo vilayet was a most important part of the great Servian Empire of the Middle Ages,' she wrote. 'The Serb of to-day looks at it as part of his birthright, and of its recapture the young men see visions and the old men dream dreams.' However, she concluded that these dreams were distractions. In Prizren, the largest city in Kosovo and an object of particular longing to Serbian nationalists, Durham found little to recall that this had once been the seat of a famous Serbian ruler. The legendary 'white castle of Tsar Lazar was but a dream in the night of the past,' she wrote. 'Around us in the daylight was the Albanian population, waiting under arms to defend the land that had been theirs in the beginning of time.'[22]

As a result of the publicity surrounding her book on Serbia, the Serbs of Kosovo assumed that Durham was still wholly on their side, and, wherever she went in Kosovo, Serbian dignitaries offered her hospitality. In Prizren, they wanted to show her round the new Orthodox seminary, not appearing to notice that she looked on this project with misgivings. 'The Director knew all about me, and regarded me as the champion of the Serbs in England,' she wrote. 'I accepted his hospitality unhappily, for I felt that so far as Prizren and its neighbourhood were concerned, the [Serbian] cause was lost, dead and gone – as lost as is Calais to England, and the English claim to Normandy.'[23] Once again she found herself cursing the Congress of Berlin for not having awarded Serbia 'the truly Serb lands' of Bosnia and Herzegovina back in 1878. Had Bosnia gone to Serbia, not to Austria, she believed, Serbian nationalism would not have been diverted down unnatural paths towards Kosovo, where the Serbs had a past but no future. By the time she concluded her trip to Kosovo, in the town of Mitrovica, she felt full of foreboding for the future of the *vilayet*, uttering her prophetic warning that the town was 'tinder waiting for a spark'.[24]

High Albania, which was published in the autumn of 1909, divided reviewers in Britain. Durham's assertive, trenchant style always did. Her last work, *Burden of the Balkans*, about Macedonia, had delighted some people but it had appalled a considerable body of opinion in England that expected books on the Balkans to confirm their own pre-existing views. As most people in England who took a strong interest in the Balkans were ardently pro-Bulgarian, Durham's different take on the root causes of the ills in Macedonia had come as a shock. As far as the *Nottingham Guardian* had been concerned, *Burden of the Balkans* had been 'a fascinating volume [...] animated and joyous',[25] a view shared by the *Daily Telegraph*, which declared it a work of 'infinite enjoyment'.[26] But the *Times Literary Supplement* complained that Durham was 'animated by a strong bias which frequently warps her judgment; she is surely not fair to the Bulgarians of Macedonia'. The book was 'both misleading and unfair'.[27] The *Glasgow Herald* was shocked by the tone of hostility to Bulgaria and by the author's admiration for the Albanians she had encountered in Macedonia. 'It is the Albanians always of whom she speaks with unqualified admiration,' the review complained. 'But the author ought to know that it is not for want of thought that the philanthropists have turned away from Albania in despair.'[28]

The critics were still more divided over *High Albania*. Like its predecessor, the book had broken with the Victorian tradition of writing about the Balkans as lands of pious Christian peasants labouring under Turkish tyranny. Many reviewers were offended. What they appeared to want were tales of derring-do from the men, information about women's jewellery, picturesque scenes from bazaars, and dollops of harmless superstition and folklore. They wanted to hear about a lost world that made them feel complacent about their own country and indignant about the plight of less fortunate lands. In *High Albania*, Durham had given them a lost world, but it was one in which people shot at each other a good deal of the time. The critics might have warmed more to *High Albania* had Durham interpolated her accounts of blood feuds with suitably moralising judgements. Instead, she seemed to stand back, which seemed doubly remiss coming from a woman. The book 'literally reeks of blood,' the *Daily News* complained in November 1909. 'On almost every page there are tales of men shot, men about to shoot, of men who glory in the tales of murders to their credit. Miss Durham seems to share their exultation in the glory of man-slaying.' The author 'revels in her tales of violence and brutality,'[29] agreed the *Nation*, which accused her of deliberately suppressing the more attractive aspects of Balkan life because she was interested primarily in carnage.[30] According to *The Outlook*, the book belonged in the waste-paper basket.[31]

Durham was not put off by the condemnations of several newspapers, doubtless seeing notoriety as preferable to obscurity. In any case, the furious attacks of some newspapers were more than counterbalanced by the passionate praise of others. The *Manchester Guardian* was ecstatic, hailing Durham's 'brilliant record of her wanderings' and adding: 'It need hardly be said that the book is thrilling.'[32]

Invitations in England to lecture on Albania and write articles came her way in the wake of the controversy. When she returned to London and responded to these requests, she made no concession to her critics in the sense of making the Albanians sound more palatable to sensitive English ears. The country was filthy and unbelievably primitive, religion was a veneer and women were of no consequence, she bluntly informed the Royal Anthropological Institute in 1910. Communal families in the mountains lived 30 or 40 together in stinking, windowless *kulas*, or towers, sharing their living spaces with sheep, goats and black clouds of buzzing flies. None of the Albanians she had met had objected to the choice of wife that had been made for them because they considered all women the same – put on earth only to work and breed. 'To eat with a woman seems to be thought very degrading,' she explained. 'The men eat first and the women eat up the bits left over afterwards at the other end of the room.' She added characteristically: 'I ate with the men.'[33]

While *High Albania* assaulted the sensibilities of a portion of her audience, it was hard for her sternest critics to deny that she had broken new ground. Before Edith Durham, no one in England had known much about Albania. Hobhouse's recollections about Byron's expedition in the 1800s seemed trite and elitist when set against this detailed, warts-and-all account of the lives and mores of the ordinary people. For all the brickbats she received, *High Albania* confirmed Durham's reputation as one of a handful of real experts on the Balkans, and the book gained her a respectful audience, ranging from the scholars of the Royal Anthropological Institute through to a swathe of Liberal MPs. Subsequent generations of readers have tended to side with the *Manchester Guardian* rather than with *The Outlook* in appreciating her account of the people of the mountains. *High Albania* was a remarkable achievement. As well as being the first detailed description in English of a little-known society that had survived almost unchanged for centuries, it was the last. Durham did not know this, of course, but the high, indestructible-looking walls surrounding the Great Mountain Land would start to crumble within only a few years of *High Albania*'s publication.

CHAPTER 7

'They never all rise in a lump'

They persist in believing I'm a queen, the queen of the 'kach-aks' – of the insurgents.
(Edith Durham, November 1911)[1]

O N HER RETURN from Kosovo to Shkodra on 5 October 1908, Durham heard that Ferdinand of Bulgaria had proclaimed himself Tsar. Four days later, the Austro-Hungarian consul in the city informed her that the Emperor had annexed Bosnia and Herzegovina. Durham was not impressed. She had seen for herself how unpopular the Austrians were in Bosnia, especially among the Serbs. She told the consul that Austria-Hungary would have been better off letting the sleeping dogs of Bosnia lie. She did not believe that Belgrade would cease nationalist agitation in Bosnia as a result of the annexation. While Austria-Hungary braced to meet the combined fury of Serbia and Russia over Bosnia, Durham also noted that Austria's action had infuriated Muslims throughout the Ottoman Empire. The loss of Bosnia had touched them greatly. In their eyes, Bosnia was a Muslim land in a way that Serbia and Bulgaria never had been. Islam had indeed rooted itself successfully in Bosnia, not just in the town. The countryside was home to a settled Muslim peasantry, mostly the descendants of converts, not immigrants. Now they had been snatched from the Sultan and placed under a Catholic emperor. The fact that the Sultan had lost all real hold over Bosnia back in 1878 did not concern them. Formal annexation was still a shock. Durham watched a hostile demonstration against Austria staged by the pious Muslims of Shkodra. Strange rumours coursed through the city, including one that the British were about to seize the city themselves. Tension mounted as a report spread that the British had already landed. In the event, Durham laconically noted, the conquistadors turned out to be a couple of English ladies who had disembarked from a steamer and wanted to see the bazaar.

Tiring of the feverish atmosphere in Shkodra, Durham fled back to Cetinje, but it was no relief. The discontent fizzing among the Muslims of Albania over the annexation was nothing compared to the hysteria gripping Montenegro, which was no longer connected to plots against the dynasty but to the prospect of war with Austria-Hungary. The Montenegrin government still suspected that Serbia had been involved in plots against the life of the Prince, but pan-Slavic solidarity necessitated a show of unity against Austria-Hungary. Besides, the annexation genuinely offended Nikola. Many Montenegrins had family, or ancestors, in Herzegovina, and the Prince had encouraged them to dream of days to come when Montenegro and Herzegovina would be one land. He felt slighted when Austria-Hungary failed to offer him any territorial compensation for the loss of this hope. The day after the annexation, Nikola issued a flowery proclamation, lamenting that 'the graves of Montenegrins who had fallen for the freedom of Herzegovina will be trod upon by foreign feet'.[2] Demonstrators attacked the Austro-Hungarian embassy in Cetinje, the Empire's commercial offices in Podgorica and the consulate in Bar. Significantly, Nikola's own daughters joined some of the protests.

When Durham arrived she found that everyone wanted to talk to her, including the diplomats and the Prince. But she felt confused and somewhat ill. The arduous journeys through the

Albanian mountains had taken much more out of her than she cared to admit. Shortly after, she left for England on a cruise ship with no one on board except for a drunken Austrian. After completing *High Albania* in England she spent the rest of 1909 there, overseeing the book's publication and trying and failing to find a cure for her worsening rheumatism and sciatica. It was not until the April of the following year that she was back in the Balkans, again steaming down the azure coast from Trieste, refreshed as always by the sight of the aquamarine sea and the lights of the Croatian ports glowing in the dark after sunset. One morning she awoke early and went out on deck to find dolphins leaping out of the water. Looking longingly at the coastline glowing pink and mauve in the dawn, her feeling of contentment was complete.[3]

Back in Shkodra in the spring of 1910, she found the atmosphere greatly changed from when she had last been there in the autumn of 1908. No one was now shouting slogans in support of the Young Turks' liberal-sounding constitution, the '*constituzi*', as Durham nicknamed it. A sullen mood gripped the city, where trust in the vague-sounding pledges of the Young Turks had curdled into disappointment. Durham went to watch the accession day celebrations of the new Sultan, Mehmed V, whom the Young Turks had installed in April 1909 to replace the dreaded Abdulhamid. The usual triumphal arches were up over town, decorated with an idiosyncratic assortment of swords, revolvers and rifles. Once more the Ottoman army units and foreign diplomats based in Shkodra staged processions, the elaborately dressed Austro-Hungarians looking especially grotesque, Durham thought, pulled along in incongruous pomp in a carriage drawn by 'one horse and one very long-eared mule'.[4]

This display of tatty flummery did not fool anyone. The wave of good feeling towards the Ottoman Empire had dissipated and Durham stole away from the processions, weighing the significance of this growing anger. The Muslim party in Albania was clearly unhappy, she concluded, still smarting over the annexation of Bosnia and uncertain about what might be coming next. On the other hand, the Catholics of the north looked openly to Austria-Hungary, hoping that the Habsburgs would now occupy Albania as well. If the annexation of Bosnia had shocked the Muslims, it had raised expectations among the Catholics. Durham heard a rumour circulating in Shkodra that in three months' time, 'something happy for Albania' would happen, 'and folk hope it is Austrian annexation'.[5] Durham thought an Austro-Hungarian invasion improbable and she was not a fan of the Habsburgs, having seen the results of their rule in Bosnia. But she sympathised with the feeling at some level. 'It couldn't be worse than the present situation,'[6] she decided.

Over the provincial border in Kosovo, the mood was angrier and more dangerous. In the spring of 1910, an armed insurrection broke out after the governor of the *vilayet* introduced an unpopular tax on goods entering towns. From Gjakova, in the west, which Durham had visited on her last trip to Kosovo, she heard reports that the insurgents had chased out the Ottoman garrison. Shkodra remained quiet but Durham was astonished to see how many guns were pouring in. While shopping in the bazaar she spotted piles of rifles and rounds of ammunition stacked casually beside bags of coffee and rice. But the Albanians appeared incapable of putting their rebellious energy to useful effect. Durham saw no sign of coordination emerging between the rebels in western Kosovo and the people of Shkodra, only a few dozen miles further west. This was the Albanian weak point. 'They never all rise in a lump,' she lamented. 'They cannot produce a native Garibaldi to organise their nation.'[7]

The traditional disunity of the Albanians, one tribe pitted against another, Muslims against Catholics in the north, Muslims against Orthodox Christians in the south, allowed the government in Constantinople to regain the initiative in Albania. In the palmy days of the Young Turk revolution the new government had given permission for schools in Albania to start teaching in Albanian. Now the authorities withdrew the concessions. Orders went out, banning the new Albanian classes and closing any schools that continued to hold them. There were reports of arrests and of outrages against women. By June 1910 Durham felt depressingly convinced that Young Turk and Old Ottoman were much the same thing. Nothing had really changed from the grim days of Abdulhamid. In some ways, the situation was worse, because the European powers were more indulgent towards Constantinople's new rulers than they had been towards the 'Red Sultan'. The powers were bamboozled, Durham thought, by the phoney talk in Constantinople about the rule of law and constitutional government. 'We did not know that "Constitution" meant that the Powers were going to let the Turks kill us,' she noted, laconically. It would be 'farcical were it not so tragic'.[8]

The fighting spread in Kosovo in the summer of 1910, as the Ottomans poured in troops and recaptured one town after another. The atmosphere became menacing in Shkodra, too. Ottoman troops began moving in to reinforce the garrison and to ensure that rebellion did not spread from Kosovo to the strategic city. Many of the soldiers came from the Empire's far-flung eastern domains, and the sight of Asiatic faces astonished and frightened the locals. The authorities ordered everyone to hand in their weapons, a decree that was extended from the city to the mountain tribes. Anyone caught disobeying was to be publicly flogged. Horses were commandeered. The Young Turks were 'too beastly,'[9] Durham wrote, disgustedly. The failure of the powers to react to any of these actions shocked her. She felt that Austria-Hungary had already lost face, which was why hardly anyone turned up at the legation in Shkodra for the Emperor Franz Joseph's birthday celebrations in August.[10] As local Catholics lost faith in Austria-Hungary's willingness to act, Italy's stock rose. Perhaps the Italians would free Albania, not Austria-Hungary, people said.

With Shkodra in a state of virtual lockdown and revolt still sputtering in Kosovo, Durham was desperate to get out and see what was going on. But her worsening health again betrayed her. The back problems that had accumulated while she was gathering material for *High Albania* had now become so severe that she was confined to bed for long periods. The attempt at a cure in England in 1909 had achieved nothing. In fact, a fall sustained there had made matters worse: she now had a seriously damaged leg as well as a bad back. It was infuriating to have to lie in bed, poring over the newspapers and watching storks flying lazily over the rooftops of Shkodra when she could have been out in the hills, knocking Albanian heads together. The state of her wounded leg frightened her. It looked as if it had been 'boiled away,' she mused.[11] Even if it got no worse, she feared she might end up with one leg considerably shorter than the other. To aggravate matters, her Albanian friends quarrelled violently over her sickbed, displaying all the Albanians' habitual fractiousness over the business of her illness. Her faithful companion, Marko Shantoya, conceived an inexplicable, murderous hatred for the local doctor, who he insisted was trying to poison her on the orders of Austria-Hungary. Marko maintained that the only way to cure her leg was to smear it in the warm fat of a freshly slaughtered pelican. Either that, or she needed to be stripped naked and wrapped in a raw sheep's hide. The northern tribesmen who also crowded into her hotel room insisted that she should do nothing at all. Like the Macedonians, they did not believe that any illness could be 'cured'; everything was down to fate, which might be nudged this way or that by the judicious use of talismans, charms and the services of witches. The Catholic clergy who accompanied the tribesmen down from the mountains disagreed. They encouraged Marko in his hatred of the doctor but had their own pet remedies. Part of the problem, Durham reflected, was that none of the Albanians truly believed that she was, in fact, ill, because she didn't 'scream like an animal', as people in the Balkans did, even when the problem was nothing more than mild toothache. Her condition took her back to her days in the hospital at Ohrid where her Macedonian patients would howl and shriek long before she did anything to them. Their bellowing had made it hard for her to tell whether her medical interventions were inflicting real pain on them or not, she reflected. The Balkan habit of screaming in anticipation of pain had made her 'too hard-hearted' towards sick people in general, she decided. As the priests, tribal chiefs, the doctor and Marko battled for supremacy over her sickbed, casting the worst aspersions on each other's motives, Durham decided she had to get away. It was too bad, leaving when Albania and Kosovo were seething and when the Ottomans were flogging people in the streets, but she was desperate for rest.

In October 1910, Durham hoisted herself out of bed and took a ship to Egypt, hoping that her numb, wasted-looking leg might improve in the hot, dry heat of the Middle East. On her tour of Bosnia and Herzegovina in 1906 Durham had expressed a fond hope that Britain might be doing a better job in Egypt than Austria-Hungary was doing in Bosnia. Now she had the opportunity to see if this was true. She soon concluded that Bosnia and Egypt were depressingly similar. As in Bosnia, so in Egypt, a foreign power bent on civilising a backward land was trampling the local culture underfoot and modernising affairs in a crass, superior fashion. Durham was amazed to see how quickly and deeply the British Empire had impressed itself on the land of the pharaohs. Huge hoardings, seemingly planted everywhere, advertised the benefits of Pears soap and Lipton's tea.[12] Egypt was like 'a vast Earls Court,' she complained, harking back to the ill-fated Balkan States Exhibition. 'Everything seems to be arranged for tourists. I don't wonder that British rule is disliked.' The pyramids were 'as bad as Margate,' she continued, 'what with hotels, tea shops, photographers, donkey boys [...] nor can one be seriously impressed with the eternal sphinx when someone is bawling through your ear, "*Napoleon – 'e pull 'is nose off!*"'.[13]

By the Christmas of 1910, however, Egypt's baking dry heat was working wonders with her leg, and although she was still lame she could at least walk. Contact with the resident British colonials, however, meanwhile hardened her growing antipathy to all empires, her own included. 'I wouldn't be a native under British rule at any price,' she wrote angrily. 'They may "do a lot of good to you", but dear God, they do let you know their contempt for you.' 'Anyone with any spunk in them would rather go to hell' than accept British rule, she added.[14]

By the spring of 1911, after several months spent recuperating in Egypt, Durham felt ready to leave her Italian-run bed and breakfast and get back to the Balkans. News from Albania filled her with optimism; her message concerning the need for unity among all the Balkan peoples against the Ottomans was taking root. While Macedonia was heaving again, King Petar of Serbia was on a visit to Italy, prompting Durham to wonder again whether, now that Austria-Hungary appeared to have abandoned its hand in the game, Italy was about to break the power of the Ottomans in Albania. Durham hoped that a new, more coordinated revolt would erupt in Albania and Kosovo and throw out the Ottomans once and for all. 'If they rise, they must all be quite ready to rise on the same day all over the country,' she told her sister in February 1911. 'Sporadic risings are useless.' She felt confident that the Montenegrins and Albanians were at last taking this point on board. 'After preaching Albano-Montenegrin entente on and off for six years, I begin to think some of my sermons have taken effect,' she declared.[15]

On her slow passage back to the Balkans via Jaffa, Beirut and Constantinople, she was pleased to discover just how famous an authority on Balkan questions she had now become. 'I had no idea I was so notorious, but it seems all the English colony wants to meet me,' she wrote in triumph from the Ottoman capital. 'The Albanian question is the question of the day.'[16] As a result there was little time to go and tour the sights. Apart from a quick trip to the Hagia Sophia and a museum, Durham happily resigned herself to giving interviews to Reuters and British newspapers on Balkan matters. She had 'done nothing except write reports and be interviewed'.[17]

She arrived back in the Balkans more of a celebrity than ever, in spite of her prolonged absence. Everyone was expecting her, one man told her, as she stepped onto the quay at the Adriatic port of Bar early in May. Everyone included the Montenegrin royal family, as Nikola was keen to resume contact. He was now no longer a prince, having since turned himself into a regular king. On 28 August 1910, marking his golden jubilee on the throne, he had upgraded his title – all part of his campaign to keep his little country abreast of Serbia. Medals were struck, a coronation ceremony arranged and invitations sent out. The authorities in Belgrade took Nikola's move in the spirit in which it was intended and sent only a modest delegation. Politicians from Serbia were significantly absent from Nikola's party. However, the Serbs did not wish it to look as if they were sulking. There was no question of King Petar going to Cetinje, but they did send the Crown Prince, Aleksandar.[18]

In obedience to the royal summons, Durham did not go to Shkodra, as she had planned, but diverted up to Cetinje, where she had 'such a reception as you cannot imagine. The whole royal family all to myself'.[19] Nikola, the stately Milena, two of the princesses and Princes Danilo and Marko all plied her with questions at once, about Egypt and her predictions about Albania, which Durham attempted to answer in both English and Serbian. The King then tried to pin his new jubilee medal on her bosom, which caused much amusement as it fell off and rolled around on the floor, at which point one of the princesses dived down to retrieve it and fastened it onto her with a safety pin.[20]

Durham was at the highpoint of her career, both in the Balkans and in England. In England, *High Albania* had achieved a form of *succes de scandale*. Durham felt so much more than a Balkan observer now. With three books in print, not to mention the numerous articles she had written for newspapers and journals, she was an established author. She had her own gospel, concerning the need for Serbs, Montenegrins and Albanians to cast aside historic ethnic and religious differences and work together to throw out the Ottomans. Unlike the British Conservatives, she had no faith in the Ottoman Empire's ability to reform itself, no reverence for empires in principle. She had not gravitated back into the Liberal camp, either. Years earlier, her work in Macedonia had made her suspicious of what she considered the Liberal fetish with the plight of the Christians in the Balkans, the Bulgarians in particular. Now she felt that many of the Liberals were rushing to barter their old faith in a big Bulgaria for an equally bogus faith in the Young Turks, falling for windy talk about religious equality and constitutions. As always, she believed, the Liberals left the Albanians out of every equation.

The respect that Durham enjoyed in 1911, a feeling of being courted, skewed her normally sound sense of judgement. Once cautious about the extent of her influence and inclined to pessimism about what she could achieve, she began to confuse praise for her books and work with active conversion to the causes in which she believed. In reality matters were not as she imagined. She had helped to awaken the British political establishment to the existence of the Albanians. But the fact that the Foreign Secretary, Sir Edward Grey, now knew where Albania was and who Durham was – his initials are visible on one of her larger missives from Shkodra in 1908[21] – did not mean he was about to commit Britain to the creation of a free Albania. Still less did it mean that he was about to commit Britain to the creation of a state that contained within its borders all those towns in the Balkans in which a majority of the population comprised Albanians.

As for the Balkans, Durham's endless 'sermons' there, as she called them, on the need for Serbian–Albanian unity, had not had as deep an impact as she imagined. The Montenegrin royal family fussed around her and appeared to hang on her advice, but once she was out of range, Nikola and his advisers went back to focusing on narrower considerations, centring on the need to seize more territory. Durham was about to find out that the Serbs and Montenegrins had no intention of liberating Albania, or of helping the Albanians to liberate themselves. The Montenegrins just wanted more land. Their plan was to encourage an Albanian revolt in order to weaken the Ottoman Empire. But they would not give serious quantities of arms to the Albanian tribesmen because they did not want the rebels to overpower the Ottoman army and set up a state. Once the Ottomans were forced onto the defensive, Montenegro intended to invade Kosovo and northern Albania and deal with the locals as it saw fit. Durham was to be disillusioned, and sooner than she could have expected.

Cetinje had changed so much in little more than a year away that Durham barely recognised the place. In his relentless determination to keep pace with Serbia, Nikola was transforming the town. Alongside the grandiose new legations that the Austro-Hungarians and the French had built for themselves, he had erected a building for the newly established parliament. There was a new bridge and a school, and a park had been laid out opposite the Grand Hotel. The barracks had been greatly enlarged and electric lighting installed in the main streets. Many of the old one-storey houses had been demolished to make way for these improvements.

The revolt on the other side of the border in Kosovo and the state of virtual siege in Shkodra, meanwhile, put the country on a war footing, and when Durham went to Podgorica, her hotel there, the Europa, was crammed with army officers. She had herself driven down to the Ottoman frontier where she found everyone in a state of nervous expectation. There were regular exchanges of gunfire across the border. Durham sat in a guardhouse, listening to the 'nervous tick-ticks of the military telegraphs – outside, the continuing rifle fire and, when the wind was in the right direction, the long swish of bullets that tear the air'. Still confident of Nikola's good intentions, Durham allowed herself to identify with the coming war and with the cause of Montenegro. The Montenegrins became 'us' in her correspondence. 'War is possible between us and Turkey,' she wrote home in May.[22]

In fact, the revolt in Kosovo was now over and by June the situation was sufficiently peaceful for the authorities to dispatch the Sultan to Kosovo for a short imperial visit, which included a tour of the site of the famous Battle of Kosovo of 1389, outside Pristina. By then the fighting in Kosovo and the disturbances in the mountains around Shkodra had displaced thousands of Albanians, and many had drifted over the border, seeking sanctuary in Montenegro. Durham decided to set up her own version of the relief fund for Macedonia. Working for the fund in 1904 had given her invaluable experience in dealing with the sick and destitute. All she lacked now was money. Although she fired off articles to British newspapers, they were not always printed. Partly, she felt, it was because the Liberals in England were still fooled by the reformist talk emanating from Constantinople. Her old colleague from the days of the Macedonian fund, Noel Buxton, was 'hopelessly in the Turks' hands,' she wrote. Unattractively, she also blamed the Jews for a pro-Turkish bias that she detected in the British press. The media were mostly controlled 'by big financiers who are mostly Jews,' she grumbled, who were 'as a body [...] pro-Muslim'.[23] Up against – at least in her mind – a grand alliance of Tories, Liberals and Jews, all bent on discouraging foreign intervention in the Balkans, Durham ploughed on with plans for a relief mission. The refugees arriving over the Montenegrin border brought horrific tales of Ottoman acts of retribution. Up in the mountains of northern Albania, she heard, they were singling out Catholics for special punishment. The priest from remote Gusinje, Father Ludwig, told her of parishioners murdered in their own homes, of churches desecrated and of orchards cut down to the roots. Others told her of waves of arrests in

Shkodra, which now sounded so dangerous that she decided she could not even visit the city. She was terrified that the Ottomans would arrest and hang her beloved Marko Shantoya, who lived in Shkodra and was incommunicado. At night she lay sleepless in her bed in Podgorica, wondering whether or when the Ottoman artillery would be playing through the row of mulberry trees outside, 'and smash the Hotel Europa'.[24]

By day, Durham put these fancies aside and got down to the business of helping refugees. Never one to take no for an answer, she soon found ways to obtain funds. A serendipitous encounter with a wealthy foreign woman netted a modest start, a donation of £25. Much more significantly, Charles Crane, a wealthy Chicago businessman she had encountered earlier in Montenegro, wired her £500.[25] It was not enough to deal with the needs of thousands of people but Durham was resourceful and economical, sweating away in the July heat in her hotel room, tearing up sheets to make rudimentary shirts. Immediate distribution of food and clothing was the priority, as many refugees were wandering round Montenegro half naked and in a state of exhaustion. Some were eating nothing more than chopped weeds and nettles. 'Their condition beggars description,' she wrote, 'haggard, wan, terrified, all in rags – absolutely destitute.'[26] After she had done with turning out a large batch of smock-like shirts, she converted her hotel room into a shoe factory, hammering away at leather hide. The stench from the sweating, freshly slaughtered hides in the heat was appalling, and to make matters worse cockroaches overran her room, swarming in and out of the piles of leather and the bags of food that she had bought to distribute. Sometimes she felt overcome with despair, 'fighting single-handed' to save a constantly swelling number of refugees whose overall condition continued to worsen, no matter how much maize she gave out, let alone how many shirts and shoes she was able to make. But after visiting a family of seven, three of whom lay dead in an improvised shack, the survivors all lying there with glassy eyes and with the distended and swollen abdomens of the starving, Durham returned to her hotel knowing that now was not the time even to think of surrender. On the contrary, she had a brainwave: she would ship in industrial quantities of block soup from the Italian army. 'If only I had enough money I could save the lot,' she wrote, feeling much more confident, at the end of July.[27]

Durham did not blame the Montenegrins for not doing more to help the milling refugees. Nikola's newly dignified kingdom was poor already, and could not be expected to take in, feed and clothe thousands of unexpected and uninvited strangers. What shocked her more was the King's almost overnight decision to make peace with the Ottomans and close down talk of imminent war. His sudden policy reversal was not totally inexplicable. Kosovo had been brought to heel and impressively large crowds of conservative Muslims had turned out to cheer the Sultan on his visits to Pristina and Skopje in June. Nikola felt he had good reason to pull in his horns. Nevertheless, his decision left the remaining Albanian rebels in Kosovo and the refugees in Montenegro looking exposed. As far as Durham was concerned, Montenegro had done its utmost to encourage an Albanian revolt, and was pulling the rug from under the rebels' feet, having decided that the time was not right to make war.

At the end of the first week of August, Durham attended a tumultuous meeting of Albanian rebel chiefs in the army barracks on the outskirts of Cetinje, where the Montenegrins coldly informed them that they had to lay down their arms and go home. In fact, they were to return whether or not they had a guarantee of safe conduct from the Ottoman authorities. Durham crept back to the hotel late that night feeling shaken and disgusted, only to be followed to her room by a group of Montenegrin officials who told her that she was the only person with sufficient authority among the Albanians to make them see sense and go home. Durham was appalled. She could see the remorseless logic of the Montenegrin case: if the King had decided that war was off, the rebels would have to go home at some stage. But she could not forgive the Montenegrins for designating her to be the bearer of such news. She had seen the acute distress and indignation of the warriors for herself at the meeting in the barracks.

The next day, Durham slipped out of the hotel early and unseen, spending most of the day hiding behind a haystack and stealing back to her room only after dark. But, back in her room, she found the head of the Montenegrin army, Janko Vukotić, a close relative to the Queen, waiting for her. Vukotić spoke bluntly. The Albanians would be turned out of Montenegro, cut off and disowned if they refused terms with the Ottomans. Durham had to go back to the barracks at dawn and clear up the business. 'I wonder how often in the world's history a foreign female has been asked by a commander in chief to make terms with insurgents,' she wrote home after Vukotić left her room.[28] She tried to snatch a few hours' rest before the meeting, but sleep did not come and she remained awake the entire night, worrying, making her way to the barracks just before six in the morning. From then until late that afternoon, in the company of a few Franciscan clerics from the northern mountain parishes, she worked the crowd, pleading and cajoling, nauseated by the task she had been obliged to undertake by people that she still considered friends. She only succeeded in her task because her fame among the northern Albanians, as well as among the Montenegrins, meant that many of them no longer merely styled her a great lady, but 'the Queen'. It was the highest honour they could bestow, and a mark of recognition that in some sense she had come to belong to them. She was 'quite accustomed now to hearing me referred to as "Queen", *kraljica*,' Durham wrote, of that tumultuous day at the barracks.[29]

Durham appreciated being designated an honorary queen, and from now on she regularly informed her family of the fact,

Plate 1 Edith Durham as a young woman: 'Escape seemed hopeless'

Plate 2 King Nikola of Montenegro and his family:
'A fine old specimen of an almost extinct type'

Plate 3 King Petar of Serbia: Durham had troubling dreams of his 'blood-stained hands'

Plate 4 Ismail Qemali and the declaration of Albanian independence, November 1912

Plate 5 William of Wied: 'A feeble stick, devoid of energy, tact or manners'

Plate 6 King Zog of Albania: 'I loathe Zog', Durham once told a friend

Plate 7 Aubrey Herbert: Declined a throne as, 'The Albanians have never paid any taxes'

Plate 8 Henry Nevinson: 'Never knew a woman to express facts with such startling vigour'

Plate 9 Robert Seton-Watson: Accused Durham of describing the Serbs as 'vermin'

Plate 10 Rebecca West: Dismissed travellers 'who return with a pet Balkan people'

Plate 11 Albanian tribesmen: 'The more I saw of the Albanians, the more I saw them worthy of help'

Plate 12 IMRO leaders in 1903: The movement's 'wire-pullers in Sofia' evoked Durham's distrust

Plate 13 Shkodra in 1897: Durham felt captivated by 'the squalor and the gorgeousness'

Plate 14 Ohrid circa 1900: 'The peasants come and go under crumbling medieval gateways'

Plate 15 Cetinje in 1895: 'It was in Cetinje that I first picked up a threat of the Balkan tangle'

Plate 16 Resen: Durham found the refugees here 'in a state of pitiable terror or sullen ferocity'

Plate 17 Macedonian freedom: Durham declared the Macedonians 'a singularly stupid breed'

Plate 18 Edith Durham School in Tirana

half seriously, half with amusement. If it gave her more authority among the Albanians, and to act on their behalf before the world, it was all to the good. In the meantime she never forgave the rulers of Montenegro for having abused the prestige that she enjoyed among the Albanians in such an unscrupulous fashion. But now a shaky peace had been restored between Montenegro and the Ottomans, she was at least able to cross the frontier, check up on matters in Shkodra and track down Marko Shantoya, who she was delighted to find had survived the troubles unscathed. Once back in the city and with Marko at her side, she decided to make a tour of the mountains, see whether the refugees were returning home safely and resume the distribution of aid to people. Money was flowing into her fund as the result of appeals planted in the *Morning Post*, *Morning Leader* and *Manchester Guardian*, some of it brought out in cash by well-wishers. One was the handsome, middle-aged journalist, Henry Nevinson, who, after meeting Durham in Shkodra, agreed to accompany her on a quick tour of the nearby Kastrati clan. The two Britons wandered around the villages in the foothills, watching the Albanians trying to rebuild roofless houses with poles and bits of grass thatch. Durham was not surprised to discover that the Ottoman authorities had not rebuilt the homes that their soldiers had torched or demolished a few months earlier. Nor had the Ottomans offered any compensation to the people they had turned into refugees. However, the government had done something by distributing a little maize, so at least the returnees were not starving as well as homeless. In the meantime she ordered quantities of timber and roofing felt from Trieste.

By the end of the month the distribution process was in full swing and Durham was busy giving out maize, planks and felt, as well as quinine and other medicines. There was never enough. Heavy planks of wood could not be carried easily up the mountains to the remoter villages. The quinine, designated for use among the malaria-ridden refugees stuck in the lowland marshes, ran out. Durham found their disappointment harrowing. People were always hungry. There was always some new village over the next hill full of 'luckless creatures eating nettles [...] the children shivering'.[30] But thousands of people made it through summer and autumn 1911 thanks to her supplies of timber, felt, maize and quinine, and their gratitude expressed itself in a new surge of devotion. 'I'm in the most odd position,' she wrote at the end of September, 'as the tribesmen persist in openly addressing me as queen and doing most lowly homage to me and can't be stopped.'[31] In fact, for all the agonising back pain and the lameness in one leg, Durham had never felt so alive. The aid mission was running well, and was hers alone. She also enjoyed the company of Nevinson, who was as open-hearted as he was good-looking. Durham was so impressed by him that she could forgive the fact that he was a particularly advanced member of the English Liberal tribe. Normally, Durham despised their earnest talk about their various causes. Emoting about Ireland, India and votes for women always got on her nerves. The soggy religiosity of many of them was another barrier. Nevinson was a prime offender in this regard, having embraced all the usual Liberal causes, and more. Apart from being a fervent supporter of suffragettes – 'ninnies' in Durham's opinion, 'whose conduct will remain a blot on the record of women'[32] – he was also, more unusually for the time, entirely relaxed about homosexual relationships, having befriended the gay rights pioneer Edward Carpenter back in the 1880s after hearing him lecture in Toynbee Hall. After the minor embarrassment of discovering that the man he assumed to be Carpenter's servant was his lover, he was a frequent guest of Carpenter's and George Merrill's in their rural home. In a touching eulogy to Carpenter, written after the latter's death in 1929, Nevinson refused to gloss over the nature of their relationship, recalling with wry amusement Carpenter's vain attempt to awaken in him a little interest in same-sex relationships. Durham was oblivious to this side of Nevinson's nature and would have been appalled. Reports of the not-infrequent tiffs between the men of Shkodra over attractive boys turned her crimson with embarrassment. She felt mortified when she learned that the teenage son of the Catholic Archbishop of Shkodra was being importuned in the street and even fought over by some older Muslim men, though she drew comfort from assuming that the existence in Albania of that particular vice, as she saw it, was entirely the result of Ottoman influence.

But Nevinson was different from the run of unmanly English Liberal male bores, she concluded. His interest in the plight of Albania seemed genuine. It also helped that his life had followed a course that, in some respects, resembled her own. Like Durham, he had been something of a lost soul until the age of about 40, since when, like her, he had packed in a series of extraordinary adventures – in his case, covering the Greek revolt in Crete, the Boer War and the 1905 revolution in Russia. After spending several weeks with him, helping refugees, Durham began daring to imagine that she had finally met a man who was capable and deserving of a part-share of her throne in the hearts of the Albanians. The fact that he was still married, albeit unhappily, seems either not to have occurred to her or not to have troubled her. Her reverie came to an abrupt end on 29 September 1911, when Italy, eager for a share in the European carve-up of Africa, declared war on the Ottoman Empire. Instead of invading Albania, as Durham at one point had vaguely hoped they might, the Italians attacked Tripoli. Nevinson hurried away to North Africa on war business.

Durham had no idea of how she really came across to members of the opposite sex at this stage in her life. On her arrival in the Balkans she still maintained a girlish bloom, which explained why various Serbs and Montenegrins had promptly offered marriage. But it was some time since she had received those offers, and her youthful air had long faded. Hard work and rough living had taken its toll and she now looked and sounded a little bizarre to her fellow countrymen and -women. As her friend and admirer Aubrey Herbert wrote not long after, 'She cuts her hair short like a man, has a cockney accent and roving eye, is clever, aggressive, competitive.'[33] Nevinson liked combative women. His first wife, Margaret Wynne Jones; his lover, Hannah 'Nannie' Dryhurst; and his other lover, Evelyn Sharp, who later became his second wife, were all left-wing, militant suffragettes. So was Jane Brailsford, whom he was desperate to take to bed but who turned him down. However, Nevinson liked his women young and pretty as well as angry and left-wing. And even someone as broad-minded as Nevinson found Durham's masculine mannerisms disconcerting. When he described her as abrupt to point of rudeness and 'her language in conversation as even more racy than the style of her books – I have never known a woman to express facts or opinions with such starling vigour',[34] it was not in a spirit of total approbation. He enjoyed riding round northern Albania with her, and fancifully likened their journeys to the royal progresses of Elizabeth I with her favourite, the Earl of Leicester. He had longed to shout out to the Albanian villagers: 'Here is your queen! Now come out and tell us what is the matter.'[35] But Elizabeth I, unlike Durham, had known how far to take artfully staged romances. Nevinson felt shocked when she broke the spell, writing to declare that parting from him had been 'more terrible than death', and adding ominously, 'I am yours to take – or leave.' Durham's doomed profession of love was 'very strange, causeless & incredible,' Nevinson noted in his diary. He had not thought of her in that light. 'What is it then that this strange, hard creature loves?' he wondered.[36]

Fortunately for their future friendship, the invitation to Nevinson to 'take' her was buried in a torrent of denunciations of the Turks and other information about Albania, which enabled him to ignore the difficult section of the letter. Diplomatically, he agreed to meet her in Rome in a few months.

While Durham dealt with Nevinson's failure to respond, Albania clamoured for attention. It was probably a relief to return. After the outbreak of war with Italy, shipping halted on the Adriatic between Italy and Albania, so no more planks and felt could be obtained via Trieste. The weather turned cold. Durham decided she would have to change her strategy if she was to keep her Albanian mission going. She abandoned hope of obtaining more supplies by ship. 'Can't import anything,' she wrote to her sister on 14 October, complaining that as a result she could only give out 'measly doles and only to the poorest families'.³⁷ Instead, she ransacked the shops of Shkodra for whatever was still to be had. The humanitarian situation of the returnees took a turn for the worse. Desperate people clustered round the door to her hotel from dawn. It was annoying to be woken by a din at six, she continued, but 'they are awfully obedient, though, and always happy and end by saying, "If our *kraljica* say so, it must be so."'³⁸ She put a brave face on her difficulties. 'I'm getting very strict,' she recorded in November, 'and say, "If they want me to be *kraljica*, they must accept what I do."' But it was hard to say 'no', as she often had to, especially 'to a woman who had walked for ten hours'.³⁹

As the weather turned icy in November, Durham decided to focus almost exclusively on the provision of warm winter clothing and to take it up the mountains herself along with Marko Shantoya. There, she reported to her uncle, they had a tremendous reception, 'as they persist in believing I'm a queen, the queen of the *kachaks* – of the insurgents'.⁴⁰ It was pleasant, being hailed also as the *kraljica inglezit*, 'the English queen', as she and Marko rode through the villages, but Durham never forgot her task. The weather was shocking by this time, rain pouring in torrents, but she struggled on, inspecting houses and handing out felt for families with no roofs, quinine for those with malaria and some bizarre-looking multi-coloured shirts that she had had made up from flannel bought in Shkodra. The more she distributed, the more people turned up. Eventually, she handed the rest of her supplies to the local parish clergy and left them to decide who needed what, returning to Shkodra to drum up new funds and goods.

Christmas in 1911 passed in a complete blur, unnoticed in Shkodra. In her hotel, Durham was more besieged than ever, the crowds at times so dense that they blocked the street. But at last her American admirer and benefactor, Mr Crane, sent a new cheque for another £200, as a result of which she was able to buy several thousands yards of cotton and have it all turned into trousers. Irritatingly, a false report got out that Crane had sent her an absolute fortune, prompting a stampede to her door. Some of the requests she heard were bizarre. One man turned up asking the *kraljica* to cure his toothache. Durham, busy turning out trousers, gave him some money and told him to buy a pair of forceps and pull out his tooth himself. By mid-January 1912, she was sending a mass of homemade clothes up the mountains that she hoped 'would warm some poor bodies'.[41] More quinine had arrived, as had another consignment of roofing material.

The Ottomans put no obstacles in her way. Now that the Empire was at war with Italy, the authorities in Constantinople were anxious to calm down the Albanians. To smooth matters and please the European powers, they promised to dispatch a reform commission, which it was hoped would grant the Albanians significant concessions. Durham put no faith in international commissions composed of worthy grandees. But she felt sufficiently relaxed about the success of her aid mission at the end of February 1912 to put in an appearance at a ball held in Shkodra by the Catholics to mark the start of Carnival.

As had happened so often in the past, the event reminded her that her Albanian admirers had both crowned and unsexed her at the same time. At the ball, she wandered around, drinking bottled beer, not knowing whether to join the men or the women. In the end, she planted herself in an armchair midway 'between the buck herd and the doe herd', as she put it.[42] But only the men came up and talked to her.

CHAPTER 8

'Boom – our big gun rang out'

I looked at my watch. It was 8am. And we were at war.
(Edith Durham, 9 October 1912)¹

SPRING COMES EARLY in the Balkans. With the advent of warm weather in March and April 1912, Durham felt able to cut back on her relief work with refugees. She dared take a holiday. Boarding ship in mid-May for Italy, she headed for Rome, and to meet Nevinson, who was also holidaying there. If any embarrassment lingered between the adventurers as a result of the love letter that Durham had sent him the previous year, the two of them put that behind them. Fortunately, she had other business to occupy her. Crowds of Italian journalists were waiting to interview her about the worsening turmoil among the Albanians, and there was even talk of obtaining a private interview with the Pope, though this *tête-à-tête* did not materialise.²

While trying to avoid a scrum of reporters and awaiting the call that never came from the Vatican, Durham and Nevinson toured the Colosseum, walked the Appian Way and took in other sights. The Roman holiday went on. But Albania called and in mid-July Durham packed, hurried to Bari and took a boat to Montenegro, alerted by the news that a fresh Albanian revolt against the Ottomans had broken out in and around Gjakova in the west of Kosovo. Once again Montenegro was back on a war footing. As was ever the case in the Balkans, an explosion in one area caused turbulence in several others. Tension all the way along the Ottoman–Montenegrin border had resulted in several frontier incidents in which Montenegrins had been shot dead. In Podgorica, the Montenegrins were up in arms and this time Durham was certain that war was unavoidable. She hurried up to Cetinje to confer with the royal family and with the British minister, Count de Salis. For years she had predicted the imminent destruction of the Ottoman Empire-in-Europe and each time it had survived. Was it finally about to self-destruct? Durham likened herself to a cat that had been sitting for too long in front of a hole, waiting for an elusive mouse to emerge. 'Something must happen soon, and something serious,' she wrote to her sister in July, at the start of a long, hot, tense summer of alarms, shootings and mobilisations.[3]

The Albanian revolt the previous year in Kosovo had, in fact, brought matters in the Balkans to a head. The four Christian states bordering the outer rim of Turkey-in-Europe – Bulgaria, Serbia, Montenegro and Greece – were now convinced that the Young Turk regime was too weak to survive another rebellion in Kosovo, and resolved to strike before an independent Albanian state emerged and seized the lands they coveted. The apparent ease with which Italy had overrun Ottoman Libya acted as a spur.

Russia was watching closely. Cheated by Austria-Hungary over the matter of the annexation of Bosnia in 1908, the Russians had decided to bring to an end Ottoman rule in Europe without regard to the interests of Austria-Hungary. In the spring of 1912 Russia encouraged all four Balkan countries to sign a series of bilateral agreements that bound them to what became known as the Balkan League. The sole purpose of these agreements was to seize and divide up the remaining Ottoman territories in Europe, leaving Constantinople and perhaps Thrace for Russia.

Serbia and Bulgaria signed an agreement on 7 March. An agreement between Bulgaria and Greece was signed in May. Greece reached agreements with Serbia and Montenegro over the summer. The mutual interest of all four states in dismembering Kosovo and Macedonia assured the success of the discussions but the lack of a precise agreement on a division of the spoils was to prove disastrous. The Serbia–Bulgaria agreement recognised Serbia's interest in Kosovo and Bulgaria's interest in Thrace but was hazy over the controversial question of Macedonia. The deal recognised Bulgaria's right to south-central Macedonia, including Ohrid, Prilep and Bitola, but the north, including Skopje, was described as a 'disputed zone', and the only agreement between Sofia and Belgrade here was that the zone might have to be put to Russian arbitration. Crucially, important elements in the Serbian military and in Serbian politics opposed the agreement, feeling it promised Bulgaria too much.[4] The agreement between Bulgaria and Greece was even more vague – the Bulgarians apparently oblivious to, or just contemptuous of, Greece's own territorial claims in Macedonia. Durham was unaware of the secret discussions taking place in far-off capitals, as were most of the governments of the great powers. She knew only of the mounting death toll on the Montenegrin border as exchanges of gunfire with the Ottomans became more frequent and as both sides began to commit atrocities. Towards the end of August 1912 she hurried down to the frontline town of Andrijevica, where she found the schoolhouse had been converted into a field hospital, housing, among others, a seven-year-old refugee whom the Ottomans had castrated.[5] From a watchtower close to the frontier she peered through a telescope at plumes of smoke rising from recently torched Serbian villages on the other side. She felt helpless. The Montenegrins, she wrote, wrongly believed that if England knew what was going on in the Balkans, it would not continue to support the status quo. The Montenegrins did not realise, she added, that Britain and the other European powers had known a great deal about what was going on in Ottoman Armenia, but had still permitted the 'Red Sultan' to massacre large numbers of Armenians 'without turning a hair'.⁶ To her embarrassment, the Montenegrin frontiersmen interpreted her arrival on the border as a sign that Britain was about to commit itself militarily to Montenegro. 'My reputation has spread among these people in the most awful way,' she wrote home on 27 August. 'They all look to me to save them. One said: You can if you will. You are the great *kraljitza*!'⁷ More disconcertingly, the head of the army, General Vukotić, suggested that she might like to mediate on their behalf with the Ottoman commander on the other side, Djavid Pasha. As she recalled, he put it: 'Would I, perhaps? [...] With a white flag the risk would not be great [...] Of course the Turks fired on it sometimes [...] but when they saw it was a woman ...'.⁸ Durham declined. She had no intention of rescuing 'old fat Yanko', as she now called him. She had not forgiven the general since he had used her – as she saw it – to get the Albanians to lay down their arms and go home. Durham neither could nor would help the general in the way that he imagined. But she still felt broadly sympathetic to Montenegro and, back in Podgorica, started alerting the British public to Montenegro's plight. Articles poured from her pen in September for the *Manchester Guardian*, *The Times* and the *Morning Chronicle*.

At dawn on 9 October 1912, a tense summer of on-and-off conflict came to an end. Assured that Serbia, Greece and Bulgaria would come immediately to its aid once it gave the signal, Nikola declared war on the Ottoman Empire. Durham, having been tipped off, rose at dawn and went by carriage to the foot of Mount Gorica, the hill above Podgorica, where she had been told that she would find Nikola posing majestically, spying out the terrain. Durham scrambled through the lush, wet grass at the base of the hill, hurrying uphill to see the hostilities officially start. The sight of the grizzled old monarch moved her profoundly. As a teenager he had fought the Turks in his uncle's army at the Battle of Grahovac in 1858. Now an old man, he was ready for battle again. Durham found herself gazing up at him, dressed resplendently in full Montenegrin costume, silhouetted against the morning sun, his son Mirko beside him.[9] She was just wondering 'if a war that might change all Europe's politics was about to begin', when it did. 'Boom – our big gun rang out from [...] the high mountains beyond us,' she recorded. 'The band struck up the Montenegrin hymn [...] the church bell rang out from the church at the foot of the hill. We shouted *zhivio!* (viva). I looked at my watch. It was 8am. And we were at war.'[10] Durham hurried off to send some telegrams.

For Durham, and almost everyone else in Montenegro, the outbreak of war came as a relief – a cooling thunderstorm after months of unbearably high pressure. But within weeks, the mood of popular enthusiasm for the conflict faded. Once Montenegro gave the signal, the other allies joined in as expected. Serbia, Bulgaria and Greece waited ten days before they declared war on the Ottoman Empire between 18 and 19 October. The First Balkan War had begun. But one consequence of the widening of the conflict was that the centre of the action shifted immediately several hundred miles away to the east and south of Nikola's small domain, towards the Bulgarian, Serbian and Greek front lines in Macedonia and Thrace. Montenegro's own little war with the Ottomans turned into a sideshow. For a few days Durham had the headlines to herself as a war correspondent for the *Manchester Guardian* and the *Daily Chronicle* – arguably the first woman war reporter in the world. But after various newspapers asked her to write about the campaign, she soon discovered to her disgust that they were cutting and even doctoring her articles. She became tired of being asked to interview the King. 'I don't know where he is for one thing,' she wrote crossly to her sister on 16 November.[11]

She decided to dedicate herself to humanitarian relief, working for the Montenegrin Red Cross in company with a British rookie volunteer, Caroline Matthews. The experience proved hellish. Unlike the hospital that Durham had run in Ohrid in Macedonia in 1904, the Montenegrin hospital was filthy, 'the floors thick in spittle and mutton bones'.[12] To her irritation the wards were also permanently packed with relatives of the sick and wounded, camping and cooking on the floor. A 'squawking crowd of dirty girls' made it hard for her to dress wounds and the staff stole things. 'The Montenegrin women are shameless thieves,' she complained.[13] Most of the patients were incurable in any case. Durham found herself retching at the sight of wounds overflowing with pus, the result of prolonged neglect. By late November, the building began filling up with incurable cases of typhus, dysentery and smallpox, the foreign Red Cross hospitals having refused to take them in.

Durham by now was anxious for the conflict to end. By the Christmas of 1912, the fighting was, in fact, more or less over because the Ottoman armies in Europe had crumbled much more quickly than anyone had anticipated. Austria-Hungary had initially greeted the outbreak of the Balkan war with discreet enthusiasm, confident that the Young Turks had rejuvenated the Ottoman Empire and would deliver Serbia a knockout blow, saving Austria the bother. German officers had been training the Ottoman army and selling it weapons for years. In the event, Germany's much talked-about modernisation of the Ottoman army made no difference. Nor did the fact that the Ottomans had patched up a peace with Italy, potentially freeing up troops that might otherwise have been kept in North Africa.

In theory, the Ottoman state ought to have been capable of seeing off a combined attack by the Christian powers in the Balkans. The Sultan's Empire had a population of 26 million. Bulgaria, the largest of its opponents, had a population of 4.3 million, while Serbia had 3 million, Greece 2.6 million and Montenegro 250,000, making about 10 million in all. Over half the 6 million inhabitants of Turkey-in-Europe were Christian, but even if these potentially disloyal subjects of the Sultan were deducted, alongside the Christian Armenians, the Sultan still had the edge in terms of pure numbers. The problem was deployment. Half the army was stationed thousands of miles away, some as far off as Yemen, and little use was made of the new railways lines in Turkey-in-Europe to move troops to the front lines, as a result of which they had to slog along the notoriously poor roads. Most importantly, the Ottomans failed to agree on a strategic plan to counter a combined attack in the Balkans. In consequence, the 300,000-or-so Ottoman troops in Thrace and Macedonia found themselves overwhelmed by the Balkan League's combined total of at least 800,000 – almost half supplied by Bulgaria.

The biggest shock came in the northern sector of Macedonia where the Serbian army dealt the Ottoman forces a crushing blow outside the town of Kumanovo on 24 October. After sweeping the Ottomans aside from this important gateway, the Serbs swept south, fanning out across Kosovo and northern and central Macedonia, including Durham's old base in Ohrid. On 30 October, King Petar of Serbia staged a triumphal entry into Skopje. Finally penetrating the north of Albania, the Serbs skirted around heavily defended Shkodra and at the end of November reached Dürres, which was less defended and some way to the south. Dipping their feet into the waters of the Adriatic, the soldiers exclaimed that Serbia had obtained access to the sea at last.

It was a tremendous achievement, but the Greeks made equally striking gains in the southern half of Macedonia. After crossing the Vardar River on 7 November, the following day the Greek army entered Thessaloniki, the headquarters of the Ottoman General Staff in Macedonia. Three days later King Constantine entered the city, much to the chagrin of the nearby Bulgarian army, which had raced to capture the city and was only just beaten to it. The Jews, the largest community among the 160,000-or-so people in Thessaloniki, who had lived peaceably for centuries under the Ottomans, were not overjoyed.[14] They preferred the Ottoman Turks to the prospect of being ruled by either Christian Greece or Bulgaria.[15]

Although disappointed in Thessaloniki and Ohrid, the Bulgarians had overrun most of Thrace and were dug in only miles from Constantinople, just to the west of Edirne. The Ottomans clung on to three garrisons: Shkodra in northern Albania, Ioannina in Macedonia, and Edirne. But the first two were now surrounded and lay deep inside enemy territory, so their fall was a matter of time, although neither Bulgaria nor Greece would lay down arms until they had actually surrendered, which forced the war to drag on into 1913.

The Montenegrins were also reluctant to end the conflict. King Nikola had started the war but had done least well out of it. He had hoped that leading the charge against the old Turkish enemy would restore Montenegro's waning prestige in the Balkans, especially in relation to Serbia. Instead the conflict exposed and highlighted the yawning disparities in the sizes and strengths of Serbia and Montenegro. With its population of about 3 million, Serbia had been able to mobilise a quarter of a million men. Tiny Montenegro, with only 250,000 people, could muster only 35,000. The small Montenegrin army enjoyed some success to the immediate west, advancing into poorly defended terrain in Kosovo where it met up with the Serbian army. But most of the conquests there had to be shared with the Serbs. Nikola had dreamt of making Prizren, a city hallowed in the memories of all Serbs, the capital of a greatly expanded Montenegro. He had even composed a song about it: 'Onward, onward, let me see Prizren!' In the event he never did see Prizren. His army did, but only once the Serbian army had occupied the city, which was not the same thing. Where the Montenegrin army fought alone against a well-defended Ottoman garrison, as it did before Shkodra, it got almost nowhere. The Ottomans had more than 25,000 men under arms in Shkodra, far too many for the Montenegrins to overwhelm. The war, therefore, failed to make a convincing case for the continued existence of a separate Serbian state in Montenegro, or silence the many voices within Montenegro calling for the union of all Serbs under Serbia. Fearing for the future of his throne if he quit the conflict with only a few conquests in western Kosovo, Nikola was all the more determined to seize Shkodra and make peace with dignity.

But the siege of Shkodra filled Durham with unease concerning Montenegro's war aims. Reports of atrocities on the front lines, this time committed by, rather than against, Serbs and Montenegrins, shook her confidence in the justice of the Serbian and Montenegrin cause. The whole conflict had become 'wildly barbaric,' she complained to her sister just before Christmas 1912, with 'wholesale slaughter and mutilations'.[16] She was particularly disturbed to come across some Ottoman prisoners in a makeshift frontline field hospital whose faces had been horribly mutilated by their captors. In a filthy hospital in Tuzi, a recently captured village on the Ottoman side of the border, Durham was horrified to discover why the heavily bandaged faces of eight captives were curiously flat. Removing the bandages she found that their noses had been cut off. She spent a week in the hospital, sweeping and cleaning, and 'wrestling with the disgusting problem of the mutilated men'.[17] In the weeks that followed, back in the hospital in Podgorica, she received confirmation that this was no isolated incident. Many of the patients among the Montenegrin soldiers boasted of having done the same thing to Muslims that they had captured. With very few exceptions they all claimed to have taken noses, she wrote: 'An old man of seventy had only taken two but excused himself on the ground of having fallen ill.'[18] She knew that if she were to reveal this crime to the newspapers it would deal a major blow to Montenegro's image in Europe, in Britain above all. With a heavy heart, she decided not to report anything, a decision that she later regretted.

Durham's aggrieved and disappointed tone did not only reflect her disgust with the way that the war had proceeded. She had lost control of events. Toiling away in a dirty hospital she had no time to visit the front lines. The Montenegrins who had hailed her as their *kraljica* only a few months earlier appeared to have forgotten all about her. She was cut off from her beloved Albania and from her companion, Marko, stuck on the other side of the front line in Shkodra.

The outbreak of war had initially gained her new fame as a woman war reporter. But as the conflict dragged on, her prestige faded. The diplomatic community in Cetinje had broken up because many of the diplomats were reluctant to stay in a war zone. The King and the princes were away fighting and were preoccupied. The British newspapers found their own full-time correspondents in the region and no longer seemed to want Durham's services. Normally so well informed about what was going on in the Balkans, she found herself out of step, struggling to keep pace. It did not help that relations with her colleague, Caroline Matthews, deteriorated dramatically. Dr Matthews had totally failed to grasp the nature and ambitions of the *kraljica*, assuming that this honorary title was just a charming affectation. Durham probably never saw the patronising tribute that Matthews wrote for a newspaper. Had she done so she would have exploded. 'Miss Durham is an ideal colleague,' Dr Matthews informed her readers in a syrupy tone. 'She is adored by the natives who treat her as a little queen and yet she is content to act as my nurse and assistant.'[19] Having misunderstood her colleague so badly, it was not surprising that her relations with Durham plummeted and that Dr Matthews soon ceased to see her as her 'ideal' workmate. Towards the end of November Durham reported home that Dr Matthews had called her a 'cat' and a 'beast' – ample proof, Durham wrote sarcastically, that she did not belong in a hospital but a lunatic asylum.[20] Durham claimed that Dr Matthews created 'terrible scenes' before she finally left in January 1913, running around and 'screaming in the streets'. She also claimed that Dr Matthews had sworn to kill her.[21] Christmas 1912 passed off in a sombre atmosphere throughout the region. The guns fell silent, all sides having undertaken to observe an internationally brokered Christmas truce. But apart from Serbia, which had already seized what it wanted, the other combatants were merely waiting for a spring thaw, Greece in order to continue the siege of Ioannina, Montenegro to continue the siege of Shkodra and Bulgaria to overrun Edirne.

What further complicated ending the war was an event in a small town in the south of Albania. On 15 November 1912 a group of Albanian patriots representing most of the districts in which Albanians lived in the Balkans assembled in the port of Vlora, hoisted the old red and black standard of the medieval hero Skanderbeg and declared the independence of Albania. They then sent a telegram to this effect to the Sultan, the ambassadors of the powers meeting in London and to the countries involved in the Balkan war. The act was not unforeseen. It was partly to forestall this that the Balkan war had started. The question was when, and where.

Durham's firsthand knowledge of Albania had long persuaded her that the time was not ripe for this step. They had 'no Garibaldi' to unite them, she had said earlier. This consideration had forced her to modify her attitude towards the Ottoman Empire over the last two or three years. She had shifted from longing for the Empire's immediate expulsion from Europe to wondering whether it might not be better for Albania if Turkey-in-Europe were to stagger on for a couple more years, if only as a kind of protective incubator for the still unformed state. But the unexpectedly rapid victories of the Serbian, Greek and Bulgarian armies in October and November 1912 rendered such speculation redundant. Now that the Balkan states had all but driven the Ottomans from Europe and left them clinging to a few isolated garrisons, it had become essential for someone to take up the baton for Albania and proclaim some sort of state before the entire territory was divided up.

The task fell to Ismail Qemali, an elderly Ottoman statesman and onetime governor of Beirut and Tripoli – certainly no Albanian Garibaldi. The fact that it was left to him to proclaim the birth of free Albania from a balcony in Vlora was a measure of just how disastrous the situation had become for the Ottoman Empire. A man of Qemali's stamp normally would never have dreamt of placing himself at the head of an independence movement. Now in his late sixties, he had spent his whole working life in the service of the Empire and had been on intimate terms with successive sultans and grand viziers whose foibles and character traits he enjoyed recording for posterity. As he recalled in his memoires, just before he left for Albania to take charge of the independence declaration, the Grand Vizier had offered him a cabinet post in Constantinople, which, as he wrote, in other circumstances he would have regarded as an honour. Even now he parted from the Grand Vizier amid mutual expressions of regret. But, as he wrote, with the Serbian army now in possession of Skopje, a city that many Albanians regarded as their own, it was no longer possible to look to the Ottoman Empire for protection. 'My place was no longer there,' he wrote, sadly, of Constantinople, 'and I owed my services entirely to my own country.'[22]

Desperate to get back to his hometown of Vlora before the Serbian army arrived, he hurried to Bucharest, which was home to a large Albanian colony, and where 15 of his fellow countrymen joined him. From Bucharest they telegrammed all the districts of Albania, announcing that the moment had come for Albania to realise its national aspirations and urging each district to appoint a delegate to attend a congress in Vlora.

From Bucharest the little band moved on by train to Budapest and Vienna, where Qemali obtained an interview with the Habsburg foreign minister, Count Berchtold, who assured them that the monarchy looked with sympathy on the Albanian national project. Austria-Hungary also provided Qemali with a vessel, understanding his need to get to Vlora as fast as possible. The journey was fraught. Sailing down the Adriatic, the Albanians found the Greek navy had blocked the harbour at Vlora, as a result of which they had to dock at Dürres. The Greek navy was there as well, but after searching their ship, the Greek officers let Qemali and his colleagues land. From there they got to Vlora on horseback.

Qemali was shocked to find out that many Albanians, even in the towns, were entirely ignorant of what had been going on in the Balkans and labouring under the pathetic illusion that the Ottoman army was about to enter Sofia and Belgrade. Fortunately the mood in Vlora was different, both more realistic and more patriotic. Here, at least, 'a holy fire of patriotism had taken possession of my native town and public enthusiasm and delight greeted us everywhere,' he recalled.[23] Qemali also found 83 delegates waiting for him in Vlora, as instructed. The congress opened at once and unanimously adopted the declaration of independence on 28 November. The deed done, they piled out of the hall and hoisted the red and black standard of Skanderbeg over the Qemali family home.

'It was an unforgettable moment for me and my hands shook with hope and pride as we fixed to the balcony of the old dwelling the standard of the last national sovereign of Albania,' he wrote. 'It seemed as if the spirit of the immortal hero passed at that moment like a sacred fire over the heads of the people.'[24]

Vlora was the logical choice for this great event, not simply because Qemali was born there. Located deep inside ethnic Albanian territory in the south-centre of the country, but not in the deep south, the town lay outside those zones in which Serbia and Greece felt a strong and immediate territorial interest. There could be no question of proclaiming Albania's independence from a city like Prizren, although Prizren was far more illustrious than Vlora and had been the birthplace of the national movement among the Albanians in the 1880s. Alas,

Prizren was already occupied by the Serbs. Even Dürres was unsafe, with Serbian soldiers paddling in the nearby sea.

Had Qemali and his colleagues confined themselves to claiming Vlora and a few surrounding towns and villages, the new state might have slipped easily into the world, unnoticed. A tiny Albania might have been acceptable even to Greece and Serbia as a buffer between them – a Balkan Luxembourg, Liechtenstein or Andorra. But this did not happen. Days after Skanderbeg's standard was hoisted over Vlora, the ambassadors of the six powers, Austria-Hungary, Germany, Italy, France, Russia and Britain, met in London. The decision to hold the meeting was unconnected to events in Albania; they met only to agree on a common position on the Balkans, now that the Balkan Christian states had abruptly ended five centuries of Ottoman rule there all on their own. Nevertheless, although Albania did not prompt the meeting, it soon found its way into the discussion. Qemali had unfurled Skanderbeg's flag just in time. Without knowing anything about Qemali, or about what he and his followers intended, Serbia's two strongest opponents, Austria-Hungary and Italy, seized on the news from Vlora to demand an offer of immediate recognition of a free Albanian state. Neither Austria-Hungary nor Italy had any altruistic concern for the rights of the Albanians. They shared only a deep anxiety about the prospect of Serbia becoming a maritime power: Italy because it coveted the Adriatic for itself, Austria-Hungary because it considered Serbia too strong already. Albania's declaration of independence was fortuitous in providing both countries with an alibi to block Serbia's maritime ambitions.

Serbia's two allies among the great powers, Russia and France, naturally felt loath to fall in with such a plan. But Germany and Britain sided with Austria-Hungary and Italy on this issue, forcing Russia and France to retreat to a second line of defence, which was to allow for the possibility of an Albanian state as long as it remained as small as possible. The statement that emerged from London in January 1913, therefore, reflected the clash of wills between the powers. It declared that they intended to recognise Albania but tellingly said almost nothing about its future frontiers.

Durham had probably done more than anyone in Britain to bring the subject of Albania to public attention through her three published books on the Balkans, steady flow of newspaper articles, lectures and humanitarian campaigns. Without her immersion in the Albanian question, their existence as a nation would have remained little known in Britain, their hazy reputation sullied by the slurs of Gladstone's heirs in the Liberal Party. Britain might then have cast its voice in 1913 on the side of Serbia, France and Russia.

But Durham was too politically versed in Balkan politics to draw any satisfaction from having played a part in the creation of a new European state. Beyond relishing being called *kraljica*, she did not dwell on what she had or had not done for Albania. As soon as she heard of the deliberations of the London Conference she felt alarmed, knowing that without speedy international recognition of borders, and without the dispatch of an international force to guarantee them, principled recognition of Albania's right to independence was worth very little. Her worst fears were soon realised. As soon as Montenegro learned of the intentions of the great powers it accelerated a military thrust against the Ottoman garrison in Shkodra, hoping a fait accompli would ensure that the city was not awarded to the new country. Durham was disgusted. It was clear to her now that Montenegro had never been fighting the Ottomans in Shkodra; it had been fighting to ensure that the city never went to Albania. Her Montenegrin friends, as she still considered them, had no right to take an indubitably Albanian city, she thought. She had not cheered on Nikola's war to end up endorsing this kind of land grab. She was 'sick to death' of being in Podgorica.[25] 'The Montenegrins talk wildly of smashing Scutari and assassinating everyone they can lay hands on – even children,' she complained. With her old companion, Marko, uppermost in her mind, she felt 'anxious for my friends'.[26]

In fact, the ambassadors in London had taken note of the Montenegrin guns battering uselessly away at Shkodra and had decided to stop them. As the Albanian expert Miranda Vickers has written, 'Austria-Hungary's principal concern was that Greece and Serbia would partition Albania [...] Foreign Minister Berchtold stressed that in no circumstance must Serbia be allowed to expand to the Adriatic [...] this principle reflected the fear that a Serbian port might some day become a Russian port.'[27]

An unscrupulous and complicated trade-off was arranged, designed to complement Austrian and Italian demands for the establishment of a viable Albanian state with Russia's demand for Serbia to receive plentiful compensation for the loss of its hoped-for outlet on the sea. This compensation was to come in the form of the whole of Kosovo. The Serbs had always hoped to reconquer the *vilayet*, seeing Kosovo as the cradle of their medieval state and referring to it as 'Old Serbia'. But Kosovo was now overwhelmingly Albanian, had been for generations, and the Albanians formed an overwhelming majority of the population in the west of the *vilayet* around Prizren and Gjakova. As a result, Austria-Hungary initially insisted that the towns of Debar, or Dibra, as the Albanians called it, and Gjakova, at the very least, should go to Albania. This was not only because almost everyone in these towns was Albanian but because the inclusion of these strategic market settlements was crucial to Albania's future economic viability.

For several weeks at the beginning of 1913 the powers tussled over the fate of Gjakova but by March the outlines of a deal had emerged by which Serbia would obtain all of Kosovo, Gjakova included, in return for abandoning its claim to an Adriatic outlet. Montenegro would not get Shkodra either. Austria-Hungary had done its best, but the Austrian ambassador Mensdorff 'had received practically no support from his

German and Italian colleagues in opposing this horse-trading and in demanding a settlement according to the merits of the case'.[28]

Years later, the British Foreign Secretary Sir Edward Grey recalled the dispute, not concealing his boredom with the quarrel and his ignorance of the town at the centre of the dispute. As he recalled:

> Serbia claimed a village called Djakova. Austria made a point of its being kept for Albania. Russia would not give way about Serbia's claims; Austria was stiff...There was deadlock. Nothing more could be done [...] Days, even a week or two, I think, passed.

Then suddenly, the Austrian ambassador, Count Mensdorff, had asked to see Grey and it was soon all over: 'Mensdorff entered briskly, even a little breathless with haste, delighted with the good news he had brought and exclaiming: "We give up Djakova!"'[29]

As the Count bustled into the room, his full-skirted frock coat had knocked over a vase of daffodils, soaking his clothes, a fairly insignificant occurrence but one that appeared to interest Grey far more than the fate of Gjakova, which was not, as he imagined, a village.

On 28 March 1913, after Austria-Hungary and Russia had adjusted their respective claims, the powers in London issued a collective note, clarifying that Shkodra would go to Albania. Abandoned by Russia as well as by Serbia, which withdrew its troops from the siege, Montenegro continued to bombard the city. Durham felt contemptuous. 'The folly and conceit of these people is sickening,' she fumed. 'All the foreign red crosses ought to withdraw.'[30] Her spirits rose when a combined fleet assembled by the powers appeared off the coast near the Montenegrin port of Bar on 5 April, but they fell again when the Montenegrins ignored the naval demonstration and continued to besiege Shkodra. However, as the city had been under attack for six months and as the sizable garrison of 25,000 had withstood everything that Montenegro had thrown at it, Durham assumed it would hold out. For all her fury with the Montenegrins, she felt sure they would have to abandon the siege in time. To her horror, at dawn on 24 April, the Ottoman Governor of Shkodra, Essad Pashe – or Pasha – Toptani, an Albanian, abruptly surrendered, allowing in the Montenegrin army and handing the keys of the city to the King's son, Prince Danilo.

Though deeply cast down by this inexplicable development, which she attributed to treachery on the part of Toptani, there was one advantage. Durham finally was able to cross from Montenegro into Shkodra the day after the surrender and restart relief work with the half-starving population. She still had some money left over from the Albanian Relief Fund that she had started the previous year. Touring houses with supplies of condensed milk and beef extract, she refused to do anything to assist the new Montenegrin authorities, agreeing to meet the city's new governor, Petar Plamenac, whom she had known for years, only to reject flatly his appeal for her to act as a go-between with the Albanians. Never again would she serve as message carrier for the Montenegrins. She no longer trusted them. Years of intimate friendship with the royal house of Petrović were over. The breach was confirmed a few weeks later when the Montenegrins were forced to abandon the captured city after the British sent a destroyer under Vice-Admiral Cecil Burney to dock on the coast near Shkodra, to enforce the decision of the London Conference concerning the future of the city. Amid reports that Austria-Hungary was mobilising troops in Bosnia, even the stubborn Montenegrins realised that the game was up. To Durham's dismay, they burned much of the city before leaving. The labyrinthine old bazaar that she had found so enchanting on her first visit in 1900 disappeared into ashes. The torching of the old heart of Shkodra sundered whatever remained of her ties to Montenegro. She felt no sympathy on hearing that the surrender of the city had shattered the royal family's prestige among the Montenegrins, who now blamed Nikola for their lacklustre war effort and fairly modest territorial gains. Years ago her heart had gone out to the beleaguered monarch and she had prayed that his long reign would not end on a note of farce. She no longer cared. In her fourth book, which she wrote on the siege of Shkodra, her verdict on their war, and on all wars, was damning. 'There are people, I believe, who still imagine that war brings forth fine qualities,' she wrote in *The Struggle for Scutari*, which was published in 1914:

> To me, it had appeared only as a sort of X-ray, which showed up pitilessly all that is most base, most foul and most bestial in human nature [...] In the name of Liberty, Civilisation and Christianity, the Montenegrin people, blood drunk, lust drunk and loot drunk, had reverted to primitive savagery – and in so doing, had lost the very small idea of discipline that they had acquired.[31]

Her new dislike of Montenegro was now so strong that it inspired a curious belated pity for the wrecked remnants of the Ottoman army now limping back to Asia Minor. Leaving Shkodra with Nevinson, who had arrived in the city on 12 June to observe Vice-Admiral Burney assume temporary control of Shkodra in the name of the powers, she headed south with him towards Dürres, which the Serbs had just evacuated. At the desolate port, the pair watched the defeated Ottoman soldiers waiting to embark for Anatolia. They formed 'a miserable little procession,' Durham noted:

> Pallid men in khaki rags, their bare feet dangling limp, clung to [...] the lean horses that bore them. Others, a shade less ill, limped after on foot. It was the last dying remnant of the

Turkish army. The transport which was to fetch them had not arrived and as the light died away they went out to pass the night on the bare ground by the shore.

'If the Turk has abused his power, he had paid for it,' she reflected.[32] Nevinson was no less affected by the sight of the starving, abandoned soldiers, stumbling along the mudflats of Dürres in the baking heat, waiting for their ship, 'their faces bloodless and reduced almost to a skull, their bodies hardly covered with their rags'.[33]

Meanwhile, everywhere in northern and central Albania they encountered evidence of the Serbian army's rampages: villages burned, olive groves torn up, the very roots of the life-giving trees destroyed. The villages were thronged with refugees who had either fled or been driven out by the Serbs from western Kosovo and the west of Macedonia. Durham visited over 1,000 burned-out families, handing out money so that they could purchase seed corn.[34] Moving south, she and Nevinson swung east on a mule track towards Ohrid in Macedonia. When Durham had managed the hospital in Ohrid in 1904 it had been a bustling town, populated mainly by exuberantly pro-Bulgarian Slavs. At the time she had found the spirit of rampant Bulgarian nationalism intolerable. It had never occurred to her that a town like Ohrid would fall to the Serbs. Now, the Serbian army was very much in control of the historic town, as well as of Bitola and the rest of north and central Macedonia.

Prevented by the powers from gaining access to the sea in Albania, the Serbs were determined to hang onto every inch of Macedonia that their armies had overrun, whether or not this broke the terms of the treaty concluded with Bulgaria in 1912 before the start of the First Balkan War. The agreement had clearly assigned Ohrid and Bitola to Bulgaria. But the fighting had forced the Bulgarians to concentrate on meeting the main thrust of the Ottoman army in Thrace, and they had not been able to stop the Serbs from moving into Macedonia's lightly defended heart. Durham found Ohrid unnervingly silent; the dismayed population showed its true feelings about the Serbian army's arrival by remaining indoors. Durham could hardly recognise the place. Only the great, brooding lake was the same, she thought.

The two travellers did not linger, tacking back south-west into Albania proper. Here they discovered that Serbia and Montenegro were not the only malevolent faeries lurking around Albania's cradle. Once they reached southern Albania they found Greek army units busy entrenching themselves in the town of Korça, creating facts on the ground and – Durham and Nevinson believed – coercing local people into taking part in pro-Greek demonstrations. Declining to grace one of these choreographed meetings, to which the Greek troops had invited them, they took direct action. Hurrying to a post office in Berat, the nearest large town not under Greek control, they sent a telegram to the London Conference in which they assured the diplomats that Korça had remained Albanian in fact and sentiment in the past, and its people 'wished to remain Albanian' in future.[35] Getting to Berat had not been easy. Durham later told her friend Harry Hodgkinson that the journey had involved a three-day march across the mountains and two nights sleeping in the open air on bare ground. At one point she claimed a Greek officer had halted her and threatened to shoot her if she advanced a step further, to which she had responded: 'You can't, I'm English.'[36] Either way, it had been worth it. The telegram proved effective. Few of the diplomats in London had much idea where Korça was, who lived there, or what they wanted. But, armed by the information contained in the telegram, and not in this instance blocked by Russia, which was more committed to Serbia than to Greece, the diplomats awarded Korça and its surroundings to Albania. 'The telegram was sent and, we hoped, helped to save Koritza,' Durham later reflected.[37]

The decision stunned the Greek government, which realised too late it had been wrong-footed by two roving Britons. Unexpectedly deprived of Korça, the Greeks found themselves shut out of the region they had hoped to annex as 'Northern Epirus'. It wasn't just the Greek government that felt appalled by the decision to move the Albanian border to the south. A large body of scholars throughout the western world who felt profoundly Hellenic in sympathy also expressed disgust. The attachment of Northern Epirus to Albania was an outrage, the Princeton professor, Jacob Schurman, fumed. It shocked him to think that people there should be 'torn from their own civilized and Christian kindred and subjected to the sway of the barbarous Mahommedans who occupy Albania'.[38]

In Berat, from where they had sent the telegram, Durham and Nevinson were relieved to find no Greek soldiers present and the new Albanian authorities in control. The contrast was obvious between the silent, depressed atmosphere in Serbian-held Ohrid and Greek-held Korça, and the jubilant atmosphere in Berat. But neither Durham nor Nevinson had illusions about the capacity of the new government to govern even the small territory it had been allocated. It had no money, no army, nor even a respectable headquarters. When Durham and Nevinson reached the provisional capital of Vlora, they were taken aback to encounter the provisional president, Qemali, and the minister of war, Mehmet Pasha, attempting to run a country from what looked like a cottage. The provisional government was a 'Gilbert and Sullivan looking body,' Durham wrote, 'though it seems to be keeping perfect order'.[39]

By July 1913, Durham had been on the road in Albania for months, inspecting, reporting and distributing aid. But the Albanian Relief Fund was now exhausted, so she and Nevinson boarded ship and returned north, Durham for Shkodra and Nevinson for England. In August and September, back in Shkodra and alone, she made further sorties into the Albanian interior. Each visit was distressing. Meeting refugees driven out of lands that Serbia or Montenegro had now seized, Durham was 'prayed to ask the King of England who has many Moslem subjects, to save these hapless Moslems from extinction'.[40] Later, when she journeyed to Elbasan, she found it semi-ruined following its brief occupation by the Serbian army, and swollen with refugees from the town of Gostivar, in western Macedonia.

Now that her money had run out Durham could do nothing for any of them. It galled her to return to Shkodra and watch sailors from the various navies of the new international force in Shkodra wandering around, oblivious to the misery of people only a few miles away. 'What rot it is for five powers to be spending the Lord knows what on these warships, admirals, soldiers, etc, hanging about Scutari while the people up country were dying of hunger,' she expostulated. The failure of the powers to decide on Albania's frontiers once and for all was 'criminal'. Without the prompt dispatch of an international commission to delineate the borders, Serbia and Montenegro would continue to 'clear off the Albanians from the debatable districts so as to show a Slav majority' before a commission finally arrived.[41]

But the business of Albania's future frontiers remained infuriatingly vague. Everything was supposedly being decided in London. But now that the powers had sorted out the trade-off between Gjakova and Shkodra, they found their attention diverted by the outbreak of the Second Balkan War, which erupted during Durham's and Nevinson's journey through central and southern Albania.

Outraged by the partition of most of Macedonia between Serbia and Greece, Ferdinand of Bulgaria suddenly attacked his erstwhile Serbian and Greek allies on 16 June 1913. The second chapter of the Balkan War was an immediate disaster for the Bulgarians. They might have held their own against the combined armies of Serbia and Greece, as the Bulgarians had a half a million troops in the field, Serbia half that number and the Greeks only half that number again. But Bulgaria failed to anticipate Romania's predatory interest in the Balkan carve-up. Romania had no land border with Turkey-in-Europe and had observed the division of the spoils, all just out of reach, with jealousy. While Bulgaria, Serbia and Greece worked together, Romania's access into the conflict was barred. Now that Bulgaria was isolated, it saw its way in. While Bulgaria mobilised its army on the southern front line in Macedonia against Greece and Serbia, Romania sent a half-million-strong force across Bulgaria's almost undefended northern border. At this point the Ottomans realised that a golden opportunity had arisen to reverse some of the territorial losses they had sustained the previous year. The Ottomans literally walked back into Edirne, which they had been force to surrender to Bulgaria on 28 March, but which Bulgaria had left undefended.

Within a month Bulgaria was overwhelmed in the south while a Romanian army advanced fast from the north in the direction of the Bulgarian capital, Sofia. In July, Ferdinand was forced to seek an armistice and sign a punitive peace treaty in Bucharest on 10 August. The treaty stripped Bulgaria of almost all the gains that it had made in the First Balkan War as well as handing Romania a slice of territory in the north of Bulgaria. Macedonia – the reason why Bulgaria had gone to the war in the first place – was lost almost entirely to them apart from a fragment around the town of Strumica. At Bucharest, Serbia and Greece expanded on the great gains they had already made in the First Balkan War while the Ottomans regained the area around Edirne. Turkey-in-Europe had survived after all, at least in Eastern Thrace.

Durham had never admired Bulgaria but she was shocked by the rapacity of the Treaty of Bucharest. Whether or not the Ottomans held on to Edirne did not concern her. Bulgaria had no obvious claim to the city in the first place and had only sought it as stepping stone to Constantinople. But the division of Macedonia between Serbia and Greece to the virtual exclusion of Bulgaria assaulted her notion of justice. Durham had criticised Bulgarian nationalism in *The Burden of the Balkans*, which she had written at a time when British Liberals tended uncritically to repeat Bulgarian claims to the whole of Macedonia. It had not occurred to her then that when Turkey-in-Europe fell, Bulgaria would receive virtually nothing at all of Macedonia. As in the case of Albania, she saw borders being fixed on the basis of sheer force, which would only create more instability in the long term. 'The one thing that can be said with certainty is that no permanent solution to the Balkan question has been arrived at,' she wrote in 1914, during the brief interval between the Treaty of Bucharest and the outbreak of World War I. 'The ethnographical questions have been ignored and a portion of each nation has been handed over to be ruled by another which it detests.'[42]

Her fears were well founded. In the years that followed the Treaty of Bucharest the Greeks Hellenised their conquests in Macedonia by resettling up to a million Greeks there, who had been expelled from Asia Minor in the 1920s. But the Serbs were not able to repeat the same feat with their gains in Macedonia and Kosovo. There were poor Bosnian Serbs and Montenegrins who fancied a new start in life on a farm elsewhere. But the number of Serbian colonists willing to start that new life in Macedonia and Kosovo was not large enough to make a permanent difference to the local demographics. Kosovo remained overwhelmingly Albanian.

The people of 'Southern Serbia', as the Serbian portion of Macedonia was now called, were forced to adopt Serbian surnames and learn Serbian in school. Their churches were taken away from the Bulgarian Exarchate and placed under the Serbian Orthodox Church. Cut off from Bulgaria, the people of Serbian Macedonia ceased in the main to look to Sofia. But they did not become Serbs, either. Bulgaria, as Durham predicted, was not reconciled to its losses. After signing the Treaty of Bucharest Bulgaria was no longer just a rival to Greece and Serbia but a sworn enemy, waiting for another opportunity to attack its neighbours. The chance occurred in exactly a year when Austria-Hungary's dispute with Serbia escalated into a European war.

Durham understood that the Second Balkan War had completely overshadowed the question of Albania in the minds of the diplomats at the London Conference, which did not bode well for Albania. She did not put much faith in the power of 'notes' dispatched by the Conference, intended to influence matters on the ground, and she suspected that without an international show of force the Greeks would remain in southern Albania while the Serbs would remain embedded in the north.

She resolved to return to England, finish the book that she had started on the siege of Shkodra and start lobbying the British parliament and the Conference on Albania's behalf in person. At the end of October 1913, she packed and left Shkodra for Trieste, and from there she embarked for London. Almost the first thing she did on her arrival was return her jubilee medal to Nikola of Montenegro – the same medal that he had tried to pin on her dress in Cetinje, which had obstinately fallen off, rolling around on the floor.

CHAPTER 9

'He is a blighter'

> Why or by whom he was chosen is a mystery. Surely those responsible must have known he is a feeble stick, devoid of energy, tact or manners and wholly ignorant of the country.
> (Edith Durham to Aubrey Herbert on King William of Albania, July 1914)[1]

DURHAM ARRIVED BACK in Britain in autumn 1913 determined to finish her fourth book, *The Struggle for Scutari*, and lobby on behalf of the Albanian ethnic minorities stranded inside the newly enlarged borders of Greece, Serbia and Montenegro. She had no faith in the promises that any of these governments said they were willing to undertake regarding the rights of minorities. Most treaties were 'hopeless rubbish'. Besides finishing her book and re-establishing contact with supporters like the MP Aubrey Herbert, there wasn't much that she could do. After the great diplomatic sparring matches between Austria-Hungary and Russia over the fates of Gjakova and Shkodra had ended, international interest in Albania drained away. Sir Edward Grey's patience with the Albanian question, never extensive, was exhausted. Durham found the doors of the Foreign Office closed to her. She continued to send them entertaining and informative cables written in her highly coloured style, but the British position was that

Albania was not the responsibility of His Majesty's Government. It was up to the Italians, or someone else, to help out.

Durham and Nevinson had snatched the southern town of Korça out of Greece's maw. But they could not solve all of Albania's territorial problems. Durham could not stop the Italians from occupying the strategic island of Sasseno, opposite Vlora, in 1914, although Albania recovered the island, eventually. As her friend Harry Hodgkinson recalled years later, Durham had contemplated doing for the island what she had done for Korça. She had 'felt it her duty to set foot in the island to protect it from all rival claimants and preserve it for the people,' he wrote. 'Stuffing an Albanian flag into her blouse and advancing to the beach she to her chagrin tried without success to induce any of the boatmen to brave a storm and take her over.'[2]

Neither she, Nevinson nor Aubrey Herbert could do anything about Albania's northern and eastern border with Serbia, which was fixed on the most disadvantageous terms. The loss of Debar in western Macedonia was every bit as serious as the loss of Gjakova in Kosovo. Debar was a strategically positioned market town, almost wholly Albanian in ethnic composition. The decision to hand it to Serbia dealt another hammer blow to the economy of central and northern Albania, which now consisted almost wholly of mountainous villages cut off from the towns in which the local people had always traded. As an Albanian contemporary noted:

> The boundary line [was placed] in such a way that the principal Albanian cities of the [old Ottoman] *vilayet* are just right on the border line, so that the market-places and the pastures passed to Serbia, while the commerce and the flocks remained within Albanian territory.[3]

The decision was not only bad for Albania. After Debar was severed from its Albanian hinterland, it entered into prolonged decline.

While Durham mulled that disaster, she was depressed to hear that the Greeks were still maintaining a military presence in the south. Under the pressure of the great powers they evacuated Korça on 1 March 1914, in return for obtaining a promise of a degree of regional autonomy. A protocol to this effect was signed a few weeks later on 14 May on the island of Corfu between the Greeks and the International Commission of Control. It conceded a good deal to the Greek side: courts and elected councils were to use both Greek and Albanian, schooling was to be in Greek where the majority of the population was Orthodox, and links between the autonomous region and the state of Albania were left vague.[4] Durham perceived that if the Greeks appeared to accede to these generous terms, it would be no more than a tactical move. The battle to unite Northern Epirus organically to Greece proper was not over, and the Greeks soon resumed the struggle using other methods.

A week after the Greeks pulled out of Korça, Albania's newly appointed German sovereign set foot in his domain, landing at Dürres. William of Wied and his wife, Sophie, arrived in considerable pomp on 8 March onboard an Austrian ship, the *Taurus*. At first all went well. The Albanians put their best foot forward. Mayors trooped onboard the *Taurus* to tender homage, a flotilla of international ships lying offshore fired salutes and the royal standard was unfurled over the so-called palace, in reality a grim-looking former Ottoman governor's residence, which had been deserted for some years. Schoolchildren trooped into the gardens to shout 'Long live the King!', and after nightfall torch-lit processions took place and mosques and other buildings were illuminated.

Behind this tatty display of pomp, the selection of William for the vacant throne was another reminder of Albania's lowly place in the calculations of the powers. As was so often the case with Albania, none of the powers had a positive interest in the country but each was determined to block proposals that came from the others. Russia, which had no intention of supplying

Muslim Albania with a prince of its own, was determined to stop the appointment of a Catholic candidate, fearing that he would be a creature of Austria. But Austria-Hungary, Albania's most determined sponsor, would not have a candidate from Italy. Qemali's provisional government vetoed the Russian idea, which was to choose a Muslim candidate from Egypt, on the grounds that the election of a Muslim monarch would compromise Albania's European identity and aspirations.

A couple of freelancers meanwhile threw their hats in the ring, including a Hungarian baron and the Duke of Montpensier, brother to the Duke of Orléans, who advanced his claim by arriving in a yacht and announcing that he would like to be King. As Qemali recalled, the Duke's arrival caused much excitement in Vlora because everyone thought the longed-for British navy had come. They were dismayed to find out that the boat belonged to a member of the long dethroned French royal family. In the event, the Duke made a favourable impression on the townsfolk during a brief walkabout but then sailed away back to Venice, never to be seen in those parts again.

After these semi-comic escapades, the crown finally descended on William of Wied, a 37-year-old captain in the German army – royalty, but of the most insignificant variety. The House of Wied was ancient and had produced a notable sixteenth-century religious leader in Archbishop Hermann of Wied, who attracted the attention of his contemporaries by trying and failing to introduce the principles of the Reformation to Cologne. Other than that, the Wieds were not especially noteworthy, the head of the house holding the rank only of count until the 1780s, when the title was upgraded to that of prince. But a few decades later the Congress of Vienna in 1815 sanctioned Wied's absorption into Prussia, after which the family retained little more than a castle and a fine title.

William had at first shown no interest in the offer of a Balkan throne. The moving force in the affair was his interfering and eccentric aunt, Elisabeth, the self-styled 'Poetess Queen' of

Romania, who wrote under the pen name of Carmen Sylva. Swathed in voluminous white mourning drapes since the death of her only child, her snow-white hair tumbling around her shoulders, this slightly frightening-looking woman spent much of her time in the Cotroceni Palace in Bucharest, presiding over salons where she encouraged her acolytes to vent their feelings as forcefully and as emotionally as possible. Apart from these female hangers-on, Elisabeth had many male fans who were entranced by her piercing grey-blue eyes, musical voice and unquestionable stage presence. But she was much given to strange fancies, such as the notion that she and her mother were two of the great psychic spirits of Europe. She had once told the Serbian minister in Bucharest, Čedomilj Mijatović, a keen admirer, that she had watched her mother levitate and float through the air down a corridor of the family castle.[5] The minister believed every word. She was 'an angel of God in silver white robes,' he gushed.[6]

Other observers, usually women, were less sympathetic. Elisabeth's niece by marriage, Marie of Edinburgh, her successor as Queen of Romania, left a hostile account of her aunt's milieu. 'The air was always vibrant with tense excitement,' Marie recalled sarcastically:

> over some topic, some new hobby, some bit of music, some embroidery, some painting, or the marvellous discovery of some new book. Nothing was ever taken calmly, everything had to be rapturous, tragic, excessive [...] Aunty [...] needed a continual audience, and this audience was trained to hang on her every word.[7]

If Elisabeth was needy, it was because she was a tragic figure, trapped in a dutiful, loveless marriage to her cold Hohenzollern husband who did not share her poetic view of the world. What would have compensated for everything was motherhood, but that option had been snatched from her. In

1874, she endured the agony of seeing her only child, Maria, die of scarlet fever, just before her fourth birthday. Elisabeth never got over the shock. The memory of Maria's awful and untimely death stimulated an obsession with the spirit world as well as worsening her chronic insomnia. At night she paced the Cotroceni Palace alone until the small hours, fleeing unseen demons, a ghostly figure hurrying along the palace corridors in her long white drapes.

As soon as Elisabeth heard of a vacancy for the throne of Albania her feverish mind was on the alert. At her bidding the Romanians forwarded William's name to the powers, and to get the enterprise moving the Queen penned an anonymous article for the *Österreichische Rundschau*. In it, she described Albania as a 'fairyland awaiting its prince' and portrayed William as the right kind of heroic knight to take on the job. Steeped in English Romantic literature – she was well read in several languages – Elisabeth thought it would be a glorious rerun of Byron's romps through Albania in the 1800s. William's wife, Sophie, whom he had married in 1906, was an eager convert to the plan. Closer to Elisabeth than her husband, Sophie had been orphaned at an early age and had partly grown up in Romania among relatives. Much of this time she had spent with Elisabeth, embracing the hothouse life of her salon and the Queen's cultivation of emotion for its own sake. In permanent mourning for her lost child, Elisabeth saw in Sophie a substitute daughter, encouraging her to marry her nephew and then plotting thrones for their two children. The impressionable and motherless Sophie fell in with the Poetess Queen's vision of Albania, as she did with everything else. Given to quoting Elisabeth's views on most aspects of life, she soon decided that she preferred the role of Balkan queen to that of wife of a German officer. According to the German Emperor, 'the ambitious, mystically excited wife of the Prince [William] saw in Albania the fulfilment of her wishes'.[8]

Emperor Wilhelm II, like most Germans, felt no great interest in Albania. Like the Russians, he thought that if anyone was to rule the country, it ought to be a Muslim. But his advice was not heeded. 'Therefore, I was not at all pleased when the choice fell upon Prince William of Wied,' he wrote later. 'The Prince knew all too little of Balkan affairs to be able to undertake this thorny task. It was particularly unpleasant to me that a German Prince should make a fool of himself there.'[9]

William ignored the Emperor's misgivings, convinced that the latter harboured a deep prejudice against Albanians. He later told the writer Joseph Swire that the Emperor's 'dislike of everything concerning Albania went so far that the Berlin foreign office avoided placing before his eyes diplomatic correspondence regarding Albania, fearing to incur His Majesty's ill humour'.[10] Deciding that he knew best, William of Wied sent a formal note of acceptance to the powers on 7 February 1914. Two weeks later the couple hosted a reception for 18 Albanian notables at the family estate in Neuwied, where the assembly declared him '*Mbret*', a title that rendered itself into English as either prince or king, as a result of which William was referred to in English as both.

Qemali, the elderly head of the provisional government, by now was longing to retire to France. Bitterly disappointed by the frontiers assigned to the new Albania he was waiting to leave as soon as the business of appointing a sovereign was complete. He was unimpressed by the appointment of William, having apparently asked Aubrey Herbert to put himself forward instead, after the two of them met in Albania in the summer of 1913. The dashing and romantic Herbert had found the prospect thrilling. 'It would be an interesting business [but...] of course with me money is the trouble,' he wrote to his brother. 'The Albanians have never paid any taxes.'[11] With regret, he told Qemali the answer had to be no, leaving the field clear for William. 'The prospect of entrusting the destinies of Albania to this unknown celebrity did not enchant me,' Qemali recalled.[12]

Durham was equally dismayed. To have a sovereign foisted on Albania by a medium-rank power like Belgium or Sweden was one thing. To receive a king at the behest of Romania, which was not a power by anyone's stretch of the imagination, was no compliment. To carry the recommendation of Romania, widely seen in Europe as a byword for corruption, was almost worse than having no recommendation. It was true that William's unofficial sponsor was Austria-Hungary, but Austria's commitment to the new King was underwhelming. According to a biographer of the Emperor Franz Joseph, the army chief Conrad and foreign minister Berchtold discussed the possibilities of William being killed in Albania in an almost jocular fashion. 'What if the prince is assassinated?' he recorded Berchtold as asking. 'Somebody else must take the throne in his place. Anyone will suit us', Conrad had allegedly replied.[13]

As soon as the publication of *The Struggle for Scutari* was settled, Durham packed her bags in England and hurried back to Albania to see what was going on. For once, she did not head for her usual base of Shkodra but continued south towards the less familiar territory of Dürres.

William and Sophie were delighted to meet the legendary Balkan expert but the meeting was not a success as far as Durham was concerned. She instantly dismissed William as a buffoon and a cipher. When she wrote about him several years later in her fifth book, *Twenty Years of Balkan Tangle*, she recalled him almost affectionately as 'a good natured St Bernard'.[14] In articles destined for publication in Britain, she also maintained a respectful tone, dutifully recording cabinet appointments and audiences granted to various clerics, and doing her best to portray the new reign in a positive light. But in her private correspondence and in the telegrams she sent to the Foreign Office she was damning, dismissing William as wholly unfitted for the post. 'I never saw a more pitiable show than Wied giving putty-medals to the wounded in the [...Dürres] hospital,' she wrote scornfully to the Foreign Office in July 1914, 'as though he were feeding nuts to monkeys. Made no speech – looking bored to death.' 'The King has a nervous laugh which he fires off at most things,' she continued. 'He asked me about some of my travels but evidently has not the vaguest comprehension what life up-country means. I believe he imagines he is roughing it.'[15]

Durham was especially scathing of the King's attempt to recreate a pared-down version of the royal courts, with which he had been familiar in Germany, in the unlikely setting of Dürres – which William seemed determined to make his royal capital solely because it was the first place in which he had set foot. Durham considered the attempt to fashion a court there an almost criminal waste of time, money and effort. While the country was being invaded from north and south, she complained that William was trying to get up his palace in Dürres 'very swagger', with 'butlers, cooks, all the paraphernalia'.[16] People in Dürres were complaining that the only thing he had done since his arrival was to appropriate the public garden for his palace.[17] She wrote in a similarly harsh tone to Aubrey Herbert. 'I have little or no sympathy with the King,' she told him. 'He is a blighter. Why or by whom he was chosen is a mystery. Surely those responsible must have known he is a feeble stick, devoid of energy, tact or manners.'[18]

The indictment rolled on to include the hapless Queen. The habits that Sophie had learned from her royal mentor in Bucharest came in for excoriating criticism. 'They are very royal – both of them,' Durham declared, 'keep a court and keep people standing in their presence. It is all ludicrous [...] her [Sophie's] only idea is to play lady bountiful, distribute flowers, put medals on the wounded and make tiny blouses of native embroidery.'[19]

It was not Sophie's fault that her efforts went down like a lead balloon. She was merely trying to replicate habits picked up in Bucharest that had served her mentor, Elisabeth, perfectly well. The Romanians did not expect their queens to involve themselves in politics, and in any case Elisabeth's total boredom with that subject was well known. Elisabeth had spent most of her spare time with her select band of women, encouraging them in romantic affairs, discussing novels, flirting with up-and-coming pianists and writers, doing needlework and illuminating books, which she and her women then presented to grateful churches and monasteries. Nothing prepared Sophie for the fact that these activities, much admired in Romania, seemed silly and superfluous in strife-torn Albania.

If Durham's harsh remarks about Sophie contained an element of spite, the other parts of her indictment contained a serious point. Immured in Dürres, William and Sophie remained strangers to the Catholic northerners, whom Durham favoured from years of personal acquaintance and considered more naturally inclined to show allegiance to a Christian king than the mainly Muslim people of the central belt and south. This was not only Durham's point of view. Qemali, who finally left Albania for Nice in January 1914, also felt that William had made a serious error by cooping himself up in such a conservative, Muslim, pro-Ottoman stronghold as Dürres. What was worse in Durham's eyes was that they had also, at least initially, allowed themselves to become virtual prisoners of Essad Pasha Toptani, the former governor of Shkodra whom Durham – and many Albanians – considered a traitor and a scoundrel for having handed the city to Montenegro the previous year.

Following his flight from Shkodra, the ex-governor had ensconced himself in Dürres, where he ingratiated himself with the royal couple. He also maintained a small private army, 'a villainous-looking company of cut-throats,' William's Anglo-Irish private secretary, Duncan Heaton-Armstrong, recalled. On William's arrival, Toptani had inveigled the King into appointing him minister for the interior and for war, after which he proceeded to spend William's foreign credits on military projects that got nowhere or were counterproductive. The King soon realised that Toptani was more of a liability than an asset and that he was almost certainly plotting to take the throne for himself. At the end of May 1914, after a brief struggle, which included bombarding his home, William had him escorted onto an Austro-Hungarian warship, the *Szigetvar*, which took him off to Italy, where Toptani continued his complicated, pointless plots with the Italians, the Ottomans and later the Serbs – with anyone who held out the prospect of making him and not William ruler of Albania. The plots continued until 1920 when, while vainly attempting to present himself to the Paris Peace Conference as the only legitimate representative of Albania, an Albanian nationalist assassinated him in front of the Hotel Continental where he was staying. But, by the time he had been expelled from Albania he had already inflicted significant damage on the prestige of the monarchy. Most Albanians loathed Toptani for his role in the surrender of Shkodra, and his months of proximity to the King discredited William, fomenting revolts up and down the country. Moreover, the King's decision to let him leave for Italy was interpreted as a sign of weakness. Heaton-Armstrong wrote that it 'made an exceedingly bad impression on his loyal subjects; they considered that the King had robbed them of their prey and had allowed himself to be outwitted by the Italian diplomats, who were generally believed to be Toptani allies'.[20] Others viewed the matter differently. From his hotel in Nice, Qemali was horrified to hear of the ructions in Dürres surrounding Toptani's dismissal, especially the fact that William's forces had trained two cannons on his house and opened fire to force him out, and that his wife had ended up waving a white bed sheet of surrender from a window to forestall further attack. Qemali thought the way the King had removed his minister was horrifyingly undignified – 'a line of action unprecedented in the annals of government'.[21] The King was turning Albania into a laughing stock, he felt.

Durham partly blamed William's private secretary for the royal couple's reluctance to abandon the relative safety of Dürres. She and Heaton-Armstrong had a confrontation on board the British warship the *Defence* – later to be sunk in the Battle of Jutland – when it docked off Dürres. As Durham recalled, the two of them were lunching with Admiral Ernest Troubridge on 28 June when she looked up at the mountains and asked whether Heaton-Armstrong wasn't 'longing to get up country and explore', to which he allegedly replied that he 'hated roughing it and hadn't the last wish to go anywhere that entailed discomfort'. According to an outraged Durham, Heaton-Armstrong admitted he had only come to Albania for the money. She struggled to contain her fury in the telegram that followed. The King's secretary belonged more 'to a Vienna café than here', she spluttered to the Foreign Office.[22] 'Who on earth appointed him?' It didn't help that Durham disliked Dürres, which was boiling-hot, malodorous in the sweltering summer heat, and full of mosquitoes. Night after night she lay awake sleepless in the town's only dilapidated hotel, her mind churning over the inadequacies of the royal couple. When she fell asleep, she was troubled by dreams of the King of Serbia's bloodstained hands and of his father-in-law, Nikola of Montenegro, weaving his spider's webs.[23]

German princes of uncertain fortune had landed in the Balkans before and turned matters round, against most people's expectations. When Ferdinand of Coburg arrived in Bulgaria to assume the vacant throne in 1887, very few seasoned Balkan observers fancied his chances, especially as he came without the approval of the powers. His predecessor, Alexander of Battenberg, had only lasted a few years before abandoning the throne under Russian pressure. Most people had given Ferdinand only months before he quit as well. Instead, by 1913, 'Foxy' Ferdinand was still on the Bulgarian throne. He had miscalculated disastrously during the Second Balkan War but had otherwise presided over Bulgaria's economic and military rebirth. His neighbour in Romania, Charles of Hohenzollern, had done equally well and in equally unpromising terrain.

However, both countries were light years ahead of the 'roadless ruin' of Albania, as Durham had once called it. It was not only because William and Sophie remained stuck in Dürres that Albania's problems piled up and buried them. Charles and Ferdinand had taken up thrones in states that functioned at some level. Bulgarians, Romanians, Greeks and Serbs – all had a developed sense of nationality, which their respective Orthodox Churches had nurtured. The peoples of these lands accepted and, however dimly, at some level remembered the office of kingship, looking back to heavily mythologised medieval soldier kings who had united them, crushed their neighbours and left behind memories of lost glory. The newly installed foreign monarchs of these countries drew on this store of folk memories to legitimise their own governments.

But the Albanians had never had a state, or a king. They had produced warriors like Skanderbeg, but he had come and gone without leaving institutions behind him. When the Albanians learned that they now had a king, it meant little to them. There was no equivalent in Albania to the Serbian Orthodox Church, which had kept alive the memory of Serbia's medieval tsars through centuries of Ottoman occupation. They had no common religion either.

Durham had spent years digesting the consequences of all of this, which was why she had modified her former hostility to the Ottoman Empire and had begun to hope that it might last a little longer, until the Albanians appeared more capable of running their own affairs. When that was no longer an option, she had trusted that the powers would send out an international force to create a little order in the new kingdom. Instead, they washed their hands of it. Once they agreed on William's appointment they forgot about Albania. Fatally, William and Sophie had not secured much in the way of international financial or physical guarantees before accepting the throne. With only a few credits arranged at high interest rates from Italy and Austria-Hungary, they soon ran out of money. The great powers remained in charge of Shkodra for the time being but they did not send any troops to guard the royal couple down south in Dürres. Instead, before the London Conference broke up, a desultory effort was made to assemble a tiny international gendarmerie. After a request to that effect was shuffled from one European capital to another, the Netherlands finally picked it up, largely because William was half Dutch – his mother had been a princess of the House of Orange. Even so, the Dutch commitment to Albania was not overwhelming. In September 1913 they agreed to supply Albania with a total of 15 policemen under the command of Colonel Lodewijk Thomson, a former military attaché in Athens.

The Dutch duly arrived in Dürres and attempted to fan out over the countryside at the head of a hastily assembled royal militia, which at its peak numbered around 2,500 men. But the rebellions, ructions and invasions by then engulfing Albania were more than a dozen Dutch police and their raw recruits could handle. When Colonel Thomson perished on 15 June 1914 in a mysterious shootout in Dürres, demands were heard in Holland for the recall of the other officers. By then, Albania was effectively parcelled up into a number of warring zones, with the Serbs lurking in parts of the northern mountains, the Greeks embedded in the south and various Muslim rebel formations in the centre, leaving the King and Queen in control of little more than Dürres and Vlora.

In the deep south, as Durham had suspected they would, the Greeks made use of the growing confusion to return to the scene. After the powers forced them to abandon the immediate goal of annexing Northern Epirus outright, they came back wearing different uniforms, claiming to be local Partisans seeking enforcement of the autonomy they had been promised under the Protocol of Corfu. After moving back into Korça on 8 July, they proclaimed the establishment of the Autonomous Region of Northern Epirus. The word 'autonomous' was pure fiction. From the start, the region was governed as an extension of metropolitan Greece, and Albanians who resisted were punished. In the Muslim central belt, meanwhile, sentiment remained strong in favour of the Ottomans and a combination of resentment against what was seen as the imposition of a Christian prince and anger about the new government's failure to liberate the peasants from the onerous rule of the landlords rendered the area ungovernable. Durham was convinced that the Muslim rebels in the centre were acting under the sponsorship of Serbia and Greece, who she believed saw the establishment of a tiny Muslim mini-state in Tirana and Dürres, possibly under Essad Pasha, as a step towards the formal partition of the rest of Albania.

While Albania fizzed with revolt and the position of the new King became desperate, the attention of the great powers was drawn to a tragedy that had just touched a much more important royal family than the house of Wied. On 28 June, the day that Durham and Heaton-Armstrong had spent arguing in the company of Admiral Troubridge over the merits of heading up-country, a young Bosnian Serb named Gavrilo Princip shot dead the Archduke Franz Ferdinand, the heir to the throne of Austria-Hungary, in Sarajevo.

Initially, the assassination did not appear a *casus belli*. The period from the 1860s to World War I was an age of assassins, when several royals fell, or very nearly fell, victim to bombs, guns and daggers. The rapid spread of socialist and anarchist ideas had rapidly eroded what remained of the culture of deference that had shielded crowned heads from popular frustration. At the same time, royals remained easy targets, as their security arrangements were often lax or non-existent. All of them, with the exception of Tsar Nicholas and his reclusive wife, Alexandra, saw publicity as the oxygen that kept dynasties alive, and most were conscientious in attending the various parliaments, diplomatic balls, military parades, church services and charitable events where their presence was expected.

Danilo of Montenegro had been assassinated, for no reason that anyone could work out, in 1860. The German Emperor, Wilhelm I, was the object of a failed assassination attempt in

Berlin in 1878. A bomb killed Alexander II of Russia in 1881. Milan of Serbia was almost shot dead in a church service in 1882. An Italian anarchist stabbed the Empress Elisabeth of Austria-Hungary to death in Geneva in 1898; he had selected her as an also-ran, having apparently come to Geneva to kill the Duke of Orléans.[24] Milan of Serbia's son, Aleksandar, and Aleksandar's wife, Draga, were slaughtered in Belgrade in 1903. The Grand Duke Serge, governor of Moscow and uncle to Tsar Nicholas, was killed in 1905 at the opera. An anarchist almost succeeded in killing Alfonso of Spain in 1906 on the day of his wedding to his English bride, Ena. The bomb missed the royal pair but killed at least 38 bystanders. Most recently, George of Greece had been shot dead in 1913 at close range by a man whose only motive appeared to be anger that the King had not given him any money.

The assassination of Franz Ferdinand, therefore, was not nearly as shocking as the murder of an important public official would be today, and the initial diplomatic reactions were mild. The future British Prime Minister, David Lloyd George, recalled the mood in London as calm. 'Our Foreign Office preserved its ordinary tranquillity of demeanour and thought it unnecessary to sound an alarm, even in the Cabinet Chamber,' he wrote:

> I cannot remember any discussion on the subject in the Cabinet until the Friday evening before the final declaration of war by Germany. We were much more concerned with the threat of imminent civil war in the North of Ireland.[25]

In Berlin, Lord Goschen, the British ambassador, wrote an anguished entry in his diary about the news from Sarajevo. It was 'awful,' he wrote – but not because it might trigger a war. It was because he had known the late Archduchess and had found her charming. 'A sad end to a very jolly week,' he lamented.[26] According to Goschen, the court in Berlin, the

Emperor included, reacted in the same way, seeing it principally as a personal misfortune for the aged Emperor, Franz Joseph, not as the likely catalyst of a great military conflict. The murder did not stop the Emperor from setting off on his annual yachting holiday in the Baltic.

Foreign diplomats were reassured by the knowledge that the Archduke's death wasn't *that* much of a personal tragedy for the Emperor. His dislike for his nephew was well known and, according to his daughter, the Archduchess Valerie, her father was shocked but otherwise unfazed by the news of the murder.[27] Franz Joseph had not forgiven the Archduke for marrying a mere countess, and he appeared to resent the fact that the suicide in 1889 of his own son, Rudolf, had forced him to accept his nephew as his heir. There was not much sign of mourning for the Archduke either at court, or in the streets of Vienna. The writer Stefan Zweig later recalled: 'People were laughing and chattering, and late in the evening music was playing again in the restaurants and cafés.'[28] The Archduke and his wife were buried with what was widely seen as indecent haste. The Austrian Foreign Ministry expressly told foreign royals not to attend the obsequies in Vienna, lest the protocol place a strain on the old Emperor, and the funeral service lasted exactly fifteen minutes.[29]

Received opinion for weeks after the dramatic event in Sarajevo was that Austria-Hungary would shrug off the assassination, bask in a glow of international sympathy and settle for a pledge from Belgrade to crack down on the Black Hand, the secret society believed to have been behind Princip's action.

Had Serbia not emerged from the First and Second Balkan Wars with such significant territorial gains, the Dual Monarchy might well have stuck to this course. However, although Austria-Hungary had blocked Serbia from obtaining access to the sea at the London Conference, Serbia had still doubled in size as a result of the Balkan Wars, making off with northern Macedonia and the whole of Kosovo.

These successes had in turn emboldened Serbian agitators in Bosnia and Herzegovina. As one modern historian of Bosnia has put it: 'The Serb student societies in Bosnia-Herzegovina grew larger and more radical with Serbian victories against the Ottoman Empire and Bulgaria in the Balkan Wars of 1912 and 1913.'[30] As a result, from 1913 the need to stop Serbia became an obsession of the war party in Vienna. If it was not stopped now, it might be too late to do so in future. Conrad, the chief of the General Staff, had been advocating a forward policy ever since his reappointment in December 1912. 'The one way out of our difficulties is to lay Serbia low without fear of the consequences,' he told Bertchtold that month.[31] On 23 July 1914, Austria-Hungary sent Serbia a ten-point ultimatum, which was worded so humiliatingly that it was said that no state could have submitted to it without compromising its independence. Point number five, which demanded that Austria-Hungary have the right to supervise the repression of nationalist groups on Serbian soil, was seen as particularly breathtaking. To Sir Edward Grey, such a request was unprecedented. An ultimatum of this sort was not only a challenge to Serbia but a challenge to the prestige in the Balkans of Russia, Serbia's sponsor among the powers. As Germany had already committed itself to fully supporting the Austria-Hungarian demands, the stage was set for a general war.

The outbreak of hostilities one month after the assassination, on 28 July, when Austria-Hungary declared war on Serbia, dealt a final, devastating blow to William's rickety throne in Albania. The Dutch had no intention of becoming involved in a conflict over Serbia and stayed out of the European conflict. Nevertheless, they still recalled their police from Albania and the international demarcation commission, which had been tasked with establishing Albania's borders, ceased to function, leaving the question of the frontiers wide open. Austria-Hungary suspended shipping to Dürres, cutting off the flow of supplies from Trieste. On 13 August the last of the royal couple's cash ran out, while the outbreak of war made it impossible for the recently established Bank of Albania to raise fresh loans. The King, Queen and Heaton-Armstrong had almost nothing left except for the remnants of their German wine cellar. That prompted Heaton-Armstrong, living up to his reputation as court jester, to suggest that the King should offer to abdicate, but only after they had all finished off the last of the wine. 'This brilliant idea was treated with scorn,' he recalled.[32]

With rebel forces only a few hundred yards away from the palace, William and Sophie threw in the towel and decided to embark on one of the few boats now docking in Dürres. At 7 a.m. on 3 September 1914, they bade farewell to Albania and boarded an Italian yacht, the *Misurata*. They had barely had time to pack, and Sophie was distressed at having to leave behind her favourite harp.

Far away, Qemali had no sympathy for their plight:

> Shut up [...] in his unlucky capital, the Prince had lost all authority and his sovereignty was non-existent. There remained none of the ten millions that had been advanced to him and which he had stupidly spent on such things as a court de cassation (High Court of Appeal) when there not even Courts of Law [in the country].
>
> Like a speculator whose business has failed, William of Wied realised that there was nothing left for him to do but to depart.

Nevertheless, many people looked on William's exit with foreboding. Even Qemali admitted that people 'watched him depart with sadness, as if he were a hope that was perishing'.[33]

Durham agreed. 'The sight was a depressing one and I would not wish any nation – even an enemy nation – to have to witness the departure of its sovereign,' she recalled. She had never held out much hope for William but, as a fighter by instinct herself, was convinced that he should have stuck it out. 'The capture of Durazzo would have been very difficult, if not impossible, thanks to its defences and the fidelity of its garrison,' she noted. 'Its defenders, almost all men of Kossovo and of South Albania, had sworn to remain absolutely faithful in all circumstances. Durazzo would therefore have been able to defend itself for a long time yet.'[34]

However, Durham herself had already gone. Her last articles from Albania that autumn were datelined 'Durazzo' but were written from London. She left shortly after finishing a last tour of the south. Reaching Vlora, the first seat of the Albanian government, she had found the town flooded with refugees from Greek-occupied districts around Korça. The sight of about 70,000 refugees, many suffering from malaria and smallpox, all hungry, almost broke her. 'A hell of misery,' she wrote.[35] Using up the last of her savings, she dealt out maize to as many refugees as she could, before leaving Vlora by boat for Brindisi at 10 p.m. on 5 August 1914.

It was only the next day, on landing in Italy, that she heard the news – to her 'shame and disgust' – that Britain had definitely entered the fray and had declared war against Germany on the side of Russia, France and, thus, Serbia.[36] For Britain to throw in its lot with the Slavic powers, led by Russia, against the Germans and Austrians, disgusted her. She left Genoa for England on 13 August.

Edith Durham was going home. The problem was, she no longer had a real home to return to. For a good part of a decade-and-a-half she had shared her life with the peoples of the Balkans. The fact that most of her hopes for the region had foundered amid the carnage and double-dealing of the Balkan Wars did not make the prospect of going back to England any less strange, or more welcoming. Sitting on the deck of the boat, listening to a boisterous crowd of returning Britons singing patriotic songs, she felt aware of how un-English she had become. 'It was years since I'd been with a large crowd of English,' she wrote. 'They seemed to me a strange race.'[37]

As they sang their bullish ditties, her thoughts drifted back to the sight of the tens of thousands of Albanian refugees camped in Vlora, sitting in the rain, many of them starving: 'and these people wanted two or three courses for breakfast. None of them had seen a war. None knew what a burnt village or a rotting corpse [...] was like'. She saw the steamer as typical of England as a whole: 'masses and masses of blind people, wilfully blind [...] filled with an overwhelming conceit'.[38]

CHAPTER 10

'For a dream's sake'

> My plans, like so many others, were completely put an end to by the Great War.
>
> (Edith Durham, 1928)[1]

DURHAM FELT MORTIFIED that Britain had declared war on Germany on the side of Serbia and Russia. 'After that I really did not care what happened,' she recalled. 'The cup of my humiliation was full.'[2] Unfortunately, the cup of humiliation was to become fuller in the years that followed. Durham was emotionally distant at best from the struggle of the Entente powers against Germany and Austria-Hungary. She felt indifferent to France and was actively hostile to Britain's two Slavic allies in the war, Russia and Serbia. After David Lloyd George, a passionate supporter of Serbia, replaced Herbert Asquith as Prime Minister in December 1916, her sense of alienation from received British opinion was complete. Awkward, angular, still committed to the high, mid-Victorian ideals she had inherited from her parents, Durham had no intention of compromising over what she saw as truth and justice for the sake of Britain's shifting foreign policy goals.

In England, Durham had hoped to continue what now had become her life's work, patiently explaining the complex religious and ethnic realities of the Balkans to the public and disabusing them of what she saw as the misleading assumption that right in the Balkans lay invariably on the side of the Christian Slavs. Instead, her newspaper and magazine articles were buried under an avalanche of pro-Serbian propaganda coming from a multitude of sources, which reached a crescendo in 1916.

In the winter of 1915 and in the New Year of 1916 a combined military assault on Serbia by Austria-Hungary, Germany and Bulgaria forced the King of Serbia, the government under Nikola Pašić and the army to flee south through the mountains of northern Albania towards the sanctuary of Corfu. Pictures and reports of the Serbian army's retreat through the snows of Albania towards the coast, frostbitten soldiers carrying the old King through the mountains on a stretcher, had an instant impact on British public opinion. A wave of sympathy for the agony of Britain's Balkan ally spawned a plethora of interlinked societies, including the Serbian Relief Fund, the Serbian Society of Great Britain and the Kossovo Day Committee. Joined by large numbers of the great and good, these societies set themselves the task of familiarising the public with Serbia's heroic past and present, especially the Battle of Kosovo in 1389, when a Serbian army under Prince Lazar had met the invading Ottomans under Murad I. Heavily mythologised over the centuries, the story of this confrontation between the outnumbered Serbs and the vast invading army of the Sultan was seen as a form of anticipation of the current war, 'Kaiser Bill' now filling the role of Sultan Murad.

The fact that most of the people now living in Kosovo were not Serbs but Albanians who bitterly resented the province's annexation to Serbia in 1912 was not remarked on. Instead, the societies organised celebrations of 'Kossovo Day' in homage to Serbia in great pomp in 1916, including a service on 7 July in St Paul's Cathedral led by the Archbishop of Canterbury.[3] To coincide with this event, the Kossovo Day Committee printed thousands of copies of a booklet, *The Lay of Kossovo*, containing short essays written in a popular, accessible style by well-known authors and historians, including G.K. Chesterton, Sir Arthur Evans and G.M. Trevelyan. The Kossovo Day Committee also distributed 30,000 copies of the Serbian national anthem.[4] *The Lay of Kossovo* was backed up by a supporting cast of other books and booklets, all written in a similar vein. They included *The Women of Serbia*, by Fanny Copeland; *Heroic Serbia*, by Victor Berard; and *The Spirit of the Serb* and *Serbia: Yesterday, Today and Tomorrow*, both by Robert Seton-Watson, a rising academic and journalist who was to become Durham's nemesis over the following decade. Seton-Watson's friend and ally, Henry Wickham Steed, the Vienna correspondent, foreign editor and later editor of *The Times*, was secretary to both the Serbian Relief Fund and the Kossovo Day Committee.

Seton-Watson's journey from friend and admirer of Germany and Austria to determined foe had taken some surprising turns. As a young man he had plunged into German-language studies and spent a good deal of time in both countries. In the Vienna of the early 1900s he had befriended Steed, then the Vienna correspondent of *The Times*. At 26, in 1906, writing for the *Scottish Review*, he summarised his firmly pro-German views, calling for greater understanding between the two Teutonic powers of Britain and Germany and throwing in a vigorous defence of Austria-Hungary. 'The Habsburg empire is the pivot of the balance of power, and its disappearance would be a European calamity,' he wrote.[5]

But, after a prolonged tour of the Hungarian half of the Habsburg Empire, he reached the opposite conclusion – a change of heart he elaborated in *Racial Problems in Hungary*, the 1908 book that made his academic reputation in England. By the time war broke out in 1914 he had become a fervent advocate of the destruction of the Habsburgs' ethnic mosaic and of its replacement by new composite nations dominated in the north by the Czechs and in the south by the Serbs. The war provided an opportunity to put his schemes into effect. 'From now on the Great Serbian state is inevitable; and *we* must create it,' he told his wife, May, on 6 August 6 1914. 'I find Steed and Strachey[6] are absolutely at one with me in this.'[7]

Seton-Watson and Wickham Steed were knowledgeable about the Balkans and Austria-Hungary. The new authors on Balkan questions knew next to nothing about the region. What they lacked in knowledge they made up for in messianic zeal. 'Hail to Kossovo Day, for it will be followed by the day of victory!', Alice and Claude Askew wrote in a typical offering in *The Lay of Kossovo*, '[t]he day when Serbia will leap up from the dust and, binding her torn locks about her forehead, will once more resume her crown'.[8] In such a climate, publicly attacking Serbia, which would have been a very congenial task for Durham, was out of the question. All she could do was try and keep the subject of Albania alive.

Against the torrent of emotive pro-Serbian booklets and posters, Durham's more nuanced, cerebral and evidence-based discussions of the rights and wrongs of the Balkans had no chance. In 1917, she recalled, 'In the whirlpool of excitement which I found when I reached England at the end of August 1914, any attempts to draw attention to the miseries of Southern Albania were hopeless.'[9] Fortunately for her peace of mind, she was out of the country for much of 1916 on another health cure in Egypt, spending part of the time working for the YMCA in Suez, to the surprise of Nevinson, who saw her there briefly on his way back to England from a war-reporting assignment. But she could not escape the hysterical atmosphere of wartime England forever. All she could do on her return was to continue ploughing on with her fifth book, *Twenty Years of Balkan Tangle*, an overview of the years she had spent in the region, which was published in 1920. In talks and articles she repeated her positive view of the Albanians' qualities. In those publications that were still prepared to give her a hearing, she reiterated that the Albanians had as much right to self-determination as any other nation. Were the powers to send a new prince to govern the Albanians, made of sterner material than William of Wied, matters would go better, she asserted.

Neither the British government, nor any other, was remotely interested. After tepidly supporting Austro-Hungarian and Italian demands for the establishment of an independent Albania in 1912 and 1913, a year later Britain was offering parcels of the new country to a variety of bidders in return for their support in the struggle against Germany. The extent of these negotiations became clear in 1917 when, to the embarrassment of the other powers, the Bolshevik revolutionaries in Russia published the terms of the secret Treaty of London of April 1915. These revelations made it clear that Britain and France were toying with giving southern Albania to Greece, most of northern Albania to Serbia, and Montenegro with the port of Vlora and its surroundings to Italy. Serbia was to get its extra slice of Albania if it remained in the fight. Greece and Italy were to receive their slabs of land if they entered the war on the side of the Entente.

The confusing course of events in Albania made it harder for the country's hardy band of British supporters, led by Durham, Nevinson and Herbert, to defend its interests. On his flight from Albania in 1914, William had consigned his powers to a regency, consisting of the three remaining delegates – Austrian, French and Italian – of the International Commission of Control. But the body had no funds and soon dispersed, and neither the Albanians nor any of their neighbours took any notice of it. The chaos in the country worsened as a variety of foreign armies occupied different areas. The Serbs extended their de facto occupation of parts of the north to include the towns of Elbasan and Pogradec, on the far side of Lake Ohrid, in effect turning the strategic lake into a Serbian pond. In December 1914, the Italians pre-empted the generous terms that the British and French were to offer them in the Treaty of London in 1915 and occupied Vlora. Later they took the port of Dürres as well. In 1916 the situation became still more confusing, when Austria-Hungary pushed Italian forces out of

Dürres while Bulgaria – the only ally of the Central Powers in the Balkans – made use of Serbia's military collapse to advance west through Macedonia to Elbasan in eastern Albania. The Italians remained on the southern coast in Vlora, moving inland to push the Greeks out of the southern town of Gjirokaster. The Greeks remained embedded in Korça. But in October 1916, fearing that Greece might surrender Korça to Bulgaria, the French army in Thessaloniki moved up from northern Greece and occupied Korça itself.

From the point of view of the local Albanians in Korça, French occupation was preferable to rule by Greece. After initially upholding Greek ascendancy in the town, the French pragmatically adjusted their position to take account of the views of the local Albanian majority, establishing a provisional mini-state called the Republic of Koritza, which came complete with its own stamps. Thus, the end of the Great War saw Albania split into a mosaic of zones, with the French still running their mini-state in Korça; the Italians entrenched in Vlora; the Serbs hunkered down in the north-east and east; and an international force, the Inter-Allied Command, led by a French general, back in Shkodra.

On the face of it, the six years that had passed since the proclamation of Albanian independence in Vlora in 1912 had been a disaster and the country was more disorderly than ever. But, in some ways, Durham felt justified in maintaining a rugged optimism about the future. At least Albania had not been wiped off the map. As she wrote in an article published in February 1918, 'a people that has shown in the past such endurance and such a capacity for surviving all foreign influence must have a future'.[10]

The balance of the war for Albania, in fact, had been a complex mass of pluses and minuses. The biggest minus was that the Great War had destroyed the country's godmother and principal foreign protector, Austria-Hungary. On the other hand it had also knocked out the Albanians' worst enemy among the powers, Tsarist Russia. From the outbreak of revolution in 1917 until World War II, Russia temporarily ceased to be an important factor in the Balkans. 'Russian policy in the Balkans,' Durham's friend, Aubrey Herbert, noted confidently in 1920, 'is, for the moment, a thing of the past.'[11] Meanwhile the aggrandisement of Serbia at the expense of Austria-Hungary took much of the heat off Albania, as Serbia's interest was now diverted towards other territory.

Apart from northern Albania the Treaty of London had offered Serbia enormous gains at the expense of the Habsburg monarchy. It was to receive the whole of Bosnia and Herzegovina and much of Slavonia. The question of access to the sea was to be solved not via a corridor running through Albania but by obtaining the whole of Dalmatia. In the end, the British and French had been compelled to abandon the Treaty, after America's high-principled president, Woodrow Wilson, refused to place America's authority behind any of these secret deals. But transatlantic disputes over the rights and wrongs of secret diplomacy did not affect the subsequent territorial settlement in the Balkans to the detriment of Serbia, Greece or Romania. Romania still obtained Greater Romania, comprising the whole of Transylvania and Bessarabia, while Greece obtained the whole of Bulgaria's Aegean Sea coastline and Serbia merged with Montenegro, Croatia and the Slovene lands to form a new entity: the Kingdom of Serbs, Croats and Slovenes, later renamed Yugoslavia.

Nikola's kingdom had ceased to exist. Serbia had ruthlessly extinguished its former ally in the war against the Central Powers. In the winter of 1915–16, the King had fled the Austro-Hungarian invasion and had taken refuge in Italy, where his daughter, Jelena, was Queen. At the same time the Serbian army had been forced to retreat to the island of Corfu. But in 1918 the Serbian army was reconstituted in northern Greece and began pushing northwards as the Central Powers collapsed. On 3 November it reached Belgrade and only three days later it entered Sarajevo in Bosnia. On 7 November, the

Serbian army entered Podgorica. The welcome was enthusiastic but the Serbs did not come to Montenegro entirely as brother Slavs and as liberators. Instead, while Nikola was still out of the country, they hastily convoked an assembly on 24 November in the building of a tobacco company in Podgorica where the assembled deputies, surrounded by Serbian troops, unsurprisingly voted to dethrone Nikola and unite Montenegro to the new Kingdom of Serbs, Croats and Slovenes. Earlier that month, still in exile, Nikola had given an interview to the Associated Press in which he expressed support in principle for union with Serbia on condition that the new state honour the equality of all its constituent parts. The outcome of the dragooned assembly in Podgorica shocked him. This was not what he had meant. The fact that he had been dethroned in the name of his own son-in-law was especially wounding.

The Entente powers accepted the fait accompli in Montenegro without demur. The King's pleas to be allowed to go home were batted aside. It was never the right time. In 1919, the representatives of his exiled government were denied separate representation to the peace talks in Versailles. Between 1920 and 1921 almost all the powers, except Italy, which followed suit in 1922, withdrew their representatives to the exiled government. The authorities in Belgrade, meanwhile, did away with anything that reminded people that Montenegro had ever existed. An abortive uprising early in 1919 gave the new authorities an excuse to round up and jail some of the more robust followers of the old regime. The following March the Montenegrin Orthodox Church was scrapped and united to the Serbian Orthodox Church. In the new centralising Yugoslav constitution adopted in June 1921, Montenegro had no place. An entity roughly corresponding to its borders survived as the *Cetinjska Oblast*, the Cetinje District. The royal palace, where Durham had exchanged views with the King, and the grand legations of Cetinje were deserted by their former occupants. Cetinje readjusted to life as an insignificant village. Nikola did not live to hear that his kingdom was now reduced to an *oblast*. He had died in March 1921 in Antibes, and was buried in the Russian church at San Remo in Italy.

From Albania's point of view, what was important about these seismic adjustments and the formation of Yugoslavia was that while the loss of Kosovo now looked permanent, Serbian pressure lessened on the north of Albania. Serbia's quest for access to the sea via northern Albania had become redundant. After Montenegro and the Croatian lands joined the new joint state, Yugoslavia had obtained a long Adriatic coastline to the north of Albania, and Serbia – or rather, Yugoslavia – altered its policy accordingly. After 1918 it ceased to hanker for Shkodra or Dürres, and while the Yugoslav military lingered in northern Albania for years, the government in Belgrade increasingly evolved towards a position of seeking to obtain influence over the whole of Albania rather than aiming to chip off part of the north and annex it.

While the formation of Yugoslavia calmed the situation on Albania's northern border, the French occupation of Korça had a similar effect in the south, impeding Greek plans to annex the region. Unlike the Serbs in regard to Shkodra, the Greeks were not immediately ready to abandon plans to absorb 'Northern Epirus'. But the Greeks also found themselves diverted. In August 1921 the Greek army suffered a catastrophic rout in Asia Minor, dealing Greek military prestige a blow from which it never entirely recovered. Shattered by the disaster and by the subsequent flight of a million-and-a-half Greeks from what was no longer the Ottoman Empire but the new state of Turkey, Greece was in no position to dictate terms to Albania in the early 1920s.

Thus, through no obvious effort of its own, Albania reached the end of World War I and survived the Treaty of Versailles without undergoing any further reduction in its territory, a state of affairs confirmed on 9 November 1921 when a conference of ambassadors reaffirmed the independence of Albania within its 1913 boundaries. At the same time, the powers ordered Yugoslavia to withdraw its last units from the north. Albania, in a sense, was free.

It was also by then a fully accepted member of the international family of nations after joining the League of Nations on 17 December 1920. An impassioned speech by Lord Robert Cecil, the South African delegate and a great friend of Herbert's, helped to swing the vote. The maverick Tory MP had been a stalwart supporter for more than a decade, a rare true believer in the ranks of Britain's aristocracy – he was the second son of the Earl of Caernarvon. A great traveller, and speaker of several languages, Herbert was boyish, affectionate and dashing. He had lived in the Ottoman capital from 1904 to 1905 as an honorary attaché of the British embassy, and:

> Years after he had left Constantinople a high window used to be pointed out from which Aubrey Herbert had dived after dinner into the Bosphorus. Even after his youth was over the apprehensive could never be quite sure at moments to what lengths he might not go.[12]

The Middle East fascinated him most, and he was a friend to T.E. Lawrence. But he was intrigued by Albania too, first visiting in 1907, again in 1911 and for a third time in 1913, by which time reports of the speeches he had delivered on Albania's behalf in the British parliament had filtered back in some form to Albania, ensuring that he received a hero's welcome.

During World War I, Herbert had tried to persuade the British government to send him and Durham back to Albania, hoping to broker an arrangement by which Albania could be put on a more secure economic and territorial footing in exchange for Italy obtaining a vague form of suzerainty. Partly because she was already on her way to Egypt, Durham did not take up the offer. Ignorant of the fact that Britain was secretly bartering away Albanian territory to Italy in the Treaty of

London, Herbert was disappointed when Grey gave his plan a cool reception.

Herbert was a driving force behind Albania's admission into the League, but there was no rivalry between him and Durham. They worked together in the Albanian Committee, the lobbying group that Herbert had established in 1913, of which Durham later beceme the Secretary. In 1918 it changed its name into the Anglo-Albanian Society.

Many Albanians were convinced that Durham's years of agitation on their behalf had also played their part in achieving the breakthrough with regard to the League of Nations. The Romanian colony sent a telegram of thanks to both Durham and Herbert, reading: 'Vous avez sauvé l'Albanie!'[13]

Albania was saved, more or less. But it had been a close thing, for long after the Americans had forced the Europeans to abandon the Treaty of London, plans to cut up Albania had continued. Harold Nicolson, one of the British peacemakers at Paris in 1919, had been busy concocting new territorial schemes as late as the summer of that year. 'Write memorandum about Albania,' he noted in his diary on 28 May 1919. '(1) Union of N. Albanians into an autonomous State under Jugoslavia [sic]; (2) Central Albania for Italy; (3) Southern Albania for Greece; (4) Koritsa to be neutralised as a centre of Albanian culture.'[14] Fortunately for Albania, nothing came of this dreadful scheme.

With Albania at peace and inside the League of Nations, the clamour grew in Albania for Durham to return and in the spring of 1921 she agreed to go. It was a last hurrah. Durham left London on 14 April for Paris and Rome, proceeding by boat from Bari to Dürres. After a quick look at William of Wied's burned-out palace she continued on to Tirana in a car belonging to some young Americans working for the Red Cross. As soon as she arrived she felt the expedition had been a mistake. Her young hosts at the Red Cross were not just different because they were American. They belonged to a different generation, a new world, and Durham recoiled from their modern mannerisms and puppy-dog friendliness. 'Albania is not like Albania with foreigners in it,' she wrote in her diary after reaching Tirana. 'Tired. Don't feel as if my Albania existed any more.'[15]

The Albanians were not much better, exhausting her with invitations to dinner and requests for her to do things that she now felt were beyond her. 'Feel like a pet animal in a cage,' she wrote on 1 May. 'Extreme hospitality overwhelms me. Don't know what to do as they all ascribe much more importance and power to me than I possess. I hear they are naming streets after me in various towns.'[16]

A feeling of being overwhelmed grew stronger as the visit progressed. The following day, after a quick meeting with the President, she wrote:

> In the evening a great procession with lights and songs came to do honour: the street full of poor grateful people all cheering. I was thunderstruck. Went on balcony and heard a speech by a young American Albanian. Was too overcome to reply properly. Thanked as best I could. It frightens me. They think that I have much more power and influence than I can ever even aspire to have.[17]

The young American Albanian who delivered the welcoming speech would have been a member of Vatra, the most important Albanian association in America and a key player in the Albanian national movement.[18] Its leader, Fan Noli, a fascinating and unusual man who combined radical politics with a deep interest in music, poetry, translation and Christianity, was in Tirana at that time, as the Albanian government has asked Vatra to appoint a delegate to parliament in recognition of its influence.

Theophan Noli, to give him his full name, was a truly cosmopolitan figure. Born in Eastern Thrace, not far from Constantinople, he had grown up in British colonial Egypt from where he emigrated to America. Living in the small Albanian Orthodox community in Massachusetts, he immersed himself in nationalist politics and in a local struggle to free the community in Boston from the suffocating cultural and religious control of the Greek Orthodox clergy. After translating the Orthodox liturgy into Albanian in Boston, Noli had had himself ordained priest in the Russian Orthodox cathedral in New York in March 1908, establishing the world's first Albanian Orthodox church back in Boston later that year. From there he roamed over the world, celebrating his newly translated liturgy in diaspora communities as far apart as Odessa and Bucharest, before visiting Albania soon after independence and celebrating his new liturgy in front of William of Wied, who of course could not understood a word.

Durham admired Noli greatly, not because she had suddenly developed an interest in theological matters or churches per se but because she saw an independent, or autocephalous, Albanian Orthodox Church as a vital breakwater against the Greek Church's Hellenising influence in southern Albania. She also keenly appreciated the fact that as a fluent English speaker and a man of wide culture, Noli was one of the few Albanian leaders able to make a favourable impression on foreign audiences and negate the common stereotype about Albanians as savages. Durham's confidence in Noli was vindicated. When he was sent to head the Albanian delegation to the League of Nations in Geneva, it was thanks also to his articulate presentation of Albania's case that it joined the League in December 1920.

While Durham enjoyed meeting Noli, the rest of her visit seemed a failure. The procession and the overpowering balcony address left her shattered, and dinner the following night with the young men of the Red Cross wore her out. 'They smoked all the time they ate,' she noted crossly in her diary. 'Deafening noise and a gramophone going...I was stunned with the row, smoke and folly. What on earth are they doing here?' By Saturday she was 'dead tired. Sick to death. Cannot bear more'.[19] She dined with Noli the following day but then escaped by car north to Shkodra.

Her experience there was no better. Albania was changing fast, and she found the town 'much modernized and made ugly', and, as soon as news got round that she was back, the mountain chiefs trooped in, begging her to see off the Serbs prowling round their villages.[20] They neither could nor would see that the Queen was exhausted – was, in fact, no more. 'Said I was powerless,' she recorded despairingly in her diary. 'They would not believe me. Said in vain I was now old and tired. They persisted till I promised to "write something"... God knows what.'[21] She felt ill, and on Thursday 12 May, only four days after arriving in Shkodra, begged her old friend, the British consul, Nicholas Summa, to get her out. 'Must get away at all costs. Heat too much,' she wrote.[22] It was her last diary entry from Albania. On the following page she tellingly wrote out a copy of the poem 'Mirage' by Christina Rossetti:

> The hope I dreamed of was a dream,
> Was but a dream; and now I wake
> Exceeding comfortless, and worn, and old,
> For a dream's sake.
>
> Lie still, lie still, my breaking heart
> My sick heart, lie still and break
> Life and the world and my own self are changed
> For a dream's sake.[23]

Edith Durham never returned to Albania, or to anywhere else in the Balkans. She was only in her late fifties but her health had been damaged beyond repair by years spent in Albania in all weathers. Now lame and in constant pain from sciatica, she found travel difficult. Almost a quarter-century of life lay ahead of her, but for the rest of it she was often housebound and unable even to leave her home in north London to attend meetings of the Anglo-Albanian Society.

But declining health was not the only reason why Durham never returned to Albania. It was also because, as she wrote in her diary, she didn't believe her Albania 'existed any more'.

In 1926, the American journalist Rose Wilder Lane came to live in Tirana, having driven there from Paris and decided to stay. Less than two decades separated Lane's arrival from the mid-point of Durham's travels in the Balkans – about the time she started to collect material for *High Albania*. It might as well have been a century. Lane's view of Albania was strikingly different from Durham's. She had visited, and been entranced by, the northern mountains in 1922, writing up her travels in a book, *Peaks of Shala*. But on her return a few years later, she described Tirana as a city much like any other city. She told her friend, Dorothy Thompson, that the Albanian government was popular when it handed out western military uniforms because the young valued this newfangled gear far above the traditional costumes of their fathers.

Lane was fully aware that something had changed, radically and recently, in Albania. With disappointment, she wrote in her journal in November 1926 that Albania was not the lost world she once had hoped to find, 'since all the peasants [...] were wearing some rag-bag kind of European clothes instead of their old white wool and black jackets. There seems to be a lack of self-respect in this precipitate abandonment of characteristic costume.' She added: 'The army has had a lot to do with it; all the young men of Albania have been put into uniforms; they get the habit of the stereotyped coat and trousers from that. Also the idea that European clothes are more civilised than Albanian.' Lane was comforted by reminding herself that it had been absurd to imagine that 'one tiny corner of the earth could stand out against the current'.[24]

Lane was not the only foreign visitor to observe this new attitude of contempt for the past. When Joseph Swire toured

Albania in the early 1930s, he wrote that many of the customs and forms of dress that Durham had described only 30 years earlier had vanished. Hardly anyone 'in these prosaic times' wore the traditional white pleated kilt, the *fustanella*, he lamented.[25] The younger Albanians seemed 'ashamed to be Albanian'.[26] He was not entirely correct. The youngsters he met were not ashamed of Albania but of a certain idea of Albania, timeless, traditional, rooted in the past – a state of affairs that was blamed now for all Albania's weaknesses.

Durham had been pained on her brief visit to encounter that new contempt for everything traditional and native. She had not wanted Albania to remain a fossil and she had not idealised the traditional Albanian way of life. She had always been appalled by the poverty, the dirt and disease, and by the stupider superstitions. She had condemned the customs of taking child brides and perpetuating blood feuds, and she had deplored the lack of education. What she did not care for in the new Albania was the phenomenon she felt she had observed in Egypt: a tendency in certain traditional societies to lose their equilibrium and ape the cheapest aspects of western society. If she didn't go back to Albania after 1921, it was not just because she was too ill to make the voyage; it was fear of what she might find there.

Herbert's premature death in 1923, two years after Durham's last visit to Albania, had cut another link. Five months before his death, his half-brother, the Earl of Caernarvon, had died shortly after discovering Tutankhamun's tomb in Egypt. By then Herbert had also gone almost blind. Out of desperation he fell for a former tutor's suggestion that if he had all or most of his teeth removed, he might regain his sight. The result was death from blood poisoning.

His death at only 43 left Durham increasingly isolated. The new shapers of British public opinion on the Balkans were Seton-Watson and Wickham Steed of *The Times*. Having argued so passionately for the creation of a united southern Slav state, unsurprisingly, when the new Yugoslavia was formed after 1918, they felt a personal stake in its success. They both saw Czechoslovakia and Yugoslavia as mighty, necessary barriers against the twin evils of German revival and Russian Bolshevism, and any criticism of the Serbs as an implied criticism of Britain's own wartime effort. Durham did not involve herself in Seton-Watson's lifelong campaign against Hungary but she refused to be silent on the subject of Yugoslavia, insofar as it impacted on the Albanians. One predictable result of this was that she found herself excluded from the various media outlets that the two men controlled.

Durham was only able to publish one article in *The New Europe*, the influential periodical that Seton-Watson established in 1916. This appeared in March 1920, by which time Durham was embroiled in a dispute over a letter she had had published in the previous volume. Although the subject, the Bektashi movement among the Muslims of Albania, sounded neutral enough, its criticism of Serbian and Greek persecution of Albanians annoyed the editor. What particularly angered him was Durham's assertion that she had visited a large Bektashi establishment in Premeti that the Greek army had later 'pillaged and burnt [...] in the summer of 1914, they too recognising that the Bektashis were a national force in Albania'. She went on to add that Bektashis were not limited to southern Albania, as many people believed. She had found them active in Prizren, in Kosovo, in 1908. 'But the Serb Orthodox Church has probably by now extirpated them,' she added.[27]

The bloodthirsty circumstances of the Serbian takeover of Prizren and its surroundings were in fact well documented. The Catholic Archbishop of Skopje had submitted a report to Rome in 1913 in which he wrote that least 400 local people had been shot dead. 'The order of the day is: everything is permitted against the Albanians – not merely permitted but willed and commanded,' he wrote.[28] As the Archbishop was an Albanian he could be accused of exaggeration, but similar accounts of Serbian behaviour came from a number of sources, including

Leon Trotsky and the international commission of inquiry set up by the Carnegie Endowment, which wrote of 'whole villages reduced to ashes, unarmed and innocent populations massacred'.[29]

In spite of that, Seton-Watson was outraged by Durham's attack on the good name of his two favourite nations, and, although he published her letter, he included a disclaimer, noting that the publication was 'not prepared to endorse Miss Durham's attacks on Greek and Serb – Ed'.[30] This unusual and humiliating addition touched off an acrimonious exchange of letters in which Durham complained that the magazine had 'practically accused me of lying'. She added: 'I have recent information that even since the armistice the Serbs have burnt and pillaged Albanian villages, Catholic as well as Moslem. But "New Europe", I know, would deny any such charges.'[31]

The argument continued for more than a decade, each accusing the other of bias and blindness towards their respective Balkan favourites. It was more than a clash between a foreign apologist for Serbia and another very similar foreign apologist for Albania. Durham had observed life in the Balkans from the bottom up. She had befriended the King of Montenegro and had appeared at court functions in Cetinje, but she had spent much more of her time in the Balkans in the company of ordinary people. While running aid operations in Macedonia and Albania she had seen the consequences for the Balkans of decisions made arbitrarily in far-away London, Paris or Berlin. Towards the end of her stay in Albania especially, she had seen people die of starvation and malaria. To Durham, Seton-Watson was a cerebral British busybody of a familiar type for whom the rearrangement of the map of Europe was a fascinating intellectual exercise. As she wrote to him in February 1929, shortly before he terminated their communication:

> You seem to regard these populations as mere pawns to be shifted on the board according to political needs. To me they

are all suffering human beings with whom I have been under fire – for whose sake I have risked smallpox and have wrestled with poisoned wounds. And with whom I have hungered and been half frozen.

She added: 'I feel it a duty to show the means by which they have been annexed and trampled on. And to call for a consideration of their cause.'[32]

Her words struck no chord with Seton-Watson. If anything his contempt for her grew as the 1920s progressed, as his own star waxed and as Durham's waned. He became ever more determined to ridicule and discredit her. An opportunity to slap her down in public fortuitously presented itself in 1925, when Durham published her sixth and penultimate book, *The Serajevo Crime*, an exploration of the background to the assassination of the Archduke Franz Ferdinand in 1914. She had been working on this topic for some time. Drawing on her fluent knowledge of Serbian, in 1924 she had also picked up on the contents of a memoir just published in Serbia by a retired minister and speaker of the Serbian parliament, Ljuba Jovanović. He had confided that the pre-war Serbian government of Nikola Pasić had known of the plans to assassinate the Archduke at least three weeks in advance of the event and had chosen not to warn the Habsburg authorities. Durham made good use of Jovanović's admissions, and of Pasić's subsequent refusal to deny them, to pin responsibility for the start of the Great War on Serbia. Soon after *The Serajevo Crime* came out, Seton-Watson, then finalising his own account of the origins of the war, savaged the book in the *Slavonic Review*, the successor magazine to *The New Europe*, which had folded in 1920. With breathtaking rudeness, he wrote: 'She has no inkling of what is meant by historical evidence, and again and again employs the method so noticeable in her earlier volume, "Twenty years of Balkan Tangle", of accepting as gospel the merest pothouse gossip or braggadocio.' Snobbishly, he continued that much of the evidence for her conclusions appeared to be based on 'the chance remarks of some obscure provincial innkeeper or ostler, or the boast of a schoolmaster or monk in the wilds of Macedonia or Albania'.[33] The verbal demolition, which went on for pages, ended with a long list of alleged grammatical and stylistic errors and included a claim that Durham had described the Serbs as 'vermin' in an address given in April 1924 to the British – later Royal – Institute of International Affairs, commonly known as Chatham House.

Whether Durham had, in fact, used the word 'vermin' in her lecture, entitled 'The Balkans as a danger point', is a moot point. There is no reference to it in the published version of her talk. Her main point was that Russia's apparent eclipse in the Balkans as a result of the Bolshevik Revolution was temporary; Russia's abiding ambition, to which it would return, was to control Eastern Europe; by siding with Serbia and Russia in the Great War, Britain had made this undesirable development more likely in the long term.[34] It was prescient enough, given what was to happen two decades later, when Russia did indeed return to the Balkans with a vengeance. But the 'vermin' tag stuck, as was intended.

While lambasting Durham in public in the pages of the *Slavonic Review*, Seton-Watson wrote to some of his many influential academic contacts to discredit her in more personal terms. The *Serajevo Crime* was a 'poisonous book, which [...] is not merely anti-Serb in a grossly unfair way but also has a quite definitely anti-British background,' he told the historian Harold Temperley in a well-aimed dart, positioning her views not only as anti-Serbian but as treacherously anti-English.[35] Seton-Watson then put the whole matter of the Great War to rights in his own book, *A Study in the Origins of the Great War*.

Durham's loss of prestige in Britain was demonstrated by the contrasting reviews that the two works received. The Royal Institute for International Affairs compared what it dismissed as 'the popping of Miss Durham's machine-gun' with

Seton-Watson's loftier ambition 'to place the murder of the Archduke in its true historical perspective'. The highly flattering review of Seton-Watson's book continued: 'As was to be expected, the book shows consummate mastery of form and matter, of literary style and of the handling of documents.'[36]

The real fault of *The Serajevo Crime* was not that it was wrong but that it was boring, which is why hardly anyone, except her embittered enemies, read it. Durham's strength as a writer had lain in her ability to marry sharp political instincts with vivid personal observations. She had brought to life complicated Balkan disputes in pithy descriptions of ordinary people in Serbia, Montenegro, Albania and Macedonia in *Through the Lands of the Serb*, *The Burden of the Balkans*, *High Albania*, *The Struggle for Scutari* and, finally, *Twenty Years of Balkan Tangle* – even if the latter was much despised by Seton-Watson. It was this quality that lifted her works above those of most other foreign writers on the Balkans, who tended to dwell on high diplomacy, or on costumes and scenes in marketplaces, and who often made use of the freedom of several hundred pages to air dull and ill-informed prejudices. But, by the time she completed *The Serajevo Crime*, Durham had been out of the Balkans for more than a decade and it showed. The book read like the memoir of an angry but tenacious lawyer who was still obsessed with revising the judgement of a long-lost court case, the precise details of which no longer really interested anyone. Durham appeared stuck in the past, obsessed with who had said or done what in the years before 1914, long after everyone else had moved on. Far from reminding people of her former significance in the Balkans, *The Serajevo Crime* confirmed her marginalisation from the scene. It was true that by 1925 only 11 years had passed since the Archduke's assassination, but it might just as well have happened a generation earlier, so much had changed in the meantime. The Hohenzollerns, Habsburgs and Romanovs, not to mention the house of Petrović in Montenegro, had all vanished. Austria-Hungary was no more,

Austria itself reduced to an impoverished rump that was little more than a client state of Mussolini's Italy. At least Austria existed in some form, a tadpole-shaped country whose vast head in Vienna dwarfed the rest of its tiny body. Montenegro was just a memory now, like Burgundy or Brittany, a onetime state reduced to a geographical expression. Its disappearance from the map was another factor that relegated Durham to a past that, quite suddenly, seemed dim and distant. Whatever her mixed feelings about Montenegro, it had been her area of special expertise. Now it was of interest only to historians.

Seton-Watson made use of a second opportunity to crush Durham in 1929 when Arnold Toynbee, the secretary of the Royal Institute of International Affairs, wrote urging him to try 'clearing things up between you and Miss Durham' and suggesting that they work together on a piece of scholarship on the Balkans. Durham, he added, had communicated a desire to end the dispute and had made 'ever so many attempts to conciliate him'. Tactlessly, Toynbee added that Durham wanted him to know that in public, on a number of occasions, she had denied that he was 'heavily subsidised by the Serb government'.[37]

An outraged Seton-Watson detected the barely veiled insult lurking in that line. 'There is open war between Miss Durham and myself,' he informed Toynbee. 'Her methods of controversy, her reckless and infamously untrue charges against all and sundry make it difficult for any friend of Jugoslavia to find any common good on which to meet.' He added:

> As for cooperation, I am amazed that you should suggest it. I am not prepared to admit her title as a serious historical student. I can only assume that you have not read her books [...] or you would surely agree that she is incapable of distinguishing between truth and merest tittle-tattle... The fact is that while always denouncing Balkan mentality, she is exactly what is meant by the word.[38]

Toynbee, nonplussed by the explosion, abandoned his peace mission.

The struggle between the two experts for mastery of the Balkan narrative was, of course, hopelessly unequal, as Durham had been the first to recognise. At times, she could joke about Seton-Watson and Wickham Steed, inventing a humorous jingle about them. 'SW, WS, the two of them made the hell of a mess,' it ran.[39] But she did not always find the combination ranged against her amusing. She sometimes felt 'frightened by what seemed personal attacks on myself,' she wrote.[40] In the Balkans, for all their macho culture, she had been treated with respect. Her single status benefited her there, placing her outside the normal plane of relations between the sexes. There she had been the *kraljica*, the Queen. In England, it seemed she was just a spinster, and thus automatically a figure of fun or an object of ridicule. In England she was almost alone, a rare champion of an obscure, chaotic country that was of negligible economic, diplomatic or strategic interest to the British Empire. She could write and talk as much as she wanted about massacres in Kosovo and about the injustice of giving Debar and Gjakova to the Serbs. Hardly anyone except Nevinson cared, and he had other causes. Seton-Watson, meanwhile, was one of several articulate champions of a country that appeared to have vindicated the trust that Britain had placed in it during the Great War. It had not fought on the wrong side, like Bulgaria; or changed sides, like Romania; or hung on the sidelines, waiting to see which side to support, like Greece. A consistent ally to Britain and France, it had been duly rewarded, had expanded vastly in size and, as Yugoslavia, had become a significant regional power. Through the help of Wickham Steed, Seton-Watson was able to repeat that point in *The Times*, one of the great pulpits of the land, as well as in his own smaller podiums, like *The New Europe* and the *Slavonic Review*. He was also first occupant of the chair of Central European studies at the School for Slavonic Studies at King's College London, an institution that he had been instrumental in founding in 1915. Many of his old friends in the Slavic nationalist movement in Austria-Hungary before the war held high office in the successor states in the 1920s and 1930s, and their glory reflected back on Seton-Watson, who was an honoured guest in Zagreb, Belgrade, Prague and Bucharest. His Czech friend, Tomáš Masaryk, had reached dizzy heights, becoming President of Czechoslovakia in 1918, a post he held until 1935. Others held less glamorous but still important positions as ministers in the governments of Yugoslavia and Romania.

Durham had no equivalent podium of significance, except for *MAN*, the organ of the Royal Anthropological Institute. In the 1930s she began writing articles for the *New Times and Ethiopia News*. Printed in the Pankhurst home in Woodford, north-east London, this slightly obscure anti-Fascist publication, which Sylvia Pankhurst had set up in 1936 following the Italian invasion of Ethiopia, was hardly an equivalent to the other *Times*. Nor is it likely that Durham's articles on Albania were widely read. Pankhurst's son, Richard, recalled that many of the paper's most dedicated readers were African nationalists whose interest in Albania can only have been tangential.[41] Considering how dismissive Durham had once been of all suffragettes, the Pankhursts in particular, it was ironic that she ended up relying in part on Sylvia to get her opinions into print. But time and adversity had prompted Durham to revise her once dismissive opinion of the Pankhursts. Richard remembered Durham as a friend to his mother[42] and, under Durham's nudging, Sylvia took up the cause of Albania, writing in June 1940 to the Foreign Secretary, Anthony Eden, to complain that Churchill's speech of 14 June had mentioned Luxembourg as an ally, but not Ethiopia or Albania. 'Surely Albania has as much right to consideration as Luxemburg [*sic*],' she complained.[43]

Having a friend in Sylvia Pankhurst was not the same as having a friend in the likes of Aubrey Herbert, however. Durham had no highly placed foreign friends, either. Fan Noli, who was a friend, briefly became Prime Minister of Albania in 1924 but did not last long. In the spring and summer of 1924 he headed a radical, reformist government that tried to take on the reactionary Muslim land-owners. But neither Italy, nor Yugoslavia, nor the Albanian land-owners, wished to see the kind of social democracy establishing itself that Noli had in mind. The land-owners opposed his land reforms while the Italians and Serbs were suspicious of his overtures to the Soviet Union. They were suspicious of popular government in Albania in general, preferring to work through a local satrap to whom they could dictate terms and who did not have to refer back to an obstreperous parliament.

The Serbs were especially keen to see a friendly dictator replace Noli in Tirana because Noli had bitterly opposed the loss of Kosovo to Serbia and had penned a long remonstrance on the subject to President Wilson in 1918. It didn't get anywhere but the Serbs remained jittery at the prospect of a progressive Albania acting as a beacon for Kosovo's oppressed Albanians. In December 1924, the land-owners' champion, an army commander named Ahmed Zogu, seized power with the help of a few thousand soldiers, mainly White Russian emigrés recruited in Belgrade. Noli fled first to Italy and then Germany. He returned for good to America in 1932, after which he devoted himself to running the Albanian Orthodox Church, and to his other great passions: music and translation, writing books on Beethoven and the French Revolution, and translating Shakespeare into Albanian. He did not return to Albania.

Not everyone missed him. 'Fan Noli is a brilliant man but he's a fool in Balkan affairs,' Rose Wilder Lane wrote in 1927, while living in Albania:

> He couldn't keep order even in the streets of Tirana. The whole country was falling to pieces under him; going back to war conditions: highwaymen and brigands everywhere; no lives or property safe...Fan Noli is typical of all the 'outside' Albanians. And they themselves are not united.

By contrast, she added, Zog 'keeps order... He is the only man who can keep the government going well enough to pay any salaries at all [...] think of it as a group of robber-baron castles of the middle ages, held together by one man.'[44] A more recent Albanian historian has concurred with that view, describing Noli as a political novice who 'had spent most of his life in the United States [...] and... was no match for consummate politicians such as Zogu or some of the former bureaucrats of the Ottoman Empire'.[45]

King Zog, as Zogu styled himself from 1928, disappointed his Serbian sponsors. At first he appeared grateful, handing over to Yugoslavia the ancient Byzantine monastery of St Naum on the shores of Lake Ohrid. It was a place familiar to Durham from her days in Ohrid hospital. She had taken her staff for a picnic there, smiling to herself as they took pot shots at grebes on the lake while she plotted redrawing the boundaries of the Balkans. It was only a sliver of territory, but its loss to Albania was still significant. A mere building and its surroundings could not be weighed against the catastrophic losses of large population centres like Debar and Gjakova, but St Naum was still a prize. Its acquisition extended Yugoslavia's share of the shore of Lake Ohrid and today it is one of the principal tourist attractions in the Republic of Macedonia.

However, following this ignominious act, Zog unhitched himself from the Serbs, signing a Treaty of Friendship and Security with Serbia's regional rival, Italy, on 27 November 1926, followed by a defence pact in 1927. Zog's decision to proclaim himself King the following year was another attempt to raise his own status, and that of Albania. It did not have much effect. The creation of a new monarchy in Europe in the late 1920s appeared an archaic gesture now that the big four dynasties in Turkey, Russia, Germany and Austria-Hungary had gone. Until 1918, an unwritten rule had remained that every new state in Europe needed to be equipped with a shipped-in royal house. Significantly, almost all the new states formed after the fall of the empires in 1917–18 – Czechoslovakia, Poland, Finland and the three Baltic states – chose republican forms of government. Yugoslavia was the exception, but Yugoslavia was Serbia writ large and so inherited the Karadjordjevićs by default. The other exception was Albania. Even there, the idea of having another king baffled many, while from America Fan Noli kept up a predictable stream of denunciations of what he called the royal 'farce'.[46]

Assuming a royal title did not increase Zog's diplomatic room for manoeuvre. He could not escape the circumstances that had brought him to power as the candidate of an outside power. Having escaped from the clutches of the Serbs, he soon felt suffocated by his new Italian allies. By the mid-1930s Italian economic and military penetration of Albania was almost complete. In August 1933, Mussolini insisted that the Italian war ministry take control of all military establishments, that an Italian expert be seconded as chief adviser to every ministry, and that Albania annul all existing commercial treaties with countries other than Italy and conclude no new ones without Italian approval. Zog resisted this long shopping list of demands but there was no escaping Italy's control in the long term. In May 1938, the Italian foreign minister, Count Ciano, wrote a memorandum for Mussolini in which he claimed that Albania's unexploited mineral resources had the potential to make Italy rich, adding that the country could support 2 million colonists once the Albanians were removed from the more fertile areas. The provision of suitable bribes to Albanian leaders would ensure that an invasion met no resistance, he continued. On 10 May, he wrote in his diary: 'In the train, the Duce discussed my memorandum on Albania with me. He agrees with my decisions and believes that the month to act will be next May. That means we shall have a year for preparations.' On 19 May, he added: 'The Duce declares that he is ready to go into Albania at once.'[47]

For months, Mussolini hung back, concerned lest an invasion of Albania push Yugoslavia into the arms of Nazi Germany, or that Yugoslavia rediscover its interest in northern Albania and demand a part-share of the country. But the ease with which Germany annexed Austria in 1938, and the so-called Sudetenland of Czechoslovakia, then occupying Prague itself, made it a matter of urgency for Italy to show it could pull off the same trick. By the spring of 1939 Mussolini judged that Yugoslavia was too preoccupied with separatist agitation in Croatia to attempt anything ambitious in Albania. In Albania itself, Ciano was keeping a keen eye on the expanding waistline of Zog's new wife, Queen Geraldine.

'There is above all a fact upon which I am counting,' he noted, caddishly. 'The coming birth of Zog's child. Zog loves his wife very much [...] I believe that he will prefer to insure to his dear ones a quiet future. And frankly I cannot imagine Geraldine running around fighting through the mountains [...] in her ninth month of pregnancy.'[48]

At 5.30 a.m. on 7 April 1939, 22,000 Italian troops supported by 400 aircraft and 300 tanks landed off the Albanian coast at Dürres, Vlora, Saranda and Shengjin. As Ciano predicted, they encountered little resistance. Most of the Albanian army's advisers were by then Italian, and Zog was too busy organising the evacuation of his wife and two-day-old son to Greece to coordinate a counter-attack. It was only once Geraldine had been sent off in the direction of Athens that the King moved to the Prime Minister's office in the afternoon and broadcast an appeal by radio urging Albanians to resist the approaching Italians to the death. As one historian has noted, the broadcast was a waste of time because 'few Albanians owned radios, so few heard the appeal; even fewer were willing to die for Zog'.[49] By 10.30 a.m. the first Italian soldiers on motorcycles, followed by small tanks, entered Tirana. To Mussolini's relief the response of the powers, with the exception of Germany, which was supportive, was almost nil. The British received no advance warning of the invasion and when it happened the Prime Minister, Neville Chamberlain, was away fishing in Scotland.[50] 'Such assurance as I ever had in the assurances of dictators is rapidly being whittled away,' he complained in a letter.[51] But the British foreign secretary, Lord Halifax, made it clear to parliament when it met in an extraordinary session on 13 April that the invasion would not affect Britain's friendly attitude towards Italy.[52] What most shocked Halifax, a deeply religious Anglican, was not the invasion but the fact that it had taken place on Good Friday, 'on the day which to most Christians is the most sacred day of the year,' he told the British MPs.[53] The subsequent British protest note was so mildly phrased that, in Ciano's opinion, the Italian foreign ministry might as well have composed it.[54] Satisfied that the West would do nothing to stop them, the Italians arranged for an Albanian delegation to travel to Rome to offer the vacant throne to King Victor Emmanuel.

The Albanians had little to fear from Ciano's imaginary wave of colonists. Far from the 2 million expected, about 30,000 Italians crossed the Adriatic to settle and work the uninviting terrain, and the Italian State ended up spending more money on its Albanian colony that it ever earned from it. 'Albania as a receptacle for Italy's excess population was a myth.'[55] Indeed, for the Albanians, the Italian occupation had one advantage. Determined to grab the whole country, the Italians averted the threat of yet another territorial partition. Yugoslavia's vague hopes of getting Italy to agree to a division of the spoils came to nothing.[56] However, Albania's independence had also come to nothing.

Durham was now in her late seventies and almost totally incapacitated. She had fallen seriously ill back in 1929, had suffered a bad fall in 1930 and had broken her shoulder in 1932. In spite of that, she continued to travel abroad in the spring when her health permitted. She visited Danzig and East Prussia in 1928, Amsterdam in 1933, Sweden in 1935 and 1936, and Belgium in 1937. Diary entries, complete with neat drawings of artefacts glimpsed through the glass panels of museums, continued to make their appearances. There had even been a cruise to Madeira and Tenerife in 1935, though this turned into a disaster. The serious and high-minded mid-Victorian did not embrace the folksy, democratic culture of the England of the 1930s, and Durham was outraged to find herself invited to take part in group activities such as fancy dress competitions and sweepstakes. The noisy gramophone in the dining room deafened her and she resented having to listen to a live radio broadcast of George V's Silver Jubilee celebrations that came complete with an – in her opinion – inane sermon. The ship was 'a sort of floating lunatic asylum', she fumed in her diary. 'No more British cruises for me.'[57]

After 1937 travel of any form became impossible and the diary came to an end that year with the briefest of notes concerning the start of a trip to Belgium. The battle on behalf of Albania in Britain continued, but had to be waged with decreasing energy from a flat in north London. She could still write. Beyond taking part in a small demonstration in London against the occupation of Albania in 1939, she could do nothing because at that point the British government was unwilling to do or say anything that might drive Italy further into Germany's arms. But her hopes were rekindled after Italy declared war on Britain and France in June 1940, and after the Italian invasion of Greece that October backfired and resulted in the Greek army advancing into Albania. The old Anglo-Albanian association that Aubrey Herbert had founded was more or less defunct, so Durham joined a new group, the Friends of Albania, campaigning for the restoration of Albanian independence. Feeling a renewed breath of wind in her sails, in 1941 she composed a long essay on Albania for the Royal Institution of Great Britain that ended with a typically warm-hearted plea. The Albanians were 'a small and fine people who want only to live their own lives on their own land,' she declared. 'In the years when I lived among them I found the Albanians loyal, grateful and kindly [...] do not let them be offered up as a human sacrifice either to appease our foes or propitiate our Allies.'[58]

Durham's reference to the propitiation of allies reflected her misgivings about the success of the Greek counter-attack. It was no good to Albania if Italian occupation gave way to its Greek counterpart. In some way the latter was the worse option. The Italians were at least committed to maintaining Albania's territorial unity. The Greeks, on the other hand, wished to chip off southern Albania – or, as they still called it, Northern Epirus – and Britain was far more sensitive to Greece's opinion on this question than Albania's. British enthusiasm for the Greek army's fierce resistance to the Italians meant that there was no question of London making any commitments concerning the borders of Albania. It was all deeply frustrating.

King Zog's flight to London posed another dilemma. After Germany invaded Yugoslavia in spring 1941, the Yugoslav royals also descended on London. But while Yugoslavia's supporters felt no compunction about rallying to the government-in-exile under King Petar, the much smaller band of Albanian supporters were divided about what to do with King Zog, whom the British refused to treat as the head of an allied government. Durham also refused to have anything to do with Zog, declining to visit him at his first residence in the Ritz or at his second home in Buckinghamshire. She was also anxious that he should not visit her in London. With that in mind, following an operation, she told her young friend Harry Hodgkinson that although she now felt better, he was not to convey the good news to Zog in case the King should venture up Haverstock Hill to pay his respects. She could never be reconciled to a man who had taken power in Tirana on the backs of White Russian mercenaries hired in Serbia, and who had driven out her friend, Fan Noli. 'I loathe Zog,' she told Hodgkinson.[59]

Meanwhile, the 'cup of humiliation' to which Durham had referred in 1914 continued to overflow from time to time. During World War II a new writer took on the subject of the Balkans and reached a far bigger audience than she or Seton-Watson had ever done. Beside this newcomer's passionate, almost religious, adoration of Serbia, Seton-Watson had been a model of intellectual restraint.

The newcomer was Rebecca West. Born in 1892, West had been too young to become caught up in the Kossovo Day Committee or the work of the other pro-Serbian clubs in Britain during World War I, though she was a friend to the Seton-Watsons and would have heard a good deal about Yugoslavia from that quarter. She maintained that her interest in Yugoslavia began in 1934, when, lying in a nursing home, she heard of the assassination of King Aleksandar in Marseille and watched a newsreel of the monarch's last moments. Struck by the pathos of the scene, she resolved to visit the country, which she did in 1936 on behalf of the British Council. After witnessing the semi-pagan sacrifice of a black lamb on a primitive altar in a field in Macedonia, she felt inspired to compose a tome of more than 1,100 pages on Yugoslavia, wound around the central theme of the Battle of Kosovo in 1389, when, according to legend, the Prophet Elijah had appeared to the Serbian Prince Lazar on the eve of the fateful battle in the guise of grey falcon, offering him two choices: military victory over the invaders at the price of spiritual perdition or heavenly victory whose price would be defeat on the battlefield.

Black Lamb and Grey Falcon was published to ecstatic reviews in 1941, deemed on a par with T.E. Lawrence's *Seven Pillars of Wisdom*, and became a much-reprinted bestseller, permanently reshaping the English-speaking world's view of the Balkans.[60] To one influential recent writer on the Balkans, it was a work of 'near perfect clairvoyance'. 'Like the Talmud,' Robert Kaplan wrote, 'one can read the book over and over again for different levels of meaning.'[61] Diplomats and United Nations peacekeepers were still quoting chunks of West's words in the 1990s as Yugoslavia fell apart, and its vehemently pro-Serbian tone played a part in shaping the West's response to the crisis, at last initially.[62] Unlike Seton-Watson, West did not engage Durham in private duels. But she attacked her for the same reasons, and just as fiercely. In the prologue to *Black Lamb*, West wrote of foreign travellers 'who return with a pet Balkan people established in their hearts as suffering and innocent, eternally the massacree and never the massacrer', adding:

> The same sort of person, devoted to good works and austerities, who is traditionally supposed to keep a cat and a parrot [...] often sets up upon the hearth the image of the Albanian, or the Bulgarian or the Serbian [...] with all the force and blandness of pious fantasy.

'The image of the Albanians as championed by Miss Durham, strongly resembles Sir Joshua Reynolds' portrait of the Infant Samuel,' she concluded, referring to the well-known painting of the prophet as an innocent child, eyes raised in adoration.[63]

It was an unfair assault from West, whose vast work fell more unambiguously into the category of pious fantasy than anything that Durham had written. Durham had spent years toiling on the ground in the Balkans. West had been there three times and had spent most of that time with a Yugoslav government minder. It was clear to Durham's trained eye that West's book was based primarily on what that minder had shown her. Unsurprisingly, she dissented from the chorus of praise and after being sent a copy to review, wrote back: 'The novelist Miss West has written an immense book on the strength of one pleasure trip to Yugoslavia, but with no previous knowledge of land or people.'[64] After she threatened to sue, West's publishers deleted Durham's name from the prologue, though it re-emerged in later editions. West remained venomous. She once wrote to a complete stranger, who had sent a compliment about her book, giving chapter and verse on Durham's more egregious errors, dismissing each of her books as 'fantastically unreliable' and recalling her 'absurd libel action'.[65]

It might have been expected that Durham, now almost 80, virtually housebound, the ridiculed champion of a forgotten nation, would succumb to despondency. But this was not so. The last years of her life saw a renewed burst of vitality, coupled with a new conviction that she would be found right in the end. Unlike World War I, which had never engaged her, the Allied cause in World War II enjoyed her complete sympathy. Ideologically, Hitler's Germany was abhorrent to her in a way that the Kaiser's had never been. And, only an Allied victory and the collapse of Fascist Italy offered hope for the restoration of Albanian independence. The privations and alarums of wartime did not affect her. She told one solicitous foreign correspondent that people in Britain had quite enough food in spite of rationing. Nor did German air raids keep her awake; she had got used to sleeping amid the sound of gunfire in the Balkan Wars.[66]

By 1942, reports from the field in the Balkans filled her with optimism. While the fall of the royalist regime in Yugoslavia in 1941 and the rise of a left-wing resistance movement under Josip Broz 'Tito' dismayed West, Durham felt elated.[67] She was now more reconciled to the continued existence of a Yugoslav state than she had been earlier – as long as it was a 'real Jugoslavia with equal rights and opportunities for all', and not, as she considered it had been, 'a mere mockery [...] a Greater Serbia under the dictatorship of the White Hand, the Crown and the Radical Party'.[68] The multi-national Partisan movement, which Durham, like many in Britain, had no idea was entirely communist-dominated, at least was committed to a federal reorganisation of the country and so had the potential to rectify the worst injustices done to Yugoslavia's minorities, she decided. 'I am greatly interested in Tito and his officers,' she declared to one of her correspondents. At the end of World War I, she continued,

> We handed over Croats, Slovenes and Montenegrins to Serb domination, willy nilly, without any plebiscite. Since then for twenty years there had been a reign of terror ... We have at last

realised this and Tito the Croat leader may at long last free them from Belgrade's tyranny [...] so we shall see a reversal of the errors of 1914–18. What a crazy world it is![69]

The cheering news from Yugoslavia was augmented by hopeful news from Albania. After the collapse of Zog's regime in 1939, armed resistance to the Italian occupation steadily gained momentum. In 1943, following the fall of Mussolini, the Italian occupation force in Albania disintegrated. German occupation promptly replaced it but, unlike the Italians, the Germans had no ambition to colonise Albania or remain there permanently. They invaded to fill the vacuum created by the departure of the Italians. From an Albanian point of view in some ways it was an improvement.

However, well-founded reports again circulated that the British were once more considering auctioning Albanian territory to Greece and Yugoslavia. The Allies had recognised both of these exiled governments as allies but Britain bizarrely continued to uphold the legality of the Italian invasion of 1939, leaving open the question of whether Albania would be reconstituted within its 1913 borders.

Although leaving her home in Glenloch Road was virtually impossible, and even a trip to the local shops left her gasping, Durham took on this new threat, targeting a flow of letters towards *The Times*, the *Manchester Guardian* and others, spreading news about the insurgency within Albania. She complained to the *New Statesman* in January 1942 that when the BBC had asked her to make a personal broadcast to Albania, they had withdrawn the invitation once she made it clear that she intended to use the opportunity to commit Britain to Albania's independence and territorial integrity. As ever, it seemed, British concern for Greek sentiments about Northern Epirus trumped any concerns about the sentiments of the Albanians. 'If justice is to survive and the Atlantic Charter to be a valid and not a mere makeshift document, let Albania's claim to be independent be recognised at once,' she wrote.⁷⁰ Making it clear that she had not lost her fighting spirit, she also wrote to the Albanian community in America, not so much suggesting as commanding an end to fratricidal intrigues and urging unity behind the struggle to liberate the country.⁷¹

In an almost elegiac tone and without a scintilla of regret, the year before she died, Durham cast her mind's eye back over the several decades that she had spent working in, and for, Albania. She was fully aware that the world, Albania included, was changing and that she might not see the outcome of the next phase. She wrote that, over 40 years earlier in January 1943,

> I first was introduced to the Albanian question [...] and promised the Albanians that I would do all I could to help them achieve liberty. It has been a long journey. Many gallant men, much younger than myself, have fallen by the way.

'The champions of freedom with whom I worked in the North [...] are all gone,' she continued. But, she went on:

> Young Albania is awake and active. I have entered my eightieth year. I can no longer spend days on horseback and climbing mountains, but I hope to see Albania restored to freedom and her frontiers extended to include the many who now are under foreign rule.⁷²

CHAPTER 11

'Albanians will never forget'

In the mountains she knew so well, her death will echo from peak to peak.

(King Zog of Albania, 1944)[1]

Durham died on 15 November 1944, at her home in Glenloch Road. In her own country she was already forgotten outside the small world of Balkan specialists, many of whom were hostile. In March 1948, Leopold Wickham Legg, editor of the *Dictionary of National Biography*, wrote to Robert Seton-Watson seeking his help in 'giving some assessment of the value of the work of Miss Mary Edith Durham in the Balkans'. He added: 'I don't know much about her, and she may not be worth including in the dictionary, so you see from this how much I should value your advice.'[2] The fact that Wickham Legg seriously thought Durham's chief denigrator was a competent authority to assess her life's work demonstrated the degree to which memories of her exploits had fallen into oblivion. Seton-Watson's reply does not survive, but given that he had boasted of being 'at war' with her, it seems unlikely he presented her endeavours in a positive light. She did not make it into the book's 1951 edition.

Though he had felt vaguely baffled by her hostility towards him, King Zog was far more generous. In a moving tribute in

The Times, he noted that when Edith Durham had first come to Albania 'the country's name was nothing more than a geographical expression'. The King, who was about to be formally dethroned, continued:

> Her whole life was devoted to Albania. She gave us her heart and she won the heart of our mountaineers, for whom she had especial sympathy. Even today, her name is treasured by them.
>
> Albanians have never forgotten – and will never forget – this Englishwoman. In the mountains she knew so well, her death will echo from peak to peak.[3]

In a joint tribute to her life and work published in December 1944 in her old organ, the *New Times and Ethiopia News*, several Albanian leaders made a similar prediction, that 'one of the first acts of free and independent Albania will be to commemorate this princess of the Albanian mountains'.[4]

Unfortunately, the new Albania was independent but by no means free, and its new rulers had no intention of commemorating princesses of any type, least of all foreign ones. Durham missed the liberation of Albania by days. Perhaps this was no bad thing, as the brutality of the liberators would have disappointed her. The last German troops left Tirana two days after her death. Eleven days later, on 28 November, Partisan forces, led by a Parisian-educated Stalinist called Enver Hoxha, entered the capital.

From this point, all hope of commemorating Durham's work was lost. There was no room under this former schoolteacher from Korça for alternative role models or sources of inspiration, with the exception of Stalin, the safely long-dead Marx and Engels, and a few ancient Albanian heroes like Skanderbeg. From November 1944 to the collapse of the Communist regime in Albania in 1991, memories of Durham were expunged. She was not attacked directly, simply reduced to a footnote. She was not the only Briton to suffer this way. Memorials to Aubrey Herbert were also done away with, starting with the street and library named after him, and the village of Herbert, which his widow, Mary, and his mother had established to house refugees from Kosovo and Macedonia.

Durham's memory in Albania would of course have experienced some form of eclipse, though it would have been less drastic under a less totalitarian regime. The Albania that she had discovered and defended over more than four decades had crumbled long before power fell into the hands of the communists. King Zog had acted as a mild break on the forces of change. But he could not check the rise of a new generation of modern nationalists who felt impatient with what they saw as their fathers' backwardness, and regarded the Albania that Durham had cherished with some contempt. This younger generation of Albanians, dressed in western clothes and full of half-digested western philosophical ideas, was highly nationalistic – a sentiment on which the communists drew when clothing Stalinism in Albanian nationalism. The communist vision of a centralised state, founded on the basis of a radical rupture with the past, roused a spirit of patriotic enthusiasm among many young people, and this idealism extended well beyond the ranks of those who considered themselves Marxist-Leninists. The new regime's literacy drives, the campaigns to outlaw the *besa* and the promotion of women's equality enjoyed broad support. The new regime did not entirely lack sympathy in émigré circles, either. Hoxha's nationalism impressed important members of the diaspora, including Durham's friend, Fan Noli, who refrained from direct public criticism of Hoxha's dictatorship. It can only be imagined what Noli, who died in 1965, would have made of Hoxha's decision two years later, to annihilate the Albanian Orthodox Church to which Noli had devoted so much of his life.

Hoxha had a cosmopolitan background. Born in 1908 to a Muslim family of land-owners and cloth merchants in

Gjirokaster, in the south of the country, he had been educated at the National Lyceé in Korça – an institution founded during the brief French regime in the town – going on to spend the next decade or so drifting from one francophone place in Europe to another after gaining a scholarship to study botany in Montpellier in 1931. Switching from Montpellier to Paris and from there to Brussels, having abandoned all thought of completing a degree, Hoxha survived on family money, taking the odd job in Albanian embassies and flirting with journalism. By the time he was 30 he had perfected his French and developed a life-long taste for expensive menswear. He returned to Albania in 1936 to pursue almost the only career available to a footloose radical dandy, that of schoolteacher, which he pursued in the same Lycée where he had been educated.

It might have been thought that all those years spent lounging in France and Belgium would have given him a truly European outlook. He was certainly the dandy of what was about to become the Soviet bloc with his tailored suits and fine manners.[5] Hoxha was also intellectually superior to most of his Eastern European comrades, 'by far the best read head of state in Eastern Europe', as one biographer put it.[6]

But Hoxha's knowledge of French plays did not make him open-minded. On the contrary, his belief in his own superior knowledge fixed in him a determination to become the Soviet bloc's ultimate pedagogue. This was a task he never laid down and in the pursuit of which he created the most paranoid and xenophobic regime in Eastern Europe. On taking power, no pretence was made at allowing a brief period of political transition from bourgeois to people's democracy along the lines pursued in Poland, Hungary, Czechoslovakia and the German Democratic Republic. Albania's great leap forward towards full Socialism was more abrupt even than Yugoslavia's. No rival political formation to Hoxha's Party of Labour, which initially styled itself the Democratic Front, was allowed to compete in the general election in December 1945, when voters had the choice of dropping a ball into a red box for the Front, or into a black box for the non-existent opposition. Hoxha noted without irony of this farce: 'There was not the slightest doubt about the victory of the candidates of the Democratic Front.'[7]

Immediately after it met in January 1946, the new constituent assembly voted to abolish the monarchy, proclaimed a people's republic and adopted a constitution modelled on Soviet lines. From the start, Hoxha intended to rule the country single-handedly, a mini-Stalin, aggregating the important posts to himself and simultaneously holding the positions of general secretary of the party, prime minister, foreign minister, defence minister and commander-in-chief. As he was only 37 in 1945 and in reasonable health, Albania was potentially in for a long haul. He remained dictator until his death in 1985.

The process of de-Stalinisation and the faint dawn of a more consumerist society in Eastern Europe passed by Albania. With the aid of his vigilant secret police, the Sigurimi, Hoxha kept Albanians under a strict watch and on the edge of their seats. Show trials in which once unimpeachably loyal communists were unmasked as traitors continued almost until Hoxha's death.

The late 1960s also saw Albania exceed anything that even Stalin had attempted in the campaign against religion. This was not the standard communist drive to minimise religious influence by intimidating believers, infiltrating churches and selectively jailing troublesome clerics. Hoxha's goal was much more radical: to extirpate religious belief and practice. After he announced the campaign on 6 February 1967, the Catholic cathedrals in Tirana, Dürres and Shkodra were seized within weeks and converted to secular purposes.[8] By the summer all 2,169 churches and mosques in the country had been closed: some 608 Orthodox churches, 327 Catholic churches, and about 1,200 mosques and other Muslim religious sites.[9] The fates of these buildings were varied. A mosque in Tirana became a shop for sign painters. The main mosque in the resort of Saranda became a warehouse. The Church of St Nicholas in Ruse was turned into apartments, while the Catholic seminary in Shkodra became a dormitory for trainee teachers and the Orthodox cathedral in Korça became a medieval art museum.[10]

Albania was proclaimed the world's first atheist state. Not even China had gone that far. To ensure that the claim was not idle, young zealots toured the country, vandalising and sometimes burning down churches and monasteries, and knocking on people's doors and demanding the surrender of any remaining religious items, such as crosses, icons and prayer books. The war on religion was not a brief fetish of Hoxha's. In 1973, news reached the West that the previous year the authorities had executed Father Shtjefën Kurti, a jailed Catholic priest in his seventies, for having baptised a fellow prisoner's baby at her request.[11] By then, all three of Albania's remaining Catholic bishops were in camps. Bishop Fishta died in one in 1973 and Ernest Coba of Shkodra followed in 1979, after a beating sustained for holding a mass in secret for fellow prisoners.[12] Only Nikollë Troshani of Dürres remained alive, in a camp near Vlora.

The Orthodox Church fared no better, despite having been treated more leniently in earlier years. Archbishop Damian Kokonesi, the head of the Church, died in prison in November 1973.[13] According to the writer Sabrina Ramet, within a few years, 'the entire surviving hierarchy of the Albanian Orthodox Church, as well as most of its priests, were held in prison'.[14]

The criminalisation of religious belief was not quite as seminal an event in Albania as it might have been in other countries, because practice of Catholicism in particular had long been almost impossible. Miranda Vickers has cited a document that noted that in 1953 only 10 of the 93 Catholic clerics active in 1945 remained at liberty. Of the other 83, 24 had been killed, 35 were in jail and the rest had died, disappeared or fled abroad.[15] At the same time, the Catholic school system had been dismantled and all seminaries, convents, orphanages and charitable organisations closed. By the mid-1950s all that remained were actual churches and a handful of clergy. As Vickers noted, Hoxha directed a special animus towards Catholics, which probably drew on a southern, Tosk bias against the northern Gegs, as well as reflecting the standard Marxist ideological hostility to the Vatican. 'The Catholic Church and its clergy were always in alliance with the reactionary regimes like those of Prince Wied, and Ahmed Zog, as well as with every foreign occupier of Albania,' Vickers quoted Hoxha as saying. 'The Muslim religion and its hierarchy were not as serious an obstacle to the struggle against the Italian occupier as the Catholic religion was.'[16]

Whatever the impact on people's interior lives of the ban on religion, it certainly had a drastic effect on Albania's urban landscape. The skylines of towns and cities changed as mosques and churches were demolished or clumsily transformed into factories, cinemas or sports centres. When the Catholic cathedral in Shkodra became a gymnasium it lost its two front towers. As one historian recalled, the abolition of religion 'stripped Albania of not only many of its cultural traditions but also the vast majority of its architectural monuments'.[17]

In April 1985, Eastern Europe's longest serving leader died of diabetes. His funeral took place on 11 April when, at 9 a.m., his coffin was placed on a gun carriage that processed through vast, weeping throngs towards Skanderbeg Square and thence to the Cemetery of the Martyrs of the Nation. Sirens wailed, guns fired salutes.

Great strides had been made in the land that Edith Durham had once called 'a roadless ruin'. During her time in Albania, about 90 per cent of the population remained illiterate. By Hoxha's death, illiteracy had vanished. Railways linked the main population centres.[18] Electricity had penetrated remote villages. Life expectancy was up, having risen from around 38 at the end of Zog's reign to around 71. Life remained austere, but by the 1980s 'every home had electricity and a radio, and more and more homes had a TV set and a refrigerator'.[19] Drainage schemes had transformed once barren hillsides and malarial swamps into orchards. Everyone had employment of some description, however footling, and rents for accommodation were nominal. Cultural life, albeit of a heavily circumscribed kind, flourished. True to Hoxha's diktat about building a wholly self-sufficient society, the country even developed its own film industry, which churned out 13 or 14 films a year in the 1970s and 1980s.[20]

But the population paid a high price for these impressive-sounding social gains in terms of loss of liberty. Hoxha perfected the most intrusive system of state surveillance in Eastern Europe, which came complete with labour camps and so-called areas of internal exile. The death penalty was prescribed for no fewer than 34 offences, which included attempted flight from the country.[21] Almost any activity could be interpreted as coming within the category of 'anti-state agitation and propaganda'.[22] Collective punishment of families for crimes committed by a single member was common.[23] Trials were farcical; there was no record of anyone being found not guilty of a political offence thanks to the activities of his or her lawyer.

Remarkably little was written in the West during the Cold War years about Albania's fate under Hoxha. The story of the era was chronicled sketchily, for reasons that Durham would have recognised: Albania's strategic irrelevance. While Hoxha kept Albania busy building mushroom-shaped concrete bunkers to ward off a non-existent invasion, the West in reality all but ignored the country. Occasional reports referred in a semi-jokey fashion to a 'hermit kingdom', as if it were some kind of Shangri-La, not a boot camp. There was no Albanian equivalent of the politically active Polish, Hungarian and Czech émigré communities, keenly following events at home and countering government narratives with their own versions of events. A large Albanian community continued to exist outside Albania, in the USA and in Yugoslavia, but the Albanians of Kosovo and Macedonia were preoccupied by their own struggles inside Yugoslavia, and some romanticised the situation inside Albania. When the Albanians of Yugoslavia were finally able to cross the border, many were shocked by what they found there.[24]

After Hoxha's death, the system he had laboured to build lingered for another half-decade under his loyal henchman and cultural affairs specialist, Ramiz Alia. As one of the main executors of the anti-religious campaign, Alia's succession appeared to guarantee the survival of Hoxha's idiosyncratic ideology. In September 1987, Alia delivered a stern speech in which he said Albania would not stray from the late leader's path. Hoxha had been 'a great man when he was alive but the greatness of his personality and deeds rises to an even loftier height now after his death,' Alia said.[25]

The words were ill chosen. In the spring of 1990 the first reports of strikes inside the country reached the West. On 28 June, a large, spontaneous protest in Tirana by several thousand people, complaining about food shortages and demanding the right to travel, destroyed the illusion of a nation still mourning Hoxha's death. After the police attacked them, thousands of the protesters invaded the precincts of the recently reopened German, French and Italian embassies. More than 3,000 entered the German embassy grounds alone. The street protests and embassy invasions 'effectively announced the end of the old regime,' a contemporary writer remarked.[26] After that, a sequence of halting and incomplete concessions confirmed a perception that the government was losing control. There was a brief lull in demonstrations in the autumn of 1990 but a new wave of protests began on the university campus in Tirana in December. The government denounced the 'dark forces'[27] at work in Albania, but then surrendered to them, and on 11 December it lifted the ban on independent political organisations, allowing for the formation of alternative parties. A date was set for a general election to be held on 31 March,

Albania's first genuinely multi-party election since the 1920s; the vote at the end of World War II hardly counted. Before the election took place, a procession of students on 20 February 1991 wound its way to Skanderbeg Square and pulled down Hoxha's 9-metre-high gilded statue.

Albania's subsequent transition towards democracy proved tumultuous by the standards of the rest of Eastern Europe, with the glaring exception of Yugoslavia, where the conflicts were not so much political as ethnic. The totalitarian character of the regime meant that its disappearance created a bigger vacuum than the fall of the monarchy had done more than a half-century earlier. Elsewhere in eastern Europe, communist governments, especially in the 1980s, had reluctantly ceded some wriggle room to other forces in society, such as writers, churches or independent trade unions. But no alternative civil society in Albania was waiting in the wings to take up its role in a free society. The Hoxha regime had crushed the life out of every independent force. Dissidents had been killed, not jailed or humiliated. As a result, when the party and the Sigurimi dissolved, the surrounding society almost collapsed alongside them, creating conditions of prolonged virtual anarchy.

Twenty years after the events of 1991, as Albania prepared to celebrate its hundredth birthday in 2012, the future looked much brighter than it had done in the dismal 1990s, but the political outlook was still uncertain, marked by almost complete deadlock between left and right, between the heirs of the former regime and its enemies.

In spite of, or perhaps because of, the mayhem that followed the fall of communism, the stock of once reviled figures of the pre-communist era grew. King Zog's son, Leka, even attempted to restore the monarchy.[28] Given that Leka had only lived in Albania for about 48 hours before his parents were forced to flee to Greece, and given that his father's reign lasted only just over a decade, it was remarkable that the monarchist cause got as many votes as it did in the referendum in 1997.[29]

Edith Durham's name was also rescued from years of oblivion. After almost half a century it was clear that many people had not forgotten their English champion. Some who felt a twinge of nostalgia for the Hoxha regime still sneered at her as a patronising foreigner who had romanticised the northern tribes. But for many others such quibbles counted for nothing. As Hoxha's name vanished from street maps, Durham's made its appearance. 'Edith Durham' or 'Miss Durham' memorials have since sprouted in a number of places. A junior school in Tirana is named after her, as are boulevards in Shkodra, Korça and other towns. There is a stone memorial near the village of Thethi in the northern mountains. There were even suggestions to name a regional airport after her.[30]

The phenomenon has not been confined to Albania. Over the border in Kosovo, Durham's name and likeness made an equally sudden reappearance. She was less associated with Kosovo than northern Albania. After all, she had been Queen of the Mountains, not Queen of the Kosovo Plain. But her denunciations of Serbian atrocities in Kosovo in the 1920s ensured that she had a following there, too, and she became an official heroine once NATO terminated Serbian rule over Kosovo in 1999, as power finally passed into the hands of Kosovo's ethnic Albanian majority. In 2009, a year after Kosovo proclaimed independence from Serbia, she appeared on the new republic's stamps – a young, severe-looking, classical Edith – Edith as a Roman matron.

She would have relished her belated rehabilitation. Never a shrinking violet, she thoroughly enjoyed her regal status among the Albanians, not because she had sought power or money but because she felt it gave her the ability to influence events in the Balkans. She would have felt vindicated, knowing that her face and name were at last being carried 'from peak to peak', as Zog had once prophesied they would be, in the 1940s.

She would have felt more vindicated by the knowledge that her predictions had proved correct. In books, lectures and articles, she had warned against the folly of allowing

Turkey-in-Europe to be divided on the basis of the military strength of the surrounding countries. For the last decades of her life, she was ridiculed as a Cassandra-like figure for trying to bring the subsequent injustices of the post-Balkan-War settlement to attention. From a modern perspective, her warnings were justified.

Seton-Watson and his friends had accused Durham of pursuing a vendetta against the Serbs for asserting that an extension of Serbian rule over large parts of the Balkans would end in bloodshed. But her words of warning on that subject were borne out. In the seven decades of its existence the Yugoslav state collapsed not once but twice, first in 1941 and again in 1991, both times with massive loss of life. The first collapse was the consequence of a German invasion, but when Yugoslavia imploded in the 1990s it did so alone, although the incoherent and contradictory responses of the western powers worsened matters. Fighting between Serbs and Croats in 1991 and again in 1995; between Bosnian Serbs, Muslims and Croats from 1992 to 1995; and between Serbs and Kosovo Albanians in 1998 to 1999 resulted in at least 20,000 dead in Croatia, around 100,000 dead in Bosnia[31] and around 10,000 dead in Kosovo[32] – a total of around 130,000. The number of people displaced by the ex-Yugoslav conflicts was larger: the Serbs displaced about 150,000 Croats in 1991 and the Croats displaced about the same number of Serbs in 1995. Over 1 million of the approximately 4.5 million inhabitants of Bosnia were forced from their homes between 1992 and 1995. The Serbian police and Yugoslav military displaced around 800,000 Kosovo Albanians in 1998 and in the spring of 1999, while about 150,000 Serbs and other non-Albanians, mainly Roma, were in turn displaced when the Albanian expellees returned home later in 1999.

That sequence of events confirmed Durham's baleful predictions about the prospects of the new state. Her more detailed predictions concerning the future of Kosovo were equally accurate. In *High Albania*, Durham had described Mitrovica in northern

Kosovo as a tinderbox, noting that an approximate ethnic boundary in the Balkans between Serbs and Albanians ran right through the town. The ethnologist in her proved prescient. In the summer of 1999, after NATO aircraft took out Serbia's military communications and forced the Serbian ruler, Slobodan Milošević, to withdraw his army and police, the Kosovo Liberation Army moved back over the Albanian border and overran one town after another. The northward and eastward advance of this guerrilla force extended as far as the northern edge of the Albanian pale of settlement, which took them to the centre of Mitrovica: to be precise, to the bridge over the Ibar, the river separating the northern and southern halves of the town. North of the Ibar the Serbs hold their own. Southwards lies an Albanian town. The people on either side of the river glare at one another, Serbian Mitrovica versus Albanian Mitrovice. More than a decade on from the 1999 conflict little has changed.[33]

The only thing that would have surprised Durham about events in Kosovo in the 1990s was the intervention of the western powers on behalf of the Albanians. She would have been more surprised still by Britain's role in the NATO air war, which undid the territorial settlement that had arisen from the Balkan Wars of 1912–13. Throughout her years in the Balkans, and for the rest of her life, Britain's indifference to her beloved Albania had frustrated her instinctive patriotism. The decision of the British Prime Minister, Tony Blair, to take on Serbia in 1999 would have enjoyed her approval. Not a Little Englander, or a pacifist, she was an exponent of the doctrine of Liberal Interventionism long before the term was invented.

Whether Durham would recognise much of today's Albania, or Kosovo, is another question. In Albania, especially in the northern mountains, she thought she had stumbled across a lost world where, as she wrote at the start of *High Albania*:

> the wanderer from the West stands awestruck [...] filled with vague memories of the cradle of his race, saying 'This did I

do some thousands of year ago [...] so thought I and so acted I in the beginning of Time.³⁴

That Albania had faded during her own lifetime and Hoxha had concreted over whatever remained. The average visitor to Albania or Kosovo is not now likely to encounter anything that fills him or her with vague memories of the dawn of his, or her, race. Many men still expect to marry virgins, and there are still a few 'sworn virgins' around, or women who claim to have taken some kind of oath to that effect.³⁵ The code of blood vengeance lingers on in the form of honour killings. For the rest, the modern Albanian reads *High Albania* with the same fascination as a western reader, observing through its pages a foreign society. Hoxha's legacy of decaying tower blocks is meanwhile ubiquitous. There is nothing to remind today's visitor to Shkodra of the romance that Durham detected there.

The fact that Hoxha obliterated so much that reminded people of the past in Albania did not make neighbouring Kosovo a repository of older values. The Albanians of Kosovo are a little more devout than their neighbours on the other side of the mountains. But they are just as careless of their traditions, if the destruction of the few remaining old buildings of Pristina is a guide. Pristina and Tirana are alike in their embrace of flashy modernity and apparent indifference to history. It is hard to imagine Durham's ghost threading its way along either city's potholed boulevards, lined with high-rise apartment blocks and identical-looking bars named after cities in America, Switzerland or Germany.³⁶ She would have been disappointed by the squalid political culture of Albania and Kosovo, as well as by their rampant corruption, which has deterred all but the most determined foreign investors.

In the end, however, it was not a naive faith in the virtuousness of Albanians that led Edith Durham to dedicate so much of her life to the cause, although she heartily admired the rugged spirit of independence and robust humour she found among the mountain people. Her fundamental motive was a belief in justice and in the right of every people to govern itself, whether the result was good or ill. To the extent that events in the late 1990s finally accorded most Albanians in the Balkans the right to shape their own destiny, she would have felt that the battle had been won.

NOTES

Introduction

1. Slobodan Milošević was born in 1941 and assumed leadership of the League of Communists of Serbia at the party's eighth plenum in 1987, propelled to victory by populist pledges to boost the position of the allegedly endangered Kosovo Serbs. Overthrown in 2000, after fomenting several wars in the former Yugoslavia, he was deported to the International Criminal Tribunal for the Former Yugoslavia, ICTY, where he died, still on trial, in 2006.
2. Azem Vllasi, born 1948, became leader of the League of Communists of Kosovo in 1986. After being toppled and arrested in 1989, he was briefly imprisoned but was released in 1990.
3. The demographic position of the Serbs in Kosovo deteriorated in the 1970s and 1980s. The first three postwar Yugoslav censuses, in 1948, 1953 and 1961, suggested that the Serbian population was holding steady at around 23 per cent. But the 1971 census revealed a sharp fall to only 18 per cent, and by 1981 the figure had dropped again, to 13 per cent. The 1991 census showed a further drop to just over 9 per cent.
4. In Serbia, Užice was named Titovo Užice. Likewise in Macedonia, Titov Veles; in Bosnia, Titov Drvar; in Vojvodina, Tito Vrbas; in Croatia, Titovo Korenica. Montenegro went furthest, renaming its capital, Podgorica, 'Titograd', dispensing with the old name entirely.
5. Serbia seized, or reclaimed, Kosovo from the Ottoman Empire – depending on one's viewpoint – in the Balkan Wars of 1912–13. Briefly annexed to Italian-ruled Albania during World War II, Tito's Partisans either conquered or liberated Kosovo – again, depending on one's viewpoint – in 1945.

  After abandoning a brief plan to unite Kosovo to Albania within an expanded Yugoslav federation, Kosovo was designated an autonomous province of Serbia inside Yugoslavia, alongside the province of Vojvodina. Tito's final constitution, adopted in 1974, strengthened the autonomy of both provinces, but created anomalies by designating them Socialist Autonomous Provinces of Yugoslavia, raising the question as to what extent either remained inside Serbia.

6. M.E. Durham, *High Albania* (London, 1985 [1909]), p. 294.
7. According to the Belgrade-based Humanitarian Law Centre and the International Commission on Missing Persons, there were 13,472 victims of the conflict from January 1998 to December 2000, of whom 9,260 were Albanians; 2,488 Serb; and 1,254 of other origin, or victims whose ethnic identity could not be ascertained.
8. By mid-2012, Kosovo had been recognised by 89 of the 193 UN member states, including 22 of the 27 European Union (EU) member states and the USA. Serbia vowed never to recognise it, citing its 2006 constitution, which described Kosovo as an integral part of the national territory. Serbia has been strongly supported by two major powers, Russia and China, as well as by five EU 'refuseniks': Greece, Cyprus, Romania, Slovakia and Spain.
9. Serbia and Kosovo signed a landmark EU-brokered agreement in April 2013 on improving relations. It did not address the issue of Kosovo's statehood but it suggested that Belgrade might be moving slowly towards the idea of recognising Kosovo at some stage.
10. M.E. Durham, *Through the Lands of the Serb* (London, 1903), *The Burden of the Balkans* (London, 1905), *High Albania* (London, 1909), *The Struggle for Scutari (Turk, Slav, and Albanian)* (London, 1914), *Twenty Years of Balkan Tangle* (London, 1920), *The Serajevo Crime* (London, 1925), *Some Tribal Origins, Laws and Customs of the Balkans* (London, 1928).
11. Mary Edith, born 1864; Arthur Ellis, born 1865; Herbert Edward, born 1866; Ellen L., born 1868; Caroline Beatrice, born 1869; Florence Margaret, born 1869; Alice L., born 1870; Frank Rogers, born 1872, Frances Hermia, born 1874.
12. Three of her siblings were mentioned in *Who Was Who, 1941–1950*: Frances Hermia, who rose to become Assistant Secretary in the Ministry of Labour; Frank Rogers; and Herbert Edward, who, after various scientific expeditions to such places as Brazil, investigating yellow fever, devoted himself to fermentation. One of Caroline Beatrice's three sons, Gregory, became a noted anthropologist.

13. For a brief résumé of Arthur Ellis's life, see his obituary, *British Medical Journal*, 19 August 1893, 447.
14. William Bateson, *William Bateson: His Essays and Addresses, with a Memoir by Beatrice Bateson* (London, 1984 [1928]), p. 69. See also Robin Henig, *The Monk in the Garden: The Lost and Found Genius of Gregor Mendel, the Father of Genetics* (New York, 2000), p. 217.
15. Alan Cock and Donald Forsdyke, *Treasure your Exceptions: The Science and Life of William Bateson* (London, 2008), p. 181.
16. Obituary of Arthur E. Durham, *British Medical Journal*, 11 May 1895, 1067–9 (p. 1067). Available at www.ncbi.nlm.nih.gov/pmc/articles/PMC2509729/?page=1 (accessed 2 September 2013).
17. Arthur Edward Durham was a distinguished surgeon at Guy's Hospital, London, becoming full surgeon in 1872 and consulting surgeon from 1894. At one time he was Vice-President of the Royal College of Surgeons. See 'Durham, Arthur Edward (1833–1895)', in *Plarr's Lives of the Fellows Online*. Available at http://livesonline.rcseng.ac.uk/biogs/E001480b.htm (accessed 2 September 2013).
18. Obituary of Arthur E. Durham, p. 1067.
19. Durham, *Twenty Years of Balkan Tangle*, p. 9.
20. Ibid., p. 81.
21. Sutherland Menzies, *Turkey Old and New*, 2 vols, Vol. 2 (London, 1880), p. 354.
22. *The Times*, 21 November 1944, quoted in M. Edith Durham, *Albania and the Albanians: Selected Articles and Letters 1903–1944*, ed. Bejtullah Destani (London, 2001), p. 243.

1 'The Balkan tangle'

1. Quoted in Jonathan Steinberg, *Bismarck: A Life* (Oxford, 2011), p. 372. Disraeli was actually quoting Bismarck.
2. G.E. Mitton, *Austria-Hungary* (London, 1914), pp. 36–7.
3. Albert Sorel, *Europe and the French Revolution* (London, 1969 [1885]), p. 473.
4. Henry Wickham Steed, *Through Thirty Years 1892–1922: A Personal Narrative*, 2 vols, Vol. 1 (London, 1924), p. 329.
5. Ibid., p. 264.
6. George Gawrych, *The Crescent and the Eagle: Ottoman Rule, Islam and the Albanians, 1874–1913* (London, 2006), p. 78.

7. 'Thus the line from Salonika to Titova Mitrovica built in 1873 was constructed specifically for easier control of potential disturbances in Macedonia.' Paul Magocsi, *Historical Atlas of East Central Europe* (Seattle, WA, 1993), p. 90.
8. George Gordon Byron Byron, *'In My Hot Youth': Byron's Letters and Journals*, ed. Leslie Marchand, 12 vols, Vol. 1 (London, 1978), p. 227.
9. Ibid., p. 228.
10. John Cam Hobhouse, *A Journey through Albania and Other Provinces of Turkey in Europe and Asia to Constantinople during the Years 1809 and 1810*, 2 vols, Vol. 1 (London, 1810), p. 8.
11. Ibid., Vol. 1, p. 32.
12. William Moneypenny, *The Life of Benjamin Disraeli, Earl of Beaconsfield*, 6 vols (London, 1804–37), Vol. 1 (1910), p. 158. See also Benjamin Disraeli, *Benjamin Disraeli: Letters, 1815–1834*, ed. J.A.W. Gunn, John Matthews, Donald M. Schurman and M.G. Wiebe (Toronto, 1982), p. 173.
13. Edward Lear, *Journals of a Landscape Painter in Albania* (London, 1851), p. 304.
14. R.W. Seton-Watson, *Disraeli, Gladstone and the Eastern Question* (London, 1935), p. 80.
15. W.E. Gladstone, *Bulgarian Horrors and the Question of the East* (London, 1876), pp. 13, 62.
16. Victoria, Queen of Great Britain, *The Letters of Queen Victoria: A Selection from Her Majesty's Correspondence and Journal between the Years 1862 and 1878*, ed. George Earle Buckle, 3 vols, Vol. 2 (London, 1926), p. 474. See also Richard Shannon, *Gladstone and the Bulgarian Agitation 1876* (London, 1963), p. 44.
17. Queen Victoria, *Letters*, Vol. 2, p. 480.
18. Seton-Watson, *The Eastern Question*, p. 314.
19. Edward Freeman, *The Ottoman Power in Europe: Its Nature, Its Growth, Its Decline* (London, 1877), pp. 311–12.
20. Alfred, Lord Tennyson, *Ballads and Other Poems* (London, 1888), p. 183.
21. Oscar Wilde, 'On the massacre of the Christians in Bulgaria', in *'Charmides' and Other Poems* (London, 1913 [1881]), p. 141.
22. William Moneypenny and G.E. Buckle, *The Life of Benjamin Disraeli*, 2 vols, Vol. 2 (London, 1929), p. 1196. See also Steinberg, *Bismarck*, p. 372.
23. Seton-Watson, *The Eastern Question*, p. 78.
24. Richard Aldous, *The Lion and the Unicorn: Gladstone vs. Disraeli* (London, 2006), p. 278. Aldous notes that the Liberal historian Edward Freeman caused a sensation in 1876 when, referring to Disraeli, he

declared: 'I am sure that we are a large enough part of the English people to make even the Jew in his drunken insolence think twice before he goes to war in our teeth.'
25. Shannon, *The Bulgarian Agitation*, p. 201, citing the *Church Times*, 25 August 1876, p. 426.
26. Georgiana Muir Mackenzie and Adeline P. Irby, *Travels in the Slavonic Provinces of Turkey-in-Europe*, 2 vols, Vol. 1 (London, 1877 [1867]), p. 221.
27. Ibid., Vol. 1, p. 227.
28. James Baker, *Turkey in Europe* (London, 1877), pp. 370–1.
29. William Stillman, *Herzegovina and the Late Uprising: The Causes of the Latter and the Remedie*s (London, 1877), p. 29.
30. Ibid., p. 154.
31. Gawrych, *Crescent and Eagle*, p. 131, citing Stanford J. Shaw, *History of the Ottoman Empire and Modern Turkey*, 2 vols, Vol. 2: *Reform, Revolution and Republic 1808–1975* (London, 1979), p. 209.
32. M.E. Durham, *Twenty Years of Balkan Tangle* (London, 1920), p. 9.

2 'The other end of nowhere'

1. Alfred, Lord Tennyson, *Ballads and Other Poems* (London, 1888), p. 183.
2. Edith Durham, letter to her mother, 20 August 1900, Royal Anthropological Institute (henceforward RAI), Box 43.
3. Durham, letter to her mother, 2 September 1900, RAI, Box 43.
4. Durham, letter to her mother, 10 September 1900, RAI, Box 43.
5. Ibid.
6. James Creagh, *Over the Borders of Christendom and Eslamiah*, 2 vols, Vol. 2 (London, 1876), p. 254.
7. Durham, letter to her mother, 10 September 1900, RAI, Box 43.
8. The Russian embassy was completed in 1903 and the French and Italian embassies in 1910. Both now are libraries. The British embassy was not completed until 1912 and is now the Academy of Music. Germany, Bulgaria and Greece rented premises, while the US consul remained ensconced in the Hotel Grand.
9. Edith Durham, 'At the Grand Hotel', undated MS, RAI, Box 45.
10. M.E. Durham, *Through the Lands of the Serb* (London, 1903), p. 17.
11. John Wilkinson, *Dalmatia and Montenegro, with a Journey to Mostar in Herzegovina and Remarks on the Slavonic Nations*, 2 vols, Vol. 1 (London, 1848), p. 430.

12. Edson Clark, *The Races of European Turkey: Their History, Condition and Prospects* (Edinburgh, 1878), pp. 377, 376.
13. William Miller, *The Balkans: Roumania, Bulgaria, Servia, and Montenegro* (London, 1896), p. 458.
14. M.E. Durham, *Some Tribal Origins, Laws and Customs of the Balkans* (London, 1928), p. 187.
15. Umberto of Italy was born in 1904, and reigned for just over a month in 1946 before the monarchy was ousted in a referendum.
16. William Miller, *The Ottoman Empire and Its Successors, 1801–1927* (Cambridge, 1936), p. 460.
17. Sutherland Menzies, *Turkey Old and New: Historical, Geographical and Statistical*, 2 vols, Vol. 2 (London, 1880), p. 309.
18. Čedomilj Mijatović, *Memoirs of a Balkan Diplomatist* (London, 1917), p. 129.
19. Herbert Vivian, *The Servian Tragedy* (London, 1904), p. 29.
20. Ibid., p. 130.
21. Ibid., p. 166.
22. Richard Shannon, *Gladstone and the Bulgarian Agitation 1876* (London, 1963), p. 278. The author notes that when Lord Houghton 'expiated to Gladstone on the "failure" of forty years of Greek independence', Gladstone felt 'stung to defend the Greek record as a "signal success"'.
23. Andrew Paton, *Highlands and Islands of the Adriatic*, 2 vols, Vol. 1 (London, 1849), p. 105.
24. Michael Palairet, *The Balkan Economies, 1800–1914: Evolution without Development* (Cambridge, 1997), p. 146.
25. William Denton, *Servia and the Servians* (London, 1869), pp. 7–8.
26. Ivo Banac, *The National Question in Yugoslavia: Origin, History, Politics* (New York, 1993 [1984]), p. 278.
27. Durham, *Lands of the Serb*, p. 126.
28. Creagh, *Over the Borders of Christendom and Eslamiah*, Vol. 2, p. 327.
29. Ibid., p. 325.
30. Durham, letter to her mother, 5 June 1901, RAI, Box 43.
31. Ibid.
32. Ibid.
33. Durham, *Lands of the Serb*, p. 191.
34. Ibid., p. 205.
35. The Peć Patriarchate consists of a complex of churches, mostly built in the thirteenth and fourteenth centuries. It was the centre of Serbian Church life from then until the Ottoman conquest in the 1450s, and

again from the mid-sixteenth to the mid-eighteenth century, when the Ottomans suppressed the see.
36. Durham, letter to her mother, 20 June 1903, RAI, Box 43.
37. Noel Malcolm, *Kosovo: A Short History* (London, 1998), p. xxxi. Malcolm downplays the idea that Kosovo formed the 'heart' of medieval Serbia, noting that the seat of the Orthodox Church was not founded there, but merely moved there after the original foundation in central Serbia was burned down.
38. M.E. Durham, *Twenty Years of Balkan Tangle* (London, 1920), p. 81.
39. Ibid., p. 324.
40. Durham, letter to her mother, 20 June 1903, RAI, Box 43.
41. Sidney Lee, *King Edward VII: A Biography*, 3 vols, Vol. 2 (London, 1927), p. 270.
42. Flora Northesk Wilson, *Belgrade, the White City of Death: Being the History of King Alexander and of Queen Draga* (London, 1903), p. 22.
43. Vivian, *Servian Tragedy*, p. x.
44. D.M. Mason, *Macedonia and Great Britain's Responsibility* (London, 1903), p. 5.
45. Durham, *Twenty Years of Balkan Tangle*, p. 93.

3 'My golden sisters of Macedonia'

1. Edith Durham, letter to her mother, 11 February 1904, RAI, Box 43.
2. Macedonia was a geographical expression and a political aspiration but not an administrative unit. Skopje, now the capital of independent Macedonia, lay inside the Ottoman *vilayet* of Kosovo.
3. Firmilian Dražić had earlier played a key role in establishing the first Serbian Orthodox Church parish in Chicago after spending six months there in 1892.
4. Richard von Mach, *The Bulgarian Exarchate: Its History and the Extent of Its Authority in Turkey* (London, 1907), pp. 13–14.
5. Leften Stavrianos, *The Balkans since 1453* (London, 2000), p. 374.
6. The relative state of the religious parties in 1907 in the Exarchate dioceses of Macedonia was as follows (E for Exarchate and P for Patriarchate):
    Skopje, 173,562 (E); 61,332 (P);
    Debar, 54,900 (E); 10,704 (P);
    Ohrid, 93,448 (E); 30,037 (P);
    Bitola, 68,528 (E); 46,134 (P);

Veles, 42,360 (E); 4,405 (P);
   Strumica, 59,992 (E); 13,299 (P);
   Nevrokop, 96,944 (E); 4,852 (P).
   See Mach, *Bulgarian Exarchate*, map at the end.
7. The Carnegie Endowment for International Peace, *Report of the International Commission to Inquire into the Causes and Conduct of the Balkan Wars* (Washington, 1914), p. 27.
8. M.E. Durham, *Burden of the Balkans* (London, 1905), p. 112.
9. Charles Jelavich, *Tsarist Russia and Balkan Nationalism: Russian Influence in the Internal Affairs of Bulgaria and Serbia, 1879–1886* (Berkeley, 1958), p. 279.
10. Ibid., p. 277, citing Sir Frederick St John to Lord Salisbury, FO 105/87, no. 41, 22 April 1888.
11. Duncan Perry, *The Politics of Terror: The Macedonian Liberation Movements 1893–1903* (London, 1988), p. 140. According to Perry some 4,694 Christian non-combatants were killed: 1,779 in Monastir *vilayet*, 2,565 in Adrianople *vilayet*, 290 in Salonika *vilayet* and 60 in Skopje *vilayet*.
12. Henry Noel Brailsford, *Macedonia: Its Races and Their Future* (London, 1906), pp. 158–9.
13. F.M. Leventhal, *The Last Dissenter: H.N. Brailsford and His World* (Oxford, 1985), p. 116: Brailsford's wife apparently married him 'on the understanding that there should be no sexual intercourse'.
14. Other members of the Balkan Committee included the Anglican bishops of Bath, Hereford, Lichfield, Liverpool and Birmingham.
15. Mosa Anderson, *Noel Buxton: A Life* (London, 1952), p. 33.
16. Robert McCormick, 'Noel Buxton, the Balkan Committee and reform in Macedonia, 1903–1914', in *Antiquity and Modernity: A Celebration of European History and Heritage in the Olympic Year 2004*, ed. Nicholas Charles Pappas (Athens, GA, 2004), pp. 151–64 (p. 152).
17. Durham, letter to her sister, Ellen ('Nellie'), 2 April 1912, RAI, Box 43.
18. Durham, letter to Nellie, 1 March 1913, RAI, Box 43.
19. Brailsford, *Macedonia: Its Races and Their Future*, p. 111.
20. Ibid., p. 112.
21. Durham, letter to Mrs Seymour, 7 January 1904, RAI, Box 43.
22. Ibid.
23. Brailsford, *Macedonia: Its Races and Their Future*, pp. 76–77.
24. Durham, letter to her mother, 22 January 1904, RAI, Box 43.
25. Durham, letter to her mother, 26 January 1904, RAI, Box 43.
26. Ibid., pp. 76–7.
27. Durham, letter to Mrs Lucas, 5 February 1904, RAI, Box 43.

28. Durham, letter to her mother, 1 February 1904, RAI, Box 43.
29. Born Georgi Sterev, 1866; died Thessaloniki, 1909. Bishop of Ohrid from 1897.
30. Durham, letter to her mother, 25 February 1904, RAI, Box 43.
31. Durham, letter to her mother, 11 February 1904, RAI, Box 43.
32. Ibid.
33. Ibid.
34. Durham, letter to her mother, 1 March 1904, RAI, Box 43.
35. Durham, *Burden of the Balkans*, p. 209.
36. Durham, letter to her mother, 12 March 1904, RAI, Box 43.
37. Durham, *Burden of the Balkans*, p. 213.
38. Durham, letter to her mother, 1 March 1904, RAI, Box 43.
39. Durham, letter to her mother, 25 February 1904, RAI, Box 43.
40. Durham, letter to Mrs Lucas, 1 March 1904, RAI, Box 43.

4 'God has sent you to save us'

1. M.E. Durham, letter to her mother, 25 April 1904, RAI, Box 43.
2. *The Thirteenth Report of the British and Foreign Bible Society* (London, 1817), p. 93.
3. George Gawrych, *The Crescent and the Eagle: Ottoman Rule, Islam and the Albanians, 1874–1913* (London, 2006), p. 90.
4. Durham, letter to her mother, 25 March 1904, RAI, Box 43.
5. Ibid.
6. 'Rough estimates placed the Albanian population at over one million Muslims, 300,000 Orthodox, and 180,000 Catholics.' See Gawrych, *Crescent and Eagle*, p. 21.
7. *The Harmsworth Encyclopaedia*, 8 vols, Vol. 1 (London, 1905), p. 131.
8. National identities were far from fixed at this time, and less important than membership of a faith community. In the 1880s, the Ioannina *vilayet* numbered about 650,000 people, a majority of whom were Orthodox Christians. Most remaining Muslims were Albanian, but so were many Christians. 'Ottoman officials seemed to regard most Orthodox in the province of Yanya [*sic*] as Albanian in ethnicity, even though many of them spoke Greek.' See Gawrych, *Crescent and Eagle*, p. 24.
9. Ibid., p. 109. According to Gawrych, the governor of Kosovo in 1897 estimated that the *vilayet* numbered 633,765 Muslims and 333,406 Christians. Most though not all of the former were Albanians, but the Muslim community also numbered significant Bosniak (Muslim Slav) and ethnic Turkish communities.

10. Ibid., p. 28.
11. Ibid., p. 83.
12. Ibid., p. 29.
13. Arthur Elliot, *The Life of George Joachim Goschen, First Viscount Goschen 1831–1907*, 2 vols, Vol. 1 (London, 1911), p. 215.
14. Alois Aehrenthal, memorandum to Charles Hardinge, 16 August 1908, Foreign Office, *Miscellaneous Papers 1906–09*, B.P. 2/3(9)
15. Dispatches to Lord Granville, 26–7 July 1880, in Elliot, *Life of George Joachim Coschen*, Vol. 1, pp. 215–16.
16. Lord Granville to the British embassies in Paris, Berlin, Rome and St Petersburg, 20 July 1888, in *The English Documents about the Albanian League of Prizren*, ed. Skënder Rizaj (Pristina, 1993), p. 323.
17. Durham, letter to Nellie, 5 April 1904, RAI, Box 43.
18. Durham, letter to her mother, 7 April 1904, RAI, Box 43.
19. Ibid.
20. M.E. Durham, *Burden of the Balkans* (London, 1905), p. 288.
21. The Scotsman David Urquhart had the same experience, long before Edith Durham, writing in the 1830s: 'I came at once upon a heap of ruins, and wandered about amongst them for some time, and under a shower of rain [...] The once proud Tepedelene [*sic*] now sheltered but one hundred and fifty and eight Greek families and, as if this amount of ruin and desolation were not sufficient, the troops there assembled were busied in levelling the fortifications.' In David Urquhart, *The Spirit of the East*, 2 vols, Vol. 2 (London, 1839), p. 277.
22. Durham, letters to her mother, 7 April 1904, RAI, Box 43.
23. Durham, letter to her mother, 9 April 1904, RAI, 43.
24. Ibid.
25. Ibid.
26. Ibid.
27. Ibid.
28. According to Gawrych, the number of pupils attending the boys' elementary school in Korça, which opened in 1887, dropped from 200 to 80 under the joint pressure of Ottoman officials and the local Greek Orthodox clergy. See Gawrych, *Crescent and Eagle*, pp. 88–9.
29. Durham, letter to her mother, 9 April 1904, RAI, Box 43.
30. Ibid.
31. Durham, letter to her mother, 7 May 1904, RAI, Box 43.
32. Durham, letter to her mother, 25 April 1904, RAI, Box 43.

5 'A fine old specimen'

1. M.E. Durham, *Twenty Years of Balkan Tangle* (London, 1920), p. 186.
2. Harry Hodgkinson, born 1913, died 1994. He visited Albania in 1937 and joined the Anglo-Albanian association on his return, befriending Edith Durham in the last few years of her life.
3. Harry Hodgkinson, 'Edith Durham and the formation of the Albanian state', in *Albania and the Surrounding World: Papers from the British–Albanian Colloquium, South East European Studies Association Held at Pembroke College, Cambridge, 29th–31st March, 1994*, Bradford Studies on South Eastern Europe 2 (Bradford, 1995), pp. 14–33 (p. 21).
4. Durham, letter to her mother, 4 May 1905, RAI, Box 43.
5. Ibid.
6. Durham, letter to William Miller, [undated, 1905?], RAI, Box 54.
7. Ibid.
8. William Miller, *The Ottoman Empire and Its Successors, 1801–1927* (Cambridge, 1936), p. 461.
9. Ibid.
10. Durham, letter to her mother, 4 May 1905, RAI, Box 43.
11. Ibid.
12. Ibid.
13. Robert Donia, *Sarajevo: A Biography* (London, 2006), pp. 69–70.
14. M.E. Durham, *Twenty Years of Balkan Tangle* (London, 1920), p. 153.
15. Durham, letter to Elsa, 16 September 1906, RAI, Box 43.
16. Durham, diary entry, 26 September 1906, RAI, Box 43.
17. Ibid.
18. Durham, letter to her uncle, Ashley Durham, 31 October 1906, RAI, Box 43.
19. Ibid.
20. Durham, *Twenty Years of Balkan Tangle*, p. 167.
21. Christian Medawar, *Mary Edith Durham and the Balkans 1900–1914*, MA thesis, McGill University, 1995, p. 28.
22. Durham, letter to Nellie, 13 June 1908, RAI, Box 43.
23. Durham, *Twenty Years of Balkan Tangle*, p. 179.
24. Durham, letter to Mr [Nicolas] Summa (British vice-consul in Shkodra), 30 April 1908, RAI, Box 43.
25. Ibid.
26. Ibid., p. 188.

27. The title of Tsar was formally offered to Ferdinand in the church at Trnovo in the name of 'the nation and the government' by the president of the Chamber of Deputies. See John Macdonald, *Czar Ferdinand and His People* (London, 1913), pp. 328–9.
28. Stephen Constant, *Foxy Ferdinand, 1861–1948: Tsar of Bulgaria* (London, 1979), p. 223.
29. Bernadotte Schmitt, *The Annexation of Bosnia 1908–1909* (Cambridge, 1937), p. 15.
30. Josip Stadler, 1843–1918, the first Roman Catholic Archbishop of Vrhbosna (Sarajevo), following the restoration of the Catholic hierarchy in Bosnia and Herzegovina in 1881.
31. Jovan Cvijić, *The Annexation of Bosnia and Herzegovina and the Serb Problem* (London, 1909), p. 9.
32. Schmitt, *Annexation of Bosnia*, p. 46.
33. Geoffrey Hosking notes that when Serbia declared war on the Ottoman Empire in 1876, a number of Russian officers clamoured to join the Serbian army, and that while the Tsarist authorities did not endorse such action in public, they tacitly permitted them to do so. See Geoffrey Hosking, *Russia and the Russians* (London, 2003), p. 275.
34. Ibid., p. 48.
35. Ibid., p. 36.
36. Henry Wickham Steed, *Through Thirty Years, 1892–1922: A Personal Narrative*, 2 vols, Vol. 1 (London, 1924), p. 283.
37. Cvijić, *Annexation of Bosnia and Herzegovina*, p. 37.
38. Francis Bridge, *From Sadowa to Sarajevo: The Foreign Policy of Austria-Hungary, 1866–1914* (London, 1972), p. 321. See also Schmitt, *Annexation of Bosnia*, p. 244.
39. Henry Pozzi, *Black Hand over Europe* (Zagreb, 1994 [1935]), p. 268.
40. Woislav Petrovitch, 'The story of the Black Hand and the Great War', in Pozzi, *Black Hand over Europe*, pp. 248–267 (p. 251).
41. Ibid., p. 252.

6 The Great Mountain Land

1. M.E. Durham, *High Albania* (London, 1909), p. 1.
2. Benjamin Disraeli, *Benjamin Disraeli: Letters, 1815–1834*, ed. J.A.W. Gunn, John Matthews, Donald M. Schurman and M.G. Wiebe (Toronto, 1982), p. 171.
3. Durham, *High Albania*, p. 25.
4. Ibid., p. 32.

5. Ibid.
6. Ibid., p. 33.
7. Ibid., p. 35.
8. Ibid., p. 55.
9. Ibid., p. 56.
10. Ibid., p. 111.
11. Ibid., p. 112.
12. Ibid., p. 210.
13. Ibid.
14. Ibid., p. 211.
15. Ibid., p. 209.
16. M.E. Durham, *Some Tribal Origins, Laws and Customs of the Balkans* (London, 1928), p. 247.
17. Ibid., p. 184.
18. Ibid.
19. Ibid., p. 62.
20. Ibid., p. 129.
21. Ibid., p. 194.
22. Ibid., p. 275.
23. Ibid.
24. Ibid., p. 294.
25. *Nottingham Guardian*, 22 March 1905, Durham collection, RAI, Box 53.
26. *Daily Telegraph*, 17 March 1905, Durham collection, RAI, Box 53.
27. *Times Literary Supplement*, 31 March 1905, Durham collection, RAI, Box 53.
28. *Glasgow Herald*, 16 March 1905, Durham collection, RAI, Box 53.
29. *The Nation*, 13 November 1909, Durham collection, RAI, Box 53.
30. *Daily News*, 6 November 1909, Durham collection, RAI, Box 53.
31. *The Outlook*, 20 November 1909, Durham collection, RAI, Box 53.
32. *Manchester Guardian*, 16 December 1909, Durham collection, RAI, Box 53.
33. M.E. Durham, 'High Albania and Its customs in 1908', *Journal of the Royal Anthropological Institute* 40 (1910), 453–72.

7 'They never all rise in a lump'

1. E.M. Durham, letter to her uncle, Ashley Durham, 17 November 1911, RAI, Box 43.
2. John Treadway, *The Falcon and the Eagle: Montenegro and Austria-Hungary, 1908–14* (West Lafayette, IN, 1983), p. 24.

3. Durham, letter to Nellie, 27 April 1910, RAI, Box 43.
4. Ibid.
5. Ibid.
6. Ibid.
7. Durham, letter to Nellie, 27 May 1910, RAI, Box 43.
8. Durham, letter to Nellie, 13 June 1910, RAI, Box 43.
9. Durham, letter to Nellie, 23 September 1910, RAI, Box 43.
10. Durham, letter to Nellie, 20 August 1910, RAI, Box 43.
11. Durham, letter to Nellie, 11 July 1910, RAI, Box 43.
12. Durham, letter to Nellie, 23 October 1910, RAI, Box 43.
13. Durham, letter to Nellie, 8 February 1911, RAI, Box 43.
14. Durham, letter to Nellie, 28 December 1910, RAI, Box 43.
15. Durham, letter to Nellie, 23 February 1911, RAI, Box 43.
16. Durham, letter to Nellie, 18 April 1911, RAI, Box 43.
17. Ibid.
18. Srdja Pavlovic, *Balkan Anschluss: The Annexation of Montenegro and the Creation of the Common South Slavic State* (West Lafayette, IN, 2008), p. 46.
19. Durham, letter to Nellie, 7 May 1911, RAI, Box 43.
20. Ibid.
21. Harry Hodgkinson, 'Edith Durham and the formation of the Albanian state', in *Albania and the Surrounding World: Papers from the British–Albanian Colloquium, South East European Studies Association Held at Pembroke College, Cambridge, 29th–31st March, 1994*, Bradford Studies on South Eastern Europe 2 (Bradford, 1995), pp. 14–33 (p. 23). Hodgkinson notes that the historian Bejtullah Destani found two letters in the Public Record Office from 1908, together comprising about 3,000 words and which, according to the minute sheet, were forwarded to John Tilley; R.P. Maxwell; and Charles Hardinge, the permanent under-secretary; as well as to Sir Edward Grey.
22. Durham, letter to her brother-in-law, Godfrey Hickson, 24 May 1911, RAI, Box 43.
23. Durham, letter to Nellie, 28 May 1911, RAI, Box 43.
24. Durham, letter to Nellie, 15 June 1911, RAI, Box 43.
25. Charles Richard Crane, 1858–1939, wealthy American businessman who took a strong interest in Eastern Europe and the Arab world.
26. Durham, letter to Nellie, 15 June 1911, RAI, Box 43.
27. Durham, letter to Nellie, 29 July 1911, RAI, Box 43.
28. Durham, letter to Nellie, 8 August 1911, RAI, Box 43.

29. Durham, letter to Nellie, 3 September 1911, RAI, Box 43.
30. Durham, letter to Nellie, 29 September 1911, RAI, Box 43.
31. Ibid.
32. Durham, letter to Nellie, 2 April 1912, RAI, Box 43.
33. Margaret FitzHerbert, *The Man Who Was Greenmantle: A Biography of Aubrey Herbert* (London, 1983), p. 117.
34. Henry Nevinson, *More Changes, More Chances* (London, 1925), p. 362.
35. Ibid., p. 363.
36. Angela John, *War, Journalism and the Shaping of the Twentieth Century: The Life and Times of Henry W. Nevinson* (London, 2000), p. 129.
37. Durham, letter to Nellie, 14 October 1911, RAI, Box 43.
38. Ibid.
39. Durham, letter to Nellie, 4 November 1911, RAI, Box 43.
40. Durham, letter to her uncle, Ashley Durham, 17 November 1911, RAI, Box 43.
41. Durham, letter to Nellie, 14 January 1912, RAI, Box 43.
42. Durham, letter to Nellie, 22 February 1912, RAI, Box 43.

8 'Boom – our big gun rang out'

1. M.E. Durham, letter to her brother-in-law, Godfrey Hickson, 9 October 1912, RAI, Box 43.
2. Durham, letter to Nellie, 20 June 1912, RAI, Box 43.
3. Durham, letter to Nellie, 31 July 1912, RAI, Box 43.
4. General Radomir Putnik, head of the Serbian army, and Nikola Pašić, head of the Radical Party and Prime Minister from the summer of 1912, both opposed the terms of the Bulgarian deal. See Richard Hall, *The Balkan Wars 1912–1913: Prelude to the First World War* (London, 2000), p. 12.
5. Durham, letter to Nellie, 23 August 1912, RAI, Box 43.
6. Ibid.
7. Durham, letter to Nellie, 27 August 1912, RAI, Box 43.
8. Durham, *The Struggle for Scutari* (London, 1914), p. 171.
9. Durham, letter to her brother-in-law, Godfrey Hickson, 9 October 1912, RAI, Box 43.
10. Ibid.
11. Durham, letter to Nellie, 16 November 1912, RAI, Box 43.
12. Ibid.
13. Durham, letter to Nellie, 7 December 1912, RAI, Box 43.

14. According to the census of 1913, of 157,889 people in Thessaloniki, 61,439 were Jews, 45,876 were listed as Ottoman (Muslim) and just under 40,000 were Greek. See Mark Mazower, *Salonica, City of Ghosts, Christians, Muslims and Jews, 1430–1950* (London, 2004), p. 303.
15. 'The Chief Rabbi put the case to me clearly and frankly when he explained that his people were Ottoman citizens, felt the keenness of the Turkish defeats as such and it was but natural that they should appear more mournful than jubilant.' W.H. Crawford Price, *The Balkan Cockpit: The Political and Military Story of the Balkan Wars in Macedonia* (London, 1914), p. 145.
16. Durham, letter to Nellie, 6 December 1912, RAI, Box 43.
17. Durham, *Struggle for Scutari*, p. 197.
18. Ibid., p. 236.
19. 'Lady Doctor at the Front', *Northern Star*, 11 January 1913, p. 5.
20. Durham, letter to Nellie, 25 November 1912, RAI, Box 43.
21. Durham, letter to Nellie, 25 January 1913, RAI, Box 43.
22. Ismail Kemal Bey, *The Memoirs of Ismail Kemal Bey*, ed. Sommerville Story (London, 1920), p. 370.
23. Ibid., p. 371.
24. Ibid., p. 372.
25. Durham, letter to Nellie, 25 January 1913, RAI, Box 43.
26. Durham, letter to Nellie, 10 March 1913, RAI, Box 43.
27. Miranda Vickers, *The Albanians: A Modern History* (London, 1995), p. 68.
28. Francis Bridge, *From Sadowa to Sarajevo: The Foreign Policy of Austria-Hungary, 1866–1914* (London, 1972), p. 350.
29. Edward Grey, *Twenty-Five Years 1892–1916*, 2 vols, Vol. 1 (London, 1925), p. 269.
30. Durham, *Struggle for Scutari*, pp. 272–3.
31. Ibid., p. 293.
32. Ibid., p. 306.
33. Nevinson, *More Changes, More Chances* (London, 1925), p. 392.
34. Durham, *Struggle for Scutari*, p. 297.
35. Angela John, *War, Journalism and the Shaping of the Twentieth Century: The Life and Times of Henry W. Nevinson* (London, 2000), p. 133.
36. Harry Hodgkinson, 'Edith Durham and the formation of the Albanian state', in *Albania and the Surrounding World: Papers from the British–Albanian Colloquium, South East European Studies Association Held at*

> *Pembroke College, Cambridge, 29th–31st March, 1994*, Bradford Studies on South Eastern Europe 2 (Bradford, 1995), pp. 14–33 (p. 27).
37. M.E. Durham, *Twenty Years of Balkan Tangle* (London, 1920), p. 247.
38. Jacob Gould Schurman, *The Balkan Wars 1912–1913* (Oxford, 1914), p. 122.
39. Durham, letter to Nellie, 8 July 1913, RAI, Box 43.
40. Durham, *Twenty Years of Balkan Tangle*, p. 248.
41. Ibid., pp. 247–9.
42. Durham, *Struggle for Scutari*, p. 315.

9 'He is a blighter'

1. Duncan Heaton-Armstrong, *The Six Month Kingdom: Albania 1914*, ed. Gervase Belfield and Bejtullah Destani (London, 2005), p. xxix.
2. Harry Hodgkinson, *The Adriatic Sea* (London, 1955), p. 227.
3. Constantine Chekrezi, *Albania Past and Present* (New York, 1919), p. 94.
4. Anon., 'Albania and Greece', *The New Europe* 3 (30 January 1919), p. 71.
5. Čedomilj Mijatović, *Memoirs of a Balkan Diplomatist* (London, 1917), p. 74.
6. Ibid., p. 73.
7. Hannah Pakula, *Queen of Romania: The Life of Princess Marie, Grand-Daughter of Queen Victoria* (London, 1984), p. 104.
8. Wilhelm II, Emperor of Germany, *The Kaiser's Memoirs: Wilhelm II, Emperor of Germany, 1888–1918*, trans. Thomas Ybarra (New York, 1922), p. 166.
9. Ibid., p. 165.
10. Joseph Swire, *Albania: The Rise of a Kingdom* (London, 1929), p. 196.
11. Margaret FitzHerbert, *The Man Who Was Greenmantle: A Biography of Aubrey Herbert* (London, 1983), p. 123.
12. Ismail Kemal Bey, *The Memoirs of Ismail Kemal Bey*, ed. Sommerville Story (London, 1920), p. 379.
13. Karl Tschuppik, *The Reign of the Emperor Francis Joseph, 1848–1916* (London, 1930), p. 459.
14. M.E. Durham, *Twenty Years of Balkan Tangle* (London, 1920), p. 269.
15. Heaton-Armstrong, *Six Month Kingdom*, p. xxix, citing FO 371 1896, fo. 193.
16. Ibid.

17. Ibid.
18. FitzHerbert, *Biography of Aubrey Herbert*, p. 125.
19. Ibid., p. 126.
20. Heaton-Armstrong, *Six Month Kingdom*, p. 67.
21. Story, *Memoirs of Kemal*, p. 383.
22. Heaton-Armstrong, *Six Month Kingdom*, pp. xxviii–xxix.
23. Durham, *Twenty Years of Balkan Tangle*, p. 272.
24. Her assassin, a Parisian-born Italian named Luigi Lucheni, was 25 at the time. Tschuppik, *Reign of the Emperor Francis Joseph*, p. 352.
25. David Lloyd George, *War Memoirs*, 6 vols, Vol. 1 (London, 1933), pp. 53–4.
26. Edward Goschen, *The Diary of Edward Goschen, 1900–1914*, ed. Christopher Howard (London, 1980), entry for 28 June 1914, p. 289.
27. Frederic Morton, *Thunder at Twilight: Vienna 1913–1914* (London, 2001), p. 267.
28. Andrej Mitrović, *Serbia's Great War, 1914–1918* (London, 2007), pp. 12–13.
29. Morton, *Thunder at Twilight*, p. 270.
30. Robert Donia, *Sarajevo: A Biography* (London, 2005), p. 119.
31. Tschuppik, *Reign of the Emperor Francis Joseph*, p. 435.
32. Heaton-Armstrong, *Six-Month Kingdom*, p. 162.
33. Story, *Memoirs of Kemal*, pp. 385–6.
34. 'The Near East', 16 September 1914, in M. Edith Durham, *Albania and the Albanians: Selected Articles and Letters 1903–1914*, ed. Bejtullah Destani (London, 2001), p. 64.
35. Durham, *Twenty Years of Balkan Tangle*, p. 276.
36. Ibid., p. 281.
37. Ibid.
38. Ibid., p. 282.

10 'For a dream's sake'

1. M.E. Durham, *Some Tribal Origins, Laws and Customs of the Balkans* (London, 1928), p. 3.
2. M.E. Durham, *Twenty Years of Balkan Tangle* (London, 1920), p. 281.
3. Tim Judah, *Kosovo: War and Revenge* (London, 2000), Introduction.
4. 'The adoption of the myth of Kosovo was no less enthusiastic in the United States, where the anniversary of Kosovo was recognized as

a day of special commemoration in June 1918.' Branimir Anzulović, *Heavenly Serbia: From Myth to Genocide* (New York, 1999), p. 148.
5. Hugh Seton-Watson, Robert W. Seton-Watson and Christopher Seton-Watson, *The Making of a New Europe: R.W. Seton-Watson and the Last Years of Austria-Hungary* (London, 1981), p. 30.
6. John St Loe Strachey, editor of the *Spectator*.
7. Seton-Watson, *Making of a New Europe*, p. 207.
8. Alice and Claude Askew, 'Kossovo Day Heroes', in *The Lay of Kossovo: Serbia's Past and Present (1389–1917)*, ed. Frederick William Harvey (London, 1917), p. 31.
9. 'The Near East', 31 August 1917, in M. Edith Durham, *Albania and the Albanians: Selected Articles and Letters 1903–1914*, ed. Bejtullah Destani (London, 2001), p. 81.
10. Durham, 'The Antiquity of Albania', in 'The Near East', 1 February 1918, p. 108.
11. Leland Buxton, *The Black Sheep of the Balkans* (London, 1920), p. 24.
12. Desmond MacCarthy, 'Aubrey Herbert', in Aubrey Herbert, *Mons, Anzac & Kut* (London, 1925). Available at www.gwpda.org/wwi-www/Mons/mons.htm (accessed 28 September 2013).
13. Durham MSS, 5 January 1921, RAI, Box 55.
14. Harold Nicolson, *Peacemaking 1919* (London, 1944 [1933]), p. 349.
15. Durham, diary entry, 30 April 1921, RAI, Box 42.
16. Durham, diary entry, 1 May 1921, RAI, Box 42.
17. Durham, diary entry, 2 May 1921, RAI, Box 42.
18. For a summary of Vatra's early years and achievements, see Avni Spahiu, 'Vatra of the Albanians of America and Noli,' *Dielli Online*. Available at http://gazetadielli.com/vatra-of-the-albanians-of-america-and-noli (accessed 26 September 2013).
19. Durham, diary entry, 7 May 1921, RAI, Box 42.
20. Durham, diary entry, 9 May 1921, RAI, Box 42.
21. Ibid.
22. Durham, diary entry, 14 May 1921, RAI, Box 42.
23. Christine Rossetti, 'Mirage', quoted by Durham following her diary entry for 22 May 1921, RAI, Box 42.
24. Rose Wilder Lane, journal entry, 1 November 1926, in Rose Wilder Lane and Helen Dore Boylston, *Travels with Zenobia: Paris to Albania by Model-T Ford* (Columbia, MO, 1983), p. 98.
25. Joseph Swire, *King Zog's Albania* (London, 1937), p. 46.
26. Ibid., p. 146.

27. 'Letter to the editor', *The New Europe*, 4 December 1919, p. 255.
28. Noel Malcolm, *Kosovo: A Short History* (London, 1998), p. 254.
29. Ibid., citing Carnegie Endowment for International Peace, *Report of the International Commission to Inquire into the Causes and Conduct of the Balkan Wars* (Washington, 1914), p. 151.
30. Seton-Watson, letter to Durham, 3 March 1920, Seton-Watson correspondence, School of Slavonic and East European Studies, SSEES, SEW 17/6/4.
31. Durham, letter to Seton-Watson, 1 March 1920, SSEES, SEW 17/6/4.
32. Durham, letter to Seton-Watson, 14 February 1929, SSEES, SEW 17/6/4.
33. Robert Seton-Watson, review of Edith Durham, *The Serajevo Crime* (London, 1925), *The Slavonic Review* 4:11 (1925), p. 520.
34. Edith Durham, 'The Balkans as a danger point', *Journal of the British Institute of International Affairs* 3:3 (May 1924), 139–44. The thrust of the article was about which races would dominate the gates of Europe: the Teutons or the Slavs. 'For the first time for centuries one race – the Serb – now dominates the Balkan peninsula, and that race is the chosen ally of Russia [...] sooner or later Russia will again press westwards and find stronger tools than before to her hand' (p. 142).
35. Seton-Watson, letter to Harold Temperley 24 April, 1926, in John Fair, *Harold Temperley: A Scholar and Romantic in the Public Realm, 1879–1939* (Newark, DE, 1992), p. 198.
36. R.G.D. Laffan, review of Robert Seton-Watson, *Sarajevo: A Study in the Origins of the Great War* (London, 1926), *Journal of the Royal Institute of International Affairs* 5:6 (November 1926), pp. 303–6.
37. Arnold Toynbee, letter to Seton-Watson, 8 February 1929, SSEES, SEW 17/6/4.
38. Seton-Watson, letter to Toynbee, 12 February 1929, SSEES, SEW 17/6/4.
39. Harry Hodgkinson, 'Edith Durham and the formation of the Albanian state', in *Albania and the Surrounding World: Papers from the British–Albanian Colloquium, South East European Studies Association Held at Pembroke College, Cambridge, 29th–31st March, 1994*, Bradford Studies on South Eastern Europe 2 (Bradford, 1995), pp. 14–33 (p. 29).
40. Durham, letter to Seton-Watson, 4 March1920, SSEES, SEW 17/6/4.
41. Richard Pankhurst, *Sylvia Pankhurst: Artist and Crusader* (London, 1979), p. 196.

42. Richard Pankhurst, *Sylvia Pankhurst: Counsel for Ethiopia* (Hollywood, 2003), p. 193.
43. Ibid., p. 186.
44. Dorothy Thompson and Rose Wilder Lane, *Dorothy Thompson and Rose Wilder Lane: Forty Years of Friendship. Letters, 1921–1960*, ed. William V. Holtz (Columbia, MO, 1991), pp. 58–9.
45. Anton Logoreci, cited in Paul Hockenos, *Homeland Calling: Exile, Patriotism and the Balkan Wars* (Ithaca, NY, 2005), p. 212.
46. Jason Tomes, *King Zog: Self-Made Monarch of Albania* (Stroud, 2007 [2003]), p. 102.
47. Owen Pearson, *Albania and King Zog: Independence, Republic and Monarchy 1908–1939* (London, 2004), p. 403.
48. Laura Fermi, *Mussolini* (Chicago, 1961), p. 387.
49. Bernd Fischer, *Albania at War, 1939–1945* (London, 1999), p. 24.
50. Anthony Eden, *The Eden Memoirs: The Reckoning* (London, 1965), p. 51.
51. Keith Feiling, *The Life of Neville Chamberlain* (London, 1946), p. 404.
52. Andrew Roberts, *The Holy Fox: A Life of Lord Halifax* (London, 2004), p. 150.
53. Edward Frederick Lindley Wood Halifax, *Speeches on Foreign Policy by Viscount Halifax*, ed. Herbert Henry Edmund Craster (Oxford, 1940), p. 250.
54. Galeazzo Ciano, *The Ciano Diaries, 1939–1943*, ed. Hugh Gibson (New York, 1947), p. 61.
55. Fischer, *Albania at War 1939–1945*, p. 258.
56. In Ciano's diaries, the Italian foreign minister mentioned several conversations with the Yugoslav Prime Minister, Milan Stojadinović, in which the latter proposed the partition of Albania. Ciano, *Diaries*, p. 29.
57. Durham, diary entry, 15 May 1935, RAI, Box 42.
58. Destani, *Albania and the Albanians*, p. 204, citing Edith Durham in *The Proceedings of the Royal Institution of Great Britain* 31 (1939–41).
59. Hodgkinson, 'Edith Durham and the formation of the Albanian state', p. 32.
60. For a description of some of those reviews, see Victoria Glendinning, *Rebecca West: A Life* (London, 1987), p. 166.
61. Robert Kaplan, *Balkan Ghosts: A Journey through History* (New York, 1993), p. 4.
62. During the 1992–5 war in Bosnia, Brendan Simms writes, 'a battered copy of Rebecca West's rabidly Serbophile travelogue, "Black Lamb

and Grey Falcon", did the rounds at the UN headquarters in Sarajevo with a label warning "UNPROFOR use only" [UNPROFOR was the UN peacekeeping mission in Bosnia]. As Michael Williams recalls of British officers, "Their reading [of it] was to reinforce their own prejudices."' See Brendan Simms, *Unfinest Hour: Britain and the Destruction of Bosnia* (London, 2001), p. 179.
63. Rebecca West, *Black Lamb and Grey Falcon* (London, 1941), p. 20.
64. John Hodgson, 'Edith Durham: Traveller and Publicist', in John Allcock and Antonia Young, *Black Lambs, Grey Falcons: Women Travellers in the Balkans* (Bradford, 1991), pp. 9–31 (p. 29).
65. Rebecca West, letter to Miss Rotherham, 11 December 1944, in *Selected Letters of Rebecca West*, ed. Bonnie Scott (London, 1999).
66. Durham, letter to Mr Pani, 12 August 1944, in Destani, *Albania and the Albanians*, 229.
67. 'To West, Churchill had decided [...] to consign Yugoslavia to Communist tyranny.' In Carl Rollyson, *The Literary Legacy of Rebecca West* (London, 1998), p. 174. Rollyson notes that West's friend, Seton-Watson, did not share her faith in the Serbian royalists, known as the Chetniks.
68. Durham papers, 'Yugoslavia', undated, presumably from the 1930s, Durham collection, RAI, Box 51.2.
69. Durham, letter to Mr Morant, undated, RAI, Box 43.
70. M.E. Durham, 'The case of Albania', *New Statesman*, 17 January 1942, quoted in Destani, *Albania and the Albanians*, p. 209.
71. Durham, letter to Faik Konitza, 29 July 1942, in ibid., p. 207.
72. M.E. Durham, 'Albania's fight for freedom', in *New Times and Ethiopia News*, 16 January 1943, in ibid., p. 210.

11 'Albanians will never forget'

1. *The Times*, 21 November 1944, in M.E. Durham, *Albania and the Albanians: Selected Articles and Letters 1903–1914*, ed. Bejtullah Destani (London, 2001), p. 243.
2. Leopold Wickham Legg, letter to Robert Seton-Watson, 20 March 1948, SSEES, SEW 17/6/4.
3. *The Times*, 21 November 1944, in Destani, *Albania and the Albanians*, p. 243.
4. *New Times and Ethiopia News*, 2 December 1944, in Destani, *Albania and the Albanians*, p. 246.

5. James O'Donnell, *A Coming of Age: Albania under Enver Hoxha* (Boulder, CO, 1999), p. 194: 'He knew how to dress well and had very refined manners [...] for the Albanians, who had always been rather an elitist people, it counted a great deal.'
6. Ibid., p. 196.
7. Enver Hoxha, *Laying the Foundations of the New Albania* (Tirana, 1984), p. 563.
8. Stephen Bowers, 'Church and state in Albania', *Religion in Communist Lands* 6:3 (1978), 148–52 (p. 148).
9. Nicholas Pano, 'The Albanian Orthodox Church', in *Eastern Christianity and the Cold War, 1945–91*, ed. Lucian Leustean (London, 2010), pp. 144–55 (p. 151).
10. Edwin Jacques, *The Albanians: An Ethnic History from Prehistoric Times to the Present* (Jefferson, NC, 1995), p. 550.
11. Amnesty International, *Albania: Political Imprisonment and the Law* (London, 1984), p. 15.
12. Janice Broun, 'The Status of Christianity in Albania', *Journal of Church and State* 28:1 (1986), 43–60 (p. 56).
13. This is unclear. There are other reports that he died at his home in Pogradec.
14. Sabrina Ramet, *Nihil Obstat: Religion, Politics and Social Change in East Central Europe and Russia* (Durham, NC, 1998), p. 217.
15. Miranda Vickers, *The Albanians: A Modern History* (London, 1995), p. 178.
16. Ibid.
17. Robert Elsie, *Historical Dictionary of Albania* (Oxford, 2004), p. lxv.
18. The first standard-gauge line from Tirana to Dürres was built with volunteer labour in 1948–9. A second line running eastwards to Elbasan and Pogradec was completed in 1980. A third line, running northwards to Shkodra, was completed in 1981. The first international connection, a 50 km line from Shkodra to Titograd in Yugoslavia, opened in 1986, but for freight traffic only.
19. Jacques, *The Albanians*, p. 540.
20. See *The Albanian Cinema Project*. Available at www.thealbaniancinema project.org/history.html (accessed 29 September 2013).
21. Amnesty International, *Albania: Political Imprisonment and the Law*, p. 31.
22. Ibid.
23. Ibid., p. 526.

24. The author had one conversation with a family in Pristina in 2004 who said they were horrified by what they found when they escaped to northern Albania in 1999, at the height of the Kosovo conflict. They spoke of being pelted with missiles and verbally abused by their hosts in Bajram Curri after being spotted returning from a shop with a crate of Coca-Cola cans – the locals apparently resenting what they saw as the Kosovo refugees' relative wealth.
25. Radio Free Europe, 24 September 1987; see 'Ramiz Alia talks about continuity in Albania despite change', *OSA Archivum*, collected by Radio Free Europe, 24 September 1987. Available at www.osaarchivum.org/greenfield/repository/osa:1e57e31a-7308–4c6e-9cfa-5ac2e89eba2f (accessed 6 October 2013).
26. Fatos Tarifa, 'Albania's road from Communism: Political and social change, 1990–1993', in *Development and Change* 26:1 (January 1995), 133–62 (p. 144).
27. Owen Pearson, *Albania as Dictatorship and Democracy* (London 2006), p. 653.
28. Born 5 April 1939, he died in Tirana, 30 November 2011.
29. In a vote held on 29 June 1997, just over 33 per cent of voters opted to restore the monarchy. The monarchist camp disputed the count, however.
30. Kristin Ohlson, 'Queen of the Highlands', *The Smart Set*. Available at http://thesmartset.com/article/article03021101.aspx (accessed 29 September 2013). Ohlson encountered many fans of Edith's on a visit to Shkodra, and also met Marko Shantoya's namesake and grandson, who told her the Communists had shot his father and stolen his beloved piano.
31. On 21 June 2007, the Research Data Center published its research on Bosnia-Herzegovina's war casualties, titled *The Bosnian Book of the Dead*. This database includes the names of 97,207 citizens of Bosnia and Herzegovina killed and missing during the 1992–5 war. See Daria Sito-Sucic and Matt Robinson, 'After years of toil, book names Bosnian war dead', available at www.reuters.com/article/2013/02/15/us-bosnia-dead-idUSBRE91E0J220130215 (last accessed 6 October 2013).
32. A joint study in 2008 by the Humanitarian Law Center (an NGO from Serbia and Kosovo), The International Commission on Missing Persons and the Missing Person Commission of Serbia concluded that 13,421 people were killed in the Kosovo conflict from 1 January 1998 to December 2000. Of that number, 10,533 were Albanians, 2,238

were Serbs, 126 were Roma, and 100 were Bosniaks and others. See *The Kosovo Memory Book 1998–2000*. Available at www.kosovskaknjiga pamcenja.org/?page_id=29&lang=de (accessed 29 September 2013).
33. In April 2013 Serbia and Kosovo signed an EU-brokered agreement on the future of Serbian districts in Kosovo, which suggested that Serbia was inching towards eventual recognition of Kosovo's independence.
34. M.E. Durham, *High Albania* (London, 1909), p. 1.
35. Ervin Qafmolla, 'Cult of virginity fades slowly in Albania', *Balkan Insight*, 18 October 2010. Available at www.balkaninsight.com/en/article/cult-of-virginity-fades-slowly-in-albania (accessed 29 September 2013).
36. See Fatmira Nikolli, 'Developers ravage Albania's historic landmarks', *Balkan Insight*. Available at www.balkaninsight.com/en/article/developers-ravage-albania-s-historic-landmarks (accessed 29 September 2013).

SELECT BIBLIOGRAPHY

Aldous, R., *The Lion and the Unicorn: Gladstone vs Disraeli*, London, 2006.
Allcock, J. and Young, A., *Black Lambs, Grey Falcons: Women Travellers in the Balkans*, Bradford, 1991.
Anderson, M., *Noel Buxton: A Life*, London, 1952.
Baker, J., *Turkey in Europe*, London, 1877.
Banac, I., *The National Question in Yugoslavia: Origin, History, Politics*, New York, 1993.
Brailsford, H., *Macedonia: Its Races and Their Future*, London, 1906.
Bridge, F., *From Sadowa to Sarajevo: The Foreign Policy of Austria-Hungary, 1866–1914*, London/Boston, 1972.
Buckle, G.E., *The Letters of Queen Victoria: A Selection from Her Majesty's Correspondence and Journal between the Years 1862 and 1878*, 3 vols, London, 1926.
Buxton, N., *The Black Sheep of the Balkans*, London, 1920.
Carnegie Endowment for International Peace, *Report of the International Commission to Inquire into the Causes and Conduct of the Balkans Wars*, Washington, 1914.
Chekrezi, C., *Albania Past and Present*, New York, 1919.
Clark, E., *The Races of European Turkey, Their History, Condition and Prospects*, Edinburgh, 1878.
Cock, V. and Forsdyke, D., *Treasure your Exceptions: The Science and Life of William Bateson*, London/Heidelberg/New York, 2008.
Constant, S., *Foxy Ferdinand, 1861–1948: Tsar of Bulgaria*, London, 1979.
Crawford Price, P., The *Balkan Cockpit: The Political and Military Story of the Balkan Wars in Macedonia*, London, 1914.
Creagh, J., *Over the Borders of Christendom and Eslamiah*, 2 vols, London, 1876.

Cviic, J., *The Annexation of Bosnia and Herzegovina and the Serb Problem*, London, 1909.

Denton, W., *Serbia and the Servians*, London, 1869.

Destani, B., ed., *M. Edith Durham, Albania and the Albanians: Selected Articles and Letters 1903–1944*, London, 2001.

Donia, R., *Sarajevo: A Biography*, London, 2006.

Durham, M.E., *Through the Lands of the Serb*, London, 1903.

—— *The Burden of the Balkans*, London, 1905.

—— *High Albania*, London, 1909.

—— *The Serajevo Crime*, London, 1925.

—— *Some Tribal Origins, Laws and Customs of the Balkans*, London, 1928.

—— *The Struggle for Scutari*, London, 1914.

—— *Twenty Years of Balkan Tangle*, London, 1920.

Elliot, A., *The Life of George Joachim Goschen, First Viscount Goschen 1831–1907*, 2 vols, London/New York, 1911.

Feiling, K., *The Life of Neville Chamberlain*, London, 1946.

Fischer, B., *Albania at War, 1939–1945*, London, 1999.

FitzHerbert, M., *The Man who was Greenmantle: A Biography of Aubrey Herbert*, London, 1983.

Freeman, E., *The Ottoman Power in Europe: Its Nature, Its Growth, Its Decline*, London, 1877.

Gawrych, G., *The Crescent and the Eagle: Ottoman Rule, Islam and the Albanians, 1874–1913*, London/New York, 2006.

Gladstone, W., *Bulgarian Horrors and the Question of the East*, London, 1876.

Glendinning, V., *Rebecca West: A Life*, London, 1987.

Grey, E., *Twenty-Five Years: 1892–1916*, 2 vols, London, 1925.

Hall, R., *The Balkan Wars 1912–1913: Prelude to the First World War*, London/New York, 2000.

Heaton-Armstrong, D., *The Six Month Kingdom: Albania 1914*, London, 2005.

Henig, R., *The Monk in the Garden: The Lost and Found Genius of Gregor Mendal, the Father of Genetics*, New York, 2000.

Hobhouse J.C., *A Journey through Albania and other Provinces of Turkey in Europe and Asia to Constantinople during the years 1809 and 1810*, 2 vols, London, 1810.

Hockenos, P., *Homeland Calling: Exile, Patriotism and the Balkan Wars*, Cornell, 2005.

Hodgkinson, H., *The Adriatic Sea*, London, 1955.

Holtz, W., ed., *Dorothy Thompson and Rose Wilder Lane: Forty Years of Friendship, Letters, 1921–1960*, Columbia/London, 1991.

Howard, C., ed., *The Diary of Edward Goschen, 1900–1914*, London, 1980.

Jacques, E., *The Albanians: An Ethnic History from Prehistoric Times to the Present*, Jefferson, 1995.

Jelavich, C., *Tsarist Russia and Balkan Nationalism: Russian Influence in the Internal Affairs of Bulgaria and Serbia, 1879–1886*, Berkeley/Los Angeles, 1958.

John, A., *War, Journalism and the Shaping of the Twentieth Century: The Life and Times of Henry W. Nevinson*, London, 2006.

Judah, T., *Kosovo: War and Revenge*, London, 2000.

Lane, R. and Boylston, H., *Travels with Zenobia: Paris to Albania by Model-T Ford*, Colombia/London, 1983.

Lear, E., *Journals of a Landscape Painter in Albania*, London, 1851.

Lee, S., *King Edward VII: A Biography*, 3 vols, London, 1927.

Leventhal, F.M., *The Last Dissenter: H.N. Brailsford and his World*, Oxford, 1985.

Mackenzie, G. and Irby, A., *Travels in the Slavonic Provinces of Turkey-in-Europe*, 2 vols, London, 1887.

Magocsi, P., *Historical Atlas of East Central Europe*, Seattle/London, 2002.

Malcolm, N., *Kosovo: A Short History*, London, 1998.

Marchand, L., *'In My Hot Youth': Byron's Letters and Journals*, 12 vols, London, 1978.

Mason, D., *Macedonia and Great Britain's Responsibility*, London, 1903.

Mazower, M., *Salonica: City of Ghosts, Christians, Muslims and Jews, 1430–1950*, London, 2004.

Medawar, C., *Mary Edith Durham and the Balkans 1900–1914*, MA thesis, McGill University, Montreal, 1995.

Menzies, S., *Turkey Old and New: Historical, Geographical and Statistical*, 2 vols, London, 1880.

Mijatović, C., *Memoirs of a Balkan Diplomatist*, London/New York, 1917.

Miller, W., *The Balkans: Roumania, Bulgaria, Servia and Montenegro*, London, 1896.

Miller, W., *The Ottoman Empire and its Successors, 1801–1927*, Cambridge, 1936.

Mitrovic, A., *Serbia's Great War, 1914–1918*, London, 2007.

Mitton, G., *Austria-Hungary*, London, 1914.

Moneypenny, W,. *The Life of Benjamin Disraeli, Earl of Beaconsfield, 1804–1837*, 6 vols, London, 1910.

Morton, F., *Thunder at Twilight: Vienna 1913–1914*, London, 2001.

Nevinson, H., *More Changes, More Chances*, London, 1925.

O'Donnell, J., *A Coming of Age: Albania under Enver Hoxha*, Boulder, 1999.

Pakula, H., *Queen of Romania: The Life of Princess Marie, Grand-daughter of Queen Victoria*, London, 1984.

Palairet, M., *The Balkan Economies, 1800–1914: Evolution Without Development*, Cambridge, 1997.

Pankhurst, R., *Sylvia Pankhurst: Artist and Crusader*, London, 1979.

Paton, A., *Highlands and Islands of the Adriatic*, 2 vols, London, 1849.

Pavlovic, S., *Balkan Anschluss: The Annexation of Montenegro and the Creation of the Common South Slavic State*, Indiana, 2008.

Pearson, O., *Albania and King Zog: Independence, Republic and Monarchy 1908–1939*, London, 2004.

—— *Albania as Dictatorship and Democracy*, London, 2006.

Perry, D., *The Politics of Terror: The Macedonian Liberation Movements 1893–1903*, London/Durham, 1988.

Pozzi, H., *Black hand Over Europe*, London, 1935.

Ramet, S., *Nihil Obstat: Religion, Politics and Social Change in East Central Europe and Russia*, London, 1998.

Rizaj, S., ed., *The English Documents about the Albanian League of Prizren*, Pristina/Istanbul/Tirana, 1993.

Roberts, A., *The Holy Fox: A Life of Lord Halifax*, London, 2004.

Schmitt, B., *The Annexation of Bosnia 1908–1909*, Cambridge, 1937.

Schurman, J.G., *The Balkan Wars 1912–1913*, Oxford/Princeton, 1914.

Scott, B., *Selected Letters of Rebecca West*, London/New Haven, 1999.

Seton-Watson, H.C., *The Making of a New Europe: R.W. Seton-Watson and the Last Years of Austria-Hungary*, London, 1981.

Seton-Watson, R.W., *Disraeli, Gladstone and the Eastern Question*, London, 1935.

Shannon, R., *Gladstone and the Bulgarian Agitation 1876*, London, 1963.

Shaw, S.E., *History of the Ottoman Empire and Modern Turkey*, 2 vols, London, 1979.

Stavrianos, L., *The Balkans since 1453*, London, 2000.

Steinberg, J., *Bismarck: A Life*, Oxford, 2011.

Stillman, W., *Herzegovina and the Late Uprising: The Causes of the Latter and the Remedies*, London, 1877.

Story, S., ed., *The memoirs of Ismail Kemal Bey*, London, 1920.

Swire, J., *Albania: Rise of a Kingdom*, London, 1929.

Tennyson, A., *Ballads and Other Poems*, London, 1880.

Tomas, J., *King Zog, Self-made Monarch of Albania*, Stroud, 2003.

Treadway, J., *The Falcon and Eagle: Montenegro and Austria-Hungary, 1908–14*, Indiana, 1983.

Urquart, D., *The Spirit of the East*, 2 vols, London, 1839.

Vickers, M., *The Albanians: A Modern History*, London/New York, 1995.

Vivian, H., *The Servian Tragedy*, London, 1904.

Von Mach, R., *The Bulgarian Exarchate: Its History and the Extent of its Authority in Turkey*, London/Neuchâtel, 1907.

Wickham Steed, H., *Through Thirty Years 1892–1922: A Personal Narrative*, 2 vols, London, 1924.

Wiebe, M., ed., *Benjamin Disraeli: Letters, 1815–1834*, Toronto/Buffalo/London, 1982.

Wilde, O., *Charmides and Other Poems*, London, 1881.

Wilkinson, J., *Dalmatia and Montenegro, with a Journey to Mostar in Herzegovina and Remarks on the Slavonic Nations*, 2 vols, London, 1848.

Wilson, N., *Belgrade, the White City of Death: Being the History of King Alexander and of Queen Draga*, London, 1903.

Ybarra, T. (tr.), *The Kaiser's Memoirs: Wilhelm II, Emperor of Germany, 1888–1918*, New York/London, 1922.

INDEX

Abdulhamid, Sultan, 57, 58, 62, 77, 83, 85, 86, 93, 111, 138, 140
Aberdeen, Earl of, 63
Adrianople, *see* Edirne
Adriatic, 12, 21, 33, 42, 43, 81, 86, 144, 155, 163, 169, 170, 172, 212
Aegean Sea, 210
Aehrenthal, Alois, 84, 113, 114
Africa, 12
Albania, Albanians, 1, 2, 6, 7, 11, 12, 13, 18, 20, 21, 28, 29, 31, 43, 45, 46, 50, 56, 76, 77–93, 104, 105, 109, 117, 139, 141, 142, 143, 145, 146–151, 154, 156, 157, 158, 160, 163, 164, 166, 177, 179, 183, 188, 192, 194, 195, 205, 207, 208, 209, 212, 228, 236, 252, 253, 254
  blood code, 121–122, 253
  borders, 19, 171–174, 177–179, 181–182, 183–185, 189, 200, 208, 212, 214, 229, 234, 239, 252
  communist takeover, 7, 120, 241–248
  education, schools, 79, 81, 82, 83, 86, 87, 91, 92, 140
  independence, 167–171, 212
  Italian/German occupation, 230–232, 233, 234, 238, 241
  language, 20, 78, 82, 83, 88, *see also* Geg; Tosk
  League of Nations, 213–214, 216
  modernisation, 218–219
  Ottoman conquest, 20
  religion, 20–21, 78, 79, 81, 82, 83, 88, 90, 120, 124–127, 129, 139, 140, 244–246, *see also* Albanian Orthodox Church; Catholic Church, in Albania; Muslims
  secret police, 244, 247
  traditional dress, 21, 23, 79, 89, 218–219, 242
  tribes, 92, 120, 123, 124, 126, 127, 130, 139, 140, 141, 146, 151, 152, 250
  virgins, 3, 130, 253
  witchcraft, 127–128
Albanian Committee, 214
Albanian Orthodox Church, 216, 228, 242, 245
Aleksandar, Prince and King of Serbia, 52, 53, 116, 144, 235
Alexander of Battenberg, King of Bulgaria, 60
Alexander II, of Russia, 52
Ali Pasha, 21–21, 23, 80, 87
Alia, Ramiz, 248
America, United States of, 79, 107, 156, 210, 214, 215, 216, 218, 228, 230, 239
Ana, Princess of Montenegro, 39
Anastasia, Princess of Montenegro, 38
Anatolia, 175
Andorra, 170
Andrijevica, 159
Anglo-Albanian Society, 214, 218, 233
Anthymos, Exarch of Bulgaria, 58, *see also* Bulgarian Exarchate
'Apis', Dragutin Dimitrijević, 116–117, *see also* Black Hand
Apollonia, 89–90
Armenia, 64, 77, 82, 160
Asia Minor, 175, 181, 212
Asquith, Herbert, 204
Athens, 21, 31, 196

Austria-Hungary, 14, 15, 16, 34, 35, 36, 45, 53, 61, 79, 83, 99, 102, 103, 104, 106, 110, 112, 113, 114, 115, 133, 136, 137, 138, 139, 140, 141, 142, 143, 146, 158, 162, 169, 170, 172, 173, 174, 182, 183, 186, 190, 192, 195, 197, 198, 199, 200, 204, 205, 206, 207, 208, 209, 210, 227, 229
Austria, Austrians, 14, 15, 17, 18, 34, 79, 83, 84, 106, 136, 138, 172, 173, 185, 199, 202, 208, 209, 224, 225, 231

Baker, Colonel James, 29
Balfour, Arthur, 94
Balkan Committee, 63, 64
Balkan League, 158, 163
Balkan States Exhibition, 100, 106–108, 118, 142
Balkan Wars, First and Second, 1912–13, 5, 6, 12, 160–168, 170, 176, 179–180, 182, 194, 199, 200, 202, 205, 237, 252
Balkans, 2, 4, 11, 13, 14, 16, 17, 18, 19, 20, 23, 24, 25, 26, 27, 28, 29, 30, 31, 32, 33, 35, 36, 37, 42, 43, 45, 47, 50, 51, 52, 54, 55, 56, 57, 58, 60, 61, 63, 64, 65, 67, 68, 69, 70, 71, 76, 78, 83, 85, 91, 93, 94, 95, 97, 98, 99, 100, 101, 102, 104, 106, 109, 110, 111, 112, 116, 118, 131, 133, 134, 135, 138, 141, 142, 143, 144, 145, 147, 153, 157, 158, 159, 162, 164, 166, 169, 170, 186, 189, 190, 194, 200, 202, 204, 205, 207, 209, 210, 213, 217, 218, 219, 221, 224, 225, 226, 228, 229, 234, 235, 236, 237, 240, 241, 250, 251, 252, 254
Bar, 42, 84, 144, 173
Beaconsfield, Lord, *see* Disraeli
Beirut, 143, 168
Bektashi sect, 220
Belgrade, 18, 19, 40, 43, 52, 57, 61, 99, 108, 114, 115, 136, 144, 159, 169, 199, 210, 212, 226, 228, 238
Berat, 88, 90, 177, 178

Berchtold, Leopold, 168, 172, 190, 200
Berlin, Congress of, 18, 27, 30, 36, 37, 42, 52, 54, 60, 84, 85, 103, 112, 114
Bessarabia, 210
Bismarck, Otto von, 27, 83, 84
Bitola (Monastir), 19, 65, 79, 81, 82, 159, 176
Black Hand, 115–116, 199
Black Sea, 19
Blair, Tony, 252
blood code, *see* Albania, blood code
Boer War, 14, 153
Bolshevism, 220, 223, *see also* communists
Bosnia and Herzegovina, 6, 17, 18, 24, 29, 30, 34, 36, 102–104, 100, 132–133, 210
Austrian annexation, 113–115, 136–137, 139, 142, 143, 158, 181, 251
Brailsford, Henry and Jane, 61, 62, 63, 64, 65, 66, 69–70, 73, 154
Britain, British, 6, 7, 14, 15, 18, 36, 47, 50, 53, 61, 85, 93, 111, 136, 142, 143, 144, 145, 147, 151, 158, 159, 160, 166, 170, 174, 183, 193, 198, 202, 204, 205, 208, 210, 213, 226, 252
British and Foreign Bible Society, 77
British Conservatives, 25, 26, 55, 63, 76, 95, 111, 145, 147
British Liberals, 24, 25, 26, 27, 28, 54–55, 61, 63, 64, 65, 76, 85, 94, 95, 100, 145, 147, 152, 171, 181
Bucharest, 168, 180, 181, 187, 191, 227
Budapest, 19, 103, 168
Bulgaria, 17, 19, 24, 25, 26, 30, 31, 37, 53, 58, 59, 60, 61, 72, 82, 94, 95, 110, 111, 133, 136, 158, 159, 160, 163, 164, 176, 179–180, 181, 194, 200, 205, 210, 226
Bulgarian 'agitation', 25–26, 54
Bulgarian Exarchate, 58–60, 72, 74, 110, 181
The Burden of the Balkans (M.E. Durham), 95, 117, 133, 181, 224
Burney, Cecil, 174, 175
Buxton, Noel, 63, 147

Byron, 21–23, 27, 28, 80, 87, 93, 135, 188
Byzantines, 18
Čačak, 48
Cambridge, 8, 9, 118–119
Canada, 93
Canon of Lek, *see* Lek
Carmen Sylva, *see* Elisabeth, Queen of Romania
Carpenter, Edward, 152
Catholic Church, 20–21, 26
  in Albania, 45, 79, 81, 83, 124–127, 129, 139, 140, 141, 147, 153, 192, 220, 244, 246–247
  in Bosnia, 102, 103–104, 113
Cecil, Lord Robert, 213
Cetinje, 32, 35, 36, 42, 43, 44, 45, 46, 47, 51, 76, 97, 107, 109, 137, 146, 149, 158, 166, 182, 211, 221
Chamberlain, Neville, 231
Chesterton, G.K., 206
Church of England, 63, 205
Church Times, 28
Churchill, Winston, 227
Ciano, Galeazzo, 230, 231, 232
Clark, Edson, 38
Clemenceau, Georges, 115
Cologne, 186
Committee of Union and Progress, *see* Young Turks
communists, 1, 2, 4, 7, 120, 237, 243, 249, *see* Albania, communist takeover
Conrad, Franz, 190, 200
conservatives, *see* British Conservatives
Constantine of Greece, 163
Constantinople, 3, 18, 19, 26, 27, 31, 78, 82, 83, 85, 87, 112, 114, 139, 140, 143, 158, 164, 168, 180, 213, 215
  Patriarchate of, 58, 59
Copeland, Fanny, 206
Corfu, 185, 196, 205, 210
Corry, Montagu, 27
Crane, Charles, 148, 153
Creagh, James, 35, 45
Croatia, Croats, 14 15, 18, 34, 138, 210, 231, 237, 238, 251

Cvijic, Jovan, 114, 115
Czechoslovakia, Czechs, 15, 102, 220, 227, 230–231, 243, 247

Daily Chronicle, 161
Daily News, 134
Daily Telegraph, 133
Dalmatia, 6, 14, 15, 30, 33–34, 35, 36, 45, 95, 102, 104, 210, *see also* Croatia
Danilo, Bishop of Montenegro, 37, *see also* Petrović dynasty
Danilo, Prince of Montenegro, 39, 104, 144, 174
Danube, 18, 42, 57
De Salis, John Francis Charles, 158
Debar, 79, 172, 184, 226, 229
Dečani, monastery of Visoki Dečani, 50, 51, 130, *see also* Serbian Orthodox Church
Denton, William, 41–42
Devič, 130
Dibra, *see* Debar
Disraeli, Benjamin, 14, 18, 23, 25, 27, 28, 30, 55, 60, 84, 119
Doçi, Prenk, 93
Draga Obrenović, Queen of Serbia, 52–54, *see also* Obrenović dynasty
Dražić, Firmilian, 57, 59–60, *see also* Skopje
Dubrovnik, 34, 104–105, 106
Dulcigno, *see* Ulcinj
Durham, Arthur Edward, 8, 9, 10
Durham, Arthur Ellis, 8
Durham, Caroline Beatrice, 8, 9, 10
Durham, Florence Margaret, 8–9
Durham, Frances Hermia, 9
Durham, Frank Rogers, 8
Durham, Herbert Edward, 8
Durham, Mary Edith,
  arrival in Balkans, 11, 14, 31–32, 42
  author's first encounter with, 1, 3
  books and writings, 3, 5, 6, 7, 12, 48, 52, 54, 95, 116, 118–119, 131, 132, 133–135, 138, 144, 171, 175, 181, 190, 207, 209, 218, 220–221, 223–224, 227, 233, 236, 239, 251, 252–253

Durham, Mary Edith – *continued*
childhood, 7–10
death, 13, 240–241
in Albania, 7, 45–47, 77–93, 97, 110,
  136–138, 141, 151–2, 155, 174, 177,
  190, 194–202, 213, 214–217, 246
in Bosnia, 34–35, 102–106, 110, 142
in Constantinople, 143–144
in Dalmatia, 33, 34, 104
in Egypt, 142–143, 213
in Italy, 157
in Kosovo, 3, 4, 51, 130–131
in Macedonia, 55–76, 95, 110, 142,
  176, 221, 229
in Montenegro, 39, 43–44, 47–48,
  51–52, 97–101, 107, 137, 144–150,
  159–166, 211, 221
in Serbia, 48–52
last years, 233–239
legacy, 250–254
as Queen, or '*kraljica*', 150–151, 155,
  160, 166, 217, 226, 254
refugee work in Albania, 174–178,
  202–203
return to Britain, 203, 226
suicidal thoughts, 10, 50–51
William of Wied, relation with, 183,
  190–191, 193–196, 201–202
women's suffrage, views on, 64, 152
Dürres, 88, 92, 94, 163, 169, 170, 176,
  185, 190, 192, 193, 194, 196, 197,
  200, 202, 208, 212, 214, 231, 244

Eden, Anthony, 227
Edirne, 19, 164, 167, 180
Edward VII, King, 53, 105, 111, 115
Egypt, 142–143, 144, 186, 207, 215, 219
Elbasan, 23, 82, 88, 90, 91, 92, 179, 208
Elisabeth, Empress of Austria, 16, 53, 198
Elisabeth, Queen of Romania, 186–188,
  191–192
Elizabeth I, Queen of England, 154
Ellis, William, 8
Ethiopia, 227, *see also New Times and
  Ethiopia News*
Evans, Sir Arthur, 206
Exarchate, Bulgarian, *see* Bulgarian
  Exarchate

Ferdinand of Coburg, King of Bulgaria,
  53, 60, 112, 136, 179, 180, 194
France, 15, 36, 53, 99, 111, 114, 115, 146,
  170, 202, 209, 210, 226, 233, 243,
  248
Franz Ferdinand, Archduke of Austria,
  30, 104, 105, 117, 197, 198, 222, 224
Franz Joseph, Emperor of Austria, 16,
  104, 113, 140, 199
Freeman, Edward, 25
fustanella, see Albania, traditional dress,
  89

Garibaldi, Giuseppe, 139, 167
Gaspari, Pietro Stefano, 20–21
Gawrych, George, 82, 83
Geg, 20, 82, 246, *see also* Albania,
  language
Germany, Germans, 8, 15, 16, 27, 36, 39,
  105, 112, 114, 120, 162, 170, 188,
  189, 194, 198, 200, 202, 204, 205,
  206, 220, 228, 229, 230, 233, 237,
  243, 248, 253
Gjakova, 130, 139, 157, 172–173, 179,
  183, 184, 226, 229
Gjirokaster, 243
Gladstone, Herbert, 63
Gladstone, William, 24, 25, 27, 28, 29,
  30, 55, 62, 63, 65, 85, 95, 171
Glasgow Herald, 133
Goschen, Lord, 83, 85, 198
Gostivar, 179
Gould, Gerald Francis, 84
Grahovac, Battle of, 161
Grand Hotel, Cetinje, 36
Granville, Lord, 85
Greece, Greeks, 7, 18, 19, 20, 21, 31,
  36, 37, 41, 58, 60, 78, 82, 88, 90,
  91, 92, 153, 158, 159, 161, 163,
  164, 170, 172, 177, 178, 179, 180,
  181, 182, 183, 185, 196, 208, 210,
  212, 214, 220, 221, 226, 231, 233,
  238, 249
Grey, Sir Edward, 7, 145, 173, 183, 200,
  202, 214
Gruda, 120, *see also* Albania, tribes,
Guardian, see Manchester Guardian
Gusinje, 147

Habsburg Empire, 14, 16, 17, 18, *see also* Austria-Hungary; Austria
Halifax, Lord, 232
Hardinge, Charles, 84
Heaton-Armstrong, Duncan, 192, 193, 194, 197, 200
Herbert, Aubrey, 7, 183, 184, 189, 208, 210, 213, 214, 219, 227, 233, 241
High Albania (M.E. Durham), 3–5, 118–135, 138, 144, 218, 224, 251, 252–253
Hobhouse, John Cam, 22–23, 27, 80, 87, 135
Hodgkinson, Harry, 97–98, 177, 184, 234
Hoti, 120, *see also* Albania, tribes
Hoxha, Enver, 241–248, 249, 250, 253
Hungary, Hungarians, 15, 16, 17, 18, 186, 206, 243, 247

Ibar, river, 252
Ignatiev, Nicholas, 58
Ilinden uprising, *see* Macedonia, uprising
India, 64
Internal Macedonian Revolutionary Organisation (IMRO), 31, 75, 110, *see also* Macedonia, uprising
International Commission of Control, 185, 208
Ioannina, 21, 22, 23, 81, 82, 86, 164, 167
Irby, Adeline, 28, 29
Ireland, 25, 64, 198
Islam, *see* Muslims
Italy, Italians, 15, 16, 20, 36, 39, 53, 86, 87, 99, 102, 114, 120, 124, 140, 143, 149, 153, 154, 155, 156, 157, 170, 172, 193, 195, 202, 208, 209, 210, 213, 214, 225, 227, 228, 229, 231, 232, 237, 248
Izvolsky, Alexander, 114

Japan, 94
Jelena of Montenegro, later Elena, Queen of Italy, 39, 210
Jews, 28, 30, 82, 102–103, 147, 163

Kaplan, Robert, 235
Karadjordjević, House of, *see* Petar Karadjordjević, King of Serbia, 39, 53, 61, 99–100, 143, 144, 163, 194, 230
Kastrati, 120, 123, 129, 151
Kelmendi, 120
Kolonja, 80
Korça, 7, 79, 177, 178, 184, 202, 212, 214, 241, 243, 245, 250
Republic of, 209, 243
Kosovo, 1, 2, 3, 4, 5, 7, 18, 29, 49, 50, 51, 52, 79, 81, 82, 85, 86, 97, 130–131, 136, 139, 142, 143, 146, 149, 158, 159, 163, 164, 172, 176, 181, 184, 199, 202, 205, 228, 241, 248, 250, 251, 252
Battle of, in 1389, 147, 205, 212, 222
Kosovo Liberation Army, 4, 252
Kossovo Day Committee, 205–206, 235
Kotor, Bay of, 35
Kragujevac, 108
Kruševo, 54
Kumanovo, 163

Lane, Rose Wilder, 218, 228
Lazar, Prince of Serbia, 132, 205, 235
Lear, Edward, 23
Lek, Canon of, 121–123, 126
Leskovac, 42
Leskovik, 80
liberals, *see* British Liberals
Lloyd George, David, 198, 204
London, 7, 8, 11, 107, 108, 118, 170, 202
Treaty of, 208, 210, 214
London Conference, 171–173, 174, 177, 179, 182, 196, 199
Luxembourg, 170

Macedonia, 5, 6, 7, 12, 18, 19, 30, 31, 56, 57–76, 94, 95, 106, 110, 111, 133, 141, 142, 143, 145, 159, 161, 162, 163, 176, 177, 179, 180, 181, 221, 224, 229, 235, 241, 248
British Relief Fund, mission to, 55, 57, 61–76, 86, 94, 147
uprising, 54–55, 60–61, 65, 72
Mackenzie, Georgiana, 28, 29

Magyars, 15, *see also* Hungary, Hungarians
Malcolm, Noel, 50
Manchester Guardian, 134, 151, 160, 161, 238
Marie, Queen of Romania, 187
Marko, Prince of Montenegro, 144
Masaryk, Tomás, 227
Matthews, Caroline, 162, 166–167
Mediterranean, 20
Mensdorff, Albert, 172–173
Menzies, Sutherland, 12, 40
Methodius, Bishop of Ohrid, 72, *see also* Bulgarian Exarchate
Mijatović, Čedomilj, 187
Milan, King of Serbia, 40–41, 198
Milena, Queen of Montenegro, 38, 47, 107, 144
Milica, Princess of Montenegro, 38
Miller, William, 38
Milošević, Slobodan, 1, 2, 4
Mirdita, 92, 93
Mirko, Prince of Montenegro, 161
Mitrovica, 1, 2, 3, 19, 130, 133, 251–252
Monastir, *see* Bitola
Montenegrin Institute, 42
Montenegrin Orthodox Church, 211
Montenegro, Montenegrins, 6, 7, 12, 26, 29, 32–43, 46–49, 51, 56, 61, 84–86, 92–94, 97, 99–101, 104, 106–109, 118–119, 137, 143–147, 149–151, 153, 157–165, 171, 173, 175, 181, 183, 208, 210, 224, 225, 237
  independence lost, 211–212
Montpensier, Duke of, 186
Morning Chronicle, 160
Morning Post, 151
Muslims, 3, 4, 19, 28, 37, 44, 45, 50, 63, 65, 74, 79, 81, 83, 85, 87, 91, 92, 95, 102, 103, 105, 110, 113, 124, 126, 127, 136, 137, 138–139, 147, 149, 153, 165, 178, 179, 186, 189, 192, 196, 197, 220, 228, 242, 246, 251
  atrocities against, 165, 220
Mussolini, Benito, 230, 231, 238

Narodna Odbrana, *see* Black Hand
Nation, 134

Natalije, Queen of Serbia, 40–41
Netherlands, 53, 196, 200
Nevinson, Henry, 6, 63, 64, 151–155, 157, 175, 176, 177, 178, 183, 207, 208
New Statesman, 238
New Times and Ethiopia News, 227, 241
Nicholas II, Tsar of Russia, 94, 100, 111, 112, 197
Nicolson, Harold, 214
Nikaj, 126, 127
Nikšić, 42
Nikola, King of Montenegro, 37–40, 44, 52, 97–99, 104, 106, 107, 108, 109, 137, 144, 146, 147, 149, 150, 160, 164, 171, 174, 175, 182, 194, 210–212, *see also* Petrović dynasty
  daughters' marriages, 38–40, 43
Niš, 19, 42
Njegusi, 102
Noli, Theophan 'Fan', 215–216, 227–229, 230, 234, 242
Northern Epirus, Greek claim to, 178, 185, 196, 212, 234, 238
Nottingham Guardian, 133

Obrenović dynasty, 52–54, 61, 100, 101
Ohrid, 23, 55, 59, 63, 69–75, 79, 81, 88, 142, 159, 162, 163, 164, 176, 177, 178, 208, 229
Orient Express, 19, 30
Orosh, abbots of, 93
Ostrog monastery, 43, 51
Ottoman Empire, Ottomans, 5, 17, 18, 19, 20, 26, 27, 30, 37, 42, 43, 48, 50, 54, 55, 57, 59, 60, 62, 63, 66, 68, 71, 75, 77, 78, 79, 82, 84, 85, 86, 91, 94, 110, 112, 113, 119, 124, 132, 136, 138, 142, 143, 146, 147, 149, 151, 156, 157, 159, 161, 162, 164, 167, 168, 169, 170, 174, 175, 176, 180, 185, 192, 195, 197, 200, 205, 212, *see also* Turkey-in-Europe; Turks
  Gladstone's denunciations of, 24, 62, 95
  revolt in, 3, 111–112, *see also* Young Turks
vilayets, 19, 22, 29, 50, 65, 81, 82, 86, 102, 132, 139, 172, 184

Pankhurst, Sylvia, 227
Paris Peace Conference, 193, 211, 212, 214
Pasha, Essad, see Toptani
Pasha, Prenk (Prenk Did Doda), 93
Pašić, Nikola, 100, 205
Patras, 21
Peć (Peje), 49, 50, 51, 130
Pejović, Krsto, 101–102, 107
Petar, King of Serbia, 39, 53, 61, 99–100, 143, 144, 163, 194, 230
Petrović dynasty, 37, 41, 99, 108, 174, 224, see also Nikola, King of Montenegro
Piedmont, 116
Pinkerton, Revd R., 78
Pirot, 42
Plamenac, Petar, 107, 108, 174
Plevna, 26
Podgorica, 42, 84, 137, 146, 148, 158, 160, 165, 171, 211
Pogradec, 208
Poland, Poles, 15, 230, 243
Postenani, 80
Prilep, 159
Princip, Gavrilo, 117, 197, 199, see also Black Hand
Pristina, 3, 130, 147, 149, 253
Prizren, 79, 82, 83, 132, 164, 169, 170, 172, 220
  League of Prizren, 85–86, 93
Prussia, 15, 186

Qemali, Ismail, 168–170, 178, 186, 189, 192, 193, 200
Queen Elisabeth, see Elisabeth, Queen of Romania
Queen Marie, see Marie, Queen of Romania

Ramet, Sabrina, 245
Reformation, 103, 120, 186
Resen (Resna), 55, 60, 61, 63, 65–72, 79, 111
Ridgeway, William, 117–118
Romania, Romanians, 8, 15, 16, 19, 20, 26, 180, 188, 190, 191, 194, 210, 214, 226, 227
Rome, 93, 124, 154, 157, 214, 220, 232

Rossetti, Christina, 217
Royal Anthropological Institute, 118–119, 134–135, 227
Royal Institute of International Affairs, 223–225
Rudolf, Crown Prince of Austria, 16
Russia, Russian Empire, 17, 18, 25, 30, 36, 37, 42, 52, 57, 60, 61, 90, 95, 99, 106, 110, 114, 136, 153, 158, 159, 170, 172, 183, 185, 186, 194, 200, 202, 204, 209–210, 220, 223, 229
Russo-Japanese War, 94, 100, 106
Russo-Turkish War, 26–27, 60

St Naum, 76, 229
Salisbury, Lord, 30, 61, 111
Salonika, see Thessaloniki
San Stefano, Treaty of, 27, 30
Sarajevo, 17, 30, 103, 105, 106, 114, 117, 197, 198, 199, 210
Saranda, 231, 245
Sava, river, 18
The Serajevo Crime (M.E. Durham), 116, 222–224
Serbia, Serbians, 1, 2, 3, 4, 5, 6, 7, 12, 15, 16, 17, 18, 19, 29, 31, 37, 39–42, 43, 45, 48, 49, 50, 51, 52, 53, 56, 57, 59, 60, 61, 72, 82, 84, 87, 97, 99, 100, 101, 102, 103, 105, 106, 107, 108, 109, 10, 111, 113, 114, 115, 116, 118, 130, 131, 132, 133, 136, 137, 143, 144, 145, 146, 153, 158, 159, 160, 161, 162, 163, 164, 165, 167, 168, 170, 171, 172, 173, 175, 176, 177, 178, 179, 180, 181, 182, 183, 184, 187, 193, 195, 196, 197, 198, 199, 200, 202, 204, 205, 206, 207, 208, 209, 210, 211, 212, 217, 221, 223, 224, 225, 228, 229, 234, 235, 237, 250, 251, 252
  aspirations
    to Bosnia, 103, 106, 113–114, 132–133, 136, 200
    to Kosovo, 2, 3, 5, 50, 97, 131, 132, 172, 184, 199, 205, 212, 220, 250–251
    to Macedonia, 59, 60, 184, 199
    to Montenegro, 211
  Durham's tour of, 48–52, 57

Serbian Orthodox Church, 17, 48, 49, 51, 211, 102, 130, 132, 181, 220
Serbian Radical Party, 99, 113, 237
Serbian Relief Fund, 205–206
Servia, *see* Serbia
Seton-Watson, Robert, 206, 219, 221–226, 234, 235, 240, 251
Shantoya, Marko, 119, 125, 128, 148, 151, 155, 166
Shkodra (Scutari, Skadar), 20, 21, 23, 77, 82, 83, 88, 92, 109, 119, 123, 124, 126, 136, 137, 138, 140, 141, 144, 145, 146, 147, 148, 151, 153, 155–156, 164, 166, 173, 178, 179, 182, 183, 190, 192, 195, 209, 212, 217, 244, 245, 250, 253
  Durham's first visit to, 45–46, 49
  Montenegrin siege of, 164–165, 167, 171, 172, 173–175, *see also* Montenegro
Sigurimi, *see* Albania, secret police
Sinas, Constantine, 77, 80, 81, 86, 88
Skanderbeg, 20, 124, 167, 169, 170, 195, 241, 246, 249
Skopje, 19, 57, 59, 65, 149, 159, 163, 220
Slavonia, 103, 210, *see also* Croatia
Slavs, 4, 16, 17, 20, 26, 29, 30, 58, 90, 94, 95, 105, 110, 137, 202, 205, 219, 226
Slavonic Review, 222–223, 226
Slovaks, 15
Slovenia, Slovenes, 2, 15, 210, 237
Sofia, 19, 74, 75, 111, 159, 169, 180
Sorel, Albert, 15
Spain, 20, 102
Split, 34
Srebrebnica, 105
Stalin, Stalinists, 241, 242, 244, *see also* Albania, communist takeover
Steed, Henry Wickham, 115, 206, 207, 219, 226
Stillman, William, 29, 30
The Struggle for Scutari (M.E. Durham), 175, 183, 190, 224
Strumica, 180
Summa, Nicholas, 217

Swire, Joseph, 189, 218–219
'Sworn virgins', *see* Albania, virgins

Taurus, 185
Tepelena, 21, 22, 23, 80, 81, 87
Tennyson, Alfred, 26, 33
Thessaloniki, 19, 163–164, 209
Thompson, Dorothy, 218
Thomson, Lodewijk, 196
Thrace, Eastern Thrace, 19, 30, 158, 159, 161, 163, 164, 176, 180, 215
Through the Lands of the Serb (M.E. Durham), 12, 48, 52, 54, 55, 87, 117, 131, 132, 224
The Times, 15, 115, 206, 226, 227, 238, 241
Times Literary Supplement, 133
Tirana, 88, 92, 197, 215, 218, 231, 234, 241, 244, 248, 249, 253, 254
Tito, Josip, 2, 237, 238
Titova Mitrovica, *see* Mitrovica
Toplica, 84
Toptani, Essad Pasha, 174, 192–193, 197
Tosk, 20, 82, 246, *see also* Albania, language
Toynbee, Arnold, 225
Transylvania, 210
Trebinje, 34, 102
Trepča, 2
Trieste, 34, 138, 151, 155, 182, 200
Tripoli, 153, 168
Trotsky, Leon, 221
Troubridge, Ernest, 194, 197
Turkey-in-Europe, 5, 12, 14, 17, 18, 19, 22, 25, 27, 28, 29, 38, 40, 50, 58, 95, 110, 112, 147, 158, 162, 163, 167, 180, 181, 212, 229, 251, *see also* Ottoman Empire
Turks, Turkish, 21, 24, 25, 26, 27, 33, 37, 47, 54, 55, 60, 65, 67, 71, 82, 85, 88, 91, 98, 105, 133, 140, 147, 154, 160, 164, 176
Tuzi, 165
Twenty Years of Balkan Tangle (M.E. Durham), 51, 55, 190, 207, 222

Ukrainians, 15
Ulcinj, 44, 49, 84, 86

United States of America, see America
Urquhart, David, 23

Vardar, river, 163
Vatra, 215
Victoria, Queen of England, 14, 25, 27, 39, 105
Vivian, Herbert, 54
Varna, 19
Versailles, see Paris Peace Conference
Vickers, Miranda, 172, 245, 246
Vienna, 15, 18, 19, 56, 78, 83, 103, 105, 114, 168, 199, 206
  Congress of, 186
vilayets, see Ottoman Empire, vilayets
Vlachs, 20, 82, 89
Vllasi, Azem, 1, 2, 4
Vlora, 80, 86, 87, 88, 89, 167, 168, 169, 170, 178, 184, 186, 196, 208, 231
Vranje, 42, 84
Vukotić, Janko, 150, 160

West, Rebecca, 235–236
Whitehead, Sir James, 53
Wied, William and Sophie of, 183, 185–186, 188–195, 200–202, 208, 214, 216, 246
Wilde, Oscar, 26

Wilhelm I, German Emperor, 197–198
Wilhelm II, German Emperor, 188–189, 199
Wilkinson, Sir John, 37
Wilson, Flora Northesk, 54
Wilson, Woodrow, 210, 228
women's suffrage, see Durham, Mary Edith, women's suffrage, views
World War I, 15, 117, 120, 181, 197, 200, 202–203, 204–210, 212, 213, 226, 237
World War II, 61, 210, 234, 237

Yanina, see Ioannina
Young Turks, 3, 112, 138, 139, 140, 145, 158, 162
Yugoslavia, 1, 2, 4, 5, 210, 212, 213, 214, 219, 220, 225, 226, 227, 228, 229, 234, 235, 236, 238, 243, 248, 249, 251

Zogu, Ahmed (King Zog), 13, 228–229, 231, 234, 238, 240–241, 246, 249, 250
Zorka, Princess of Montenegro, 39, see also Petar, King of Serbia
Zweig, Stefan, 199